The Cost of Institutions

The Cost of Institutions

Information and Freedom in Expanding Economies

Jacob P. Rodriguez,
Steven R. Loomis, and Joseph G. Weeres

THE COST OF INSTITUTIONS
© Jacob Rodriguez, Steven Loomis, Joseph Weeres, 2007

First published in 2007 by
PALGRAVE MACMILLAN™
175 Fifth Avenue, New York, N.Y. 10010 and
Houndmills, Basingstoke, Hampshire, England RG21 6XS.
Companies and representatives throughout the world.

PALGRAVE MACMILLAN is the global academic imprint of the Palgrave Macmillan division of St. Martin's Press, LLC and of Palgrave Macmillan Ltd. Macmillan® is a registered trademark in the United States, United Kingdom and other countries. Palgrave is a registered trademark in the European Union and other countries.

ISBN-10: 1-4039-7969-3
ISBN-13: 978-1-4039-7969-8

Library of Congress Cataloging-in-Publication Data

Rodriguez, Jacob.

The cost of institutions : information and freedom in expanding
     economies / Jacob Rodriguez, Steven Loomis, Joseph Weeres.
        p. cm.
     Includes bibliographical references and index.
     ISBN 1-4039-7969-3 (alk. paper)
      1. Institutional economics. 2. Knowledge management. I. Loomis,
     Steven. II. Weeres, Joseph G., 1939-III. Title.

     HB99.5.R64 2007
     330—dc22   2006036370

A catalogue record for this book is available from the British Library.

Design by Macmillan India Ltd.

First edition: June 2007

10 9 8 7 6 5 4 3 2 1

Printed in the United States of America.

For Michelle
For Ena, Sophia, and Stephen
For Lee

Contents

List of Sidebars

Acknowledgments

We are very deeply grateful to Anthony (Toby) Wahl, senior editor at Palgrave Macmillan, for the kind patience that he showed to us throughout the writing of this book. It has been a delightful experience to be associated with a man of such uncommon integrity. Our warmest and sincerest thanks, Toby.

We extend warm appreciation to our students who are presently finding innovative ways to use the theory advanced in this book, and to the G. W. Aldeen Memorial Fund of Wheaton College that helped to finance part of this project.

Introduction

This book is about the evolution of institutions and the economy. In it we have developed a new analytical framework for explaining the ways in which institutions affect what we value and believe, what we strive for, the performance of economies, and the intricacies of human exchange. In essence most of the book shows how an economy whose costs exceed its benefits may nevertheless continue to expand.

The analysis presented in these pages develops the basic idea that as institutions attempt to support the expansion of markets with rules (property rights, etc.), they are compelled by scarcity to trade off higher-cost (particular) information for lower-cost (universal) information. This division of information, in turn, highly distorts the information field of markets, altering preferences, hopes and fears, meanings, and factor prices and proportions, in effect setting a least-cost direction to production.

The main point of our argument, about which we try to be explicit from the outset, is that the separation of information results in loss of the capacity to preserve individual liberty, and so it functions as a causal mechanism to raise the total sum of costs in the social order. If true, this contention suggests reconsideration of the relation between market growth and costs. It means, above all, that economic analysis cannot sustain the claim that the expansion of markets tends to zero costs. On the contrary, this book will show that the evolving rule (institutional) structure of market expansion is on net balance a cost-increasing mechanism in that it makes individuals less free to choose.

We believe it is a powerful evidence for this book that it can explain so many domains of experience and observed features of market activity. As a statement of general theory, it has a logic that transcends the context of particular nations and confronts questions that seem common to all. Is there a specific direction to developing economies? Are property rights becoming more or less secure? Does market growth correspond to the development of complex social reality? Why does the state (government) continue to grow? Why can it not effectively limit its own powers and interventions? Will democracy be workable in the long run? Can markets overcome the impossibility results of social choice? What constitutes rationality in an expanding market? Does an expanding economy make people more or less free? We now have plausible answers to these and other longstanding questions.

These considerations will be discussed presently, but first we must take a forward glance at some of the key terms that will be used throughout the book. Their definitions will give a sense of the overall argument.

- *Expansion* refers to growth in the size of market structures—an increase in the volume or quantity of production and trade. It is a rise in the scale of operations (output and trade) that is filtered through and supported by institutional rules, property rights, customs, etc. In these pages we argue that the rising volume of trade within institutions alters the cost of information, and this, in turn, alters production probabilities, the set of preferences, the locus of decision making, the calculus of self-interest, and the ideological construction of the social good.

- *Institutions* are the formal and informal rules and conventions that govern the process of collective action, production, and exchange. Douglass North (1990: 3) said they are "the humanly devised constraints that shape human interaction."[1] Indeed we regard institutions as integral features of the productive base of the economy; they form the capital assets of society and function to guide the allocation of scarce resources. As Samuel Bowles (2004: 48) phrased it, "Institutions influence who meets whom, to do what tasks, with what possible courses of action, and with what consequences of actions jointly taken."[2]

- *The division of information* is the act of trading off particular information for universal information. It is a dynamical process traceable through institutional rules, regulations, customs, values, ideas, language, symbols, etc. It is the cumulative experience of millions of interacting individuals who make production and consumption decisions regarding future scarcities under conditions of uncertainty. In other words, the division of information is an aggregative consequence of individual choice orderings under expansion, the countless decisions to trade off some preferred values and ends for other preferred values and ends. With cost (in money or other terms) as a guide, the trade-offs decided upon induce change in the provision of rules and maximizing opportunities, the direction of learning and trials, the discourse and logic—all the existing formal and informal constraints of the institution. Indeed, what is going on inside all of this activity, at a level much harder to observe, is the perpetual yielding of higher-cost information to lower-cost information. In terms of increasing scale, the same pattern of trading off one kind of information for another applies to complexity in all institutional settings; it persists in the face of various disturbances and continues through time on its low-cost trajectory. This book points to the division of information as the specific mechanism by which institutional expansion gets priced below its social cost; it is the article upon which liberty stands or falls.

- *Particular information* refers to data that are mostly qualitative in nature; it is inherently variable, irregular, uncertain, and hard to measure. In general, it is the kind of information that cannot yield precise definitions, which has no exact boundaries to measure, and is unpredictable. Particular information pertains mainly to the nonlinear types of behavior, to the unique, dynamic elements of living or physical systems; it is, perhaps, most applicable to complex social phenomena and the field of human relations where extensive variation tends to dominate the component parts of the data. This information finds expression in personal distinctions, independence, emotions, improvisation, value judgments, moral principles, acts of will—all the essential aspects and distinct individualities that make up human personality and the intricacies of human interaction. In this book the term "particular information" also applies to its social construction, which finds expression in the institutional rules of the smaller market; for example, policies designed for local or smaller numbers, for communities, cultures, even states, countries, or nation-states, as opposed to universal rule sets that are organized around the wider collective or the global, that is, the larger market and sphere of trade.

- *Universal information* refers to data that are mostly quantitative in nature; it tends to be constant, common, linear, and measurable. In the realm of universal information we can expect to find categories that correspond to standardization, consolidation, and integration; it is fundamentally compatible with a capacity for generating order and stability, prediction, fixed patterns of logical structures, and precise planning and control. In rules, laws, norms, customs, language, values, ideas, and so forth, universal information tends to deal with instances of the type (i.e., abstract and general forms), not the particular or individual. When we speak of the universalizing trend that parallels expanding markets we also mean the social construction of this information. That is to say, as trade grows outside the purview of the existing rule structure, the arena of institutional rules must enlarge and embrace the new circle of trade. This requires a reformulation of the rules—substituting more universal information for particular information. In other words, the rules must become more universal—conform to collective interests—before they can animate plans for further expansion. As the new set of rules organize around the larger market, the old rule set, which once was seen as universal information, now becomes seen as particular information.

Next we want to call attention to the question that this combination of universal and particular information presses for an answer: namely, what accounts for the cost difference between these two classes of information?

- *The cost of information* accompanies choice—the decisions to trade off one desire, need, or goal for another. These choices in turn define and transform production probabilities. To understand the reasons for the cost difference between universal and particular information, we need only reflect a moment on what makes information more or less costly in the productive system. Information is less costly (in financial or other terms) to the degree that it (1) successfully connects cause and effect, (2) yields a sense of certainty, (3) exhibits clear utility, (4) complements profitable activities, (5) uses relatively fewer resources to ascertain its costs and benefits, (6) increases legibility, verification, and enforcement, and (7) is comparatively easy to acquire, process, reproduce, and transmit.

    Expanding markets prefer universal information—embedded in rules, customs, norms, values, etc.—because it matches up with these characteristics and functions to lower the cost of production. Its properties tend to make communication easier and enable calculation and trade to move forward toward impersonal exchange. It is the type of information that can model regularity, yield a high degree of certainty, and can, and often is, described in quantitative terms. Hence the value of universal information consists mainly in the opportunities it provides for cooperative outcomes, efficiency in production, and gains from trade, all of which lower the cost of decision making, which may be where its chief advantage lies.

    By contrast, it is the dynamic terms—variable, indefinite, and nonlinear—that capture the essence of the higher-cost sources of information. Its correspondence to the field of human activity means that its costs and benefits are hard to determine. They are, generally, not capable of being demonstrated by common mathematical techniques. Indeed, particular information tends to be at variance with the features and aims of growth. It entails the possibility of the conflict of values, of an incompatibility between the vast variety of claims and differing purposes of diverse groups of human beings. These particularities are the sources of friction and noise within the institution. The use of this information can obstruct the pattern of unity and coherence of views; it can lead to higher production costs, which, as a consequence, has an inhibiting effect on growth.

The point here is that the selection of information is primarily driven by cost. It is expense that deters an institution from increasing the volume of particular information. As the scale of trade goes up, the competition for scarce resources intensifies, which causes the institution to choose the cheaper (universal) way. This move toward universal measures and standards allows for stable, controllable expansion. The same measurements, the same rules and laws, the same terminology and viewpoint, the same fair conditions lead to a convergence of means and ends and to a wider sphere of trade. This opens the way for a more streamlined (technical) structure of production. On the whole, as scale goes up, production will ascend from the concrete to the general; from more to less variation; from an irregular, dynamic model to a more fixed and static model. The price of generating a higher volume of production and trade is an impersonal drive that forces a choice between universal information and particular information. This choice is an inescapable trade-off, and not merely an option, if expansion is going to take place and be sustained.

- *Freedom* in this book means freedom from outside interference, from coercion, from man-made obstacles that prevent human action. It means the right not to be infringed upon within a certain minimum area, the right and opportunity to act as well as not to act, to choose and not to be chosen for. Freedom also includes the positive notion— that is, the freedom to, the basic sense of which is the freedom to shape, to make the best of one's self, to achieve a definite condition. It generally implies active participation, to alter things in a certain way, the individual and collective conquest of that which obstructs you.

These (positive and negative) conceptions of freedom exist in complex relation and are necessary preconditions for the success of individual endeavors and for successful (virtuous or ideal) human existence. These principles seem to hold no matter where or how the "individual" or "group" is represented in the social hierarchy: an individual person, an individual community, an individual nation-state; likewise, a collective community, a collective nation-state, a collective transnational agency. The terms "individual" and "collective" are relative to context, and this appears to hold, too, for the exercise of agency and liberty.

It is worth remarking further that we take it to be self-evident that the capacity for choice is intrinsic to rationality and to the dignity and status of the human individual. The freedom to choose between possibilities is one of the essential demands of human nature and is part of the very conception of what it is to be a normal human being. Into the details of the question of human nature we do not propose to go. We only wish here to point out what reason demands: that to contract the area of choice is to deny humanity to the human agent; it is to degrade the true essence of man and the idea of persons as self-directed beings. If such a claim is conceded then we shall have to admit that to confine individual liberty to an ever-limited range, that is, to decrease the sum of individual freedom, is to transmit an unredeemable cost onto the individual and society. And no amount of efficiency, output, or trade—indeed no other factor—can compensate for its loss.

With these definitions we come directly to a brief word on methodology. Our epistemological approach to this project has been nontechnical, theoretical, and in the rich tradition of F. A. Hayek and others. We rely upon the reader's common reason and good judgment to recognize that if basic philosophical axioms and the logic of argument are denied a priori to a project such as ours, then what is left is merely descriptive, quantitative data and technical analysis, hardly an inviting vista to see and uncover the important ontological factors hidden within the economy. In any event, we do not embrace the positivist vision of social reality chiefly because such a vision cannot capture the meanings behind phenomena, its many differing variables, its structure of relations, its multiplicity of events, and its divergent levels of causation.

Our work identifies significant facts (e.g., rising costs within the economy), it matches these facts to a mechanism operating within expanding institutions (i.e., the division of information), and articulates a new theoretical framework (or paradigm) by which to examine these phenomena.[3] Relying primarily on deductive analysis, our method emphasizes the interrelated principles of internal consistency and logical coherence. If theory meets these criteria, there can be no *logical* objection raised against it. Of course, meeting this initial standard of evaluation does not yet validate the plausibility of theory. Plausibility would require the additional and higher epistemic burden of truth-correspondence—that there exists within the articulation an adequately warranted set of cause-and-effect relationships, in this case corroborated by certain economic and informational mechanisms and actual phenomena taking place within social reality.[4] We should note that for the truth-correspondence criterion to be met there is simply no epistemological requirement that it be met via a strict technical or positivist methodology. A criterion of verifiability may also be met by the accurate and nonarbitrary narrative accounts of reality itself.

While recognizing that we encounter challenges owing to the principle of falsifiability, as do many theories, these do not constitute fatal flaws in our approach since they merely imply what has been known for centuries: a priori theoretical frameworks are often the rails upon which academic disciplines approach the pursuit of knowledge (see Kuhn 1996). Therefore, we assume, as Weber did, that empirical observation or study depends on an underlying prior theorizing anyway;[5] we are simply cutting to the chase and examining these embedded theories relative to phenomena. And though our theory has broad explanatory power, we are under no epistemic burden to explain everything: just the phenomena that we do in fact explain.[6] As Sen (2002: 611) has noted, "Complete articulation need not be set up as an enemy of useful articulation."

Our dynamic theory is one of deductive inference that does evaluate—successfully we believe—empirical content. It emphasizes the identity of causal mechanisms and forces that affect social (political and economic) conditions. As many know, in trying to model complex social phenomena, that is, a complex adaptive order, all that is possible is conditional prediction. At best we can describe the principle (or set of principles) by which complex social phenomena (e.g., rising costs in the economy) works and predict broad patterns of behavior. In other words, explanatory strength comes at the cost of less-predictive power. Our book broadens the field of complex phenomena to be explained by studying the means-ends relationship and the essential causes of the state of the market and complex social phenomena in general.

As to procedure, ours begins with the presupposition that when individual agents act in the social sphere, their choice of behavior is often an amalgam of causal factors and conditions. For this reason, the complex idea of freedom is our starting point of analysis for human affairs. This entails the interaction of individual elements and capacities relative to social complexity, specifically the rights and liberties of individual persons. Individual freedom is the proper basis for assessment of cost in the socioeconomic system. As such, we are making an individual, freedom-based (and informationally grounded) assessment of economic expansion. We are most interested in what happens to the particular and dynamic properties of information within institutions, and we cannot get at nor explain these phenomena within the narrow parameters of a technical method.

Consider this final point. We are not opponents of growth; in many ways we avidly yield to the many obvious benefits of institutional expansion. Indeed, we shall be completely misunderstood if we are supposed to be calling for restrictions on economic development. Our caveat, one too often avoided, is the hard question concerning the costs rising against the individual in the social system that needs to be answered. One economist goes so far as to distill the formula in this manner: "People respond to incentives—all the rest is commentary." Well, part of that commentary might just be critical to understanding the causal conditions surrounding the structure of incentives and that which must be traded off in the process. We must not pretend to ignore the trade-off of individual liberty for growth, the particular for the universal, complexity for simplicity, for to do so is to engage in a most unfortunate reductionism as well as to undermine any prospect for recapturing inherently valuable human information.

We have divided the book, roughly speaking, into three sections. The first part, chapters 1 and 2, presents the general theoretical argument and diagnostic examples of the theory. The middle part of the book, chapters 3 through 5, presents the example of education. So far as we can tell, this marks the most comprehensive institutional analysis ever done on the system of education. The last part is chapter 6. Here we give a more complete view of the theory and its wide implications for the social order.

In chapter 1, "Expansion under Uncertainty," and throughout this book, we identify an information constraint operating within the rule-making function of institutions that makes it impossible to find a just order—the "right rules"—whereby all competing claims can reach a state of rational cooperation. Institutions invariably transmit costs to markets through the rules they enact. Simply put, our thesis is that scale alters the cost of utilizing information.

This thesis cuts across much of the work in institutional economics and public choice theory that sees the problem of institutions as one of collective decision making—a difficulty in aggregating individual preferences that results in the infringement of the interest of the individual on the collective. Our work complements this research. But it locates the problem differently, and therefore arrives at different conclusions. Cost, not just self-interest and collective choice, is at the heart of the decision problem. It is the rational adjustment to cost differences in information that increases the flow of information in one direction and decreases it in another. The informational priority of scale gives direction to institutional expansion. It favors standardization and more centralized decision units. It shifts the reference point for judging value within the institution toward the collective and away from the individual. Chapter 2, "The State: An Information Theory," shows through several examples how this process aligns the growth of markets with a bigger state.

These rules of production benefit the production of goods whose inputs can suffer standardization without much loss in quality. However, not all goods conform to this requirement. For many, the agency of the individual is central to the production of the good.

Enter here, in chapters 3 through 5, the special case of education. The system of education becomes an object of analysis in this book because it so clearly affirms the role and requirements of individual liberty and shows the explanatory force of this theory.

In chapter 3, Establishing Direction in Education Production," we illustrate the practical effects of expansion on the direction of production and on perceptions of the complex human good. We show that the requirements of education expansion force the institution to trade off higher-cost information for lower-cost information in production; in other words, while education preserves the universals (attainment), it denies the particulars (knowledge and skills) full access to the productive agenda.

Chapter 4, "The Individual and the Collective in Education," argues that the long-term trend in education is toward delegitimizing the individual as a unique process of production. The progressive expansion of education creates a process in which the starting point for education continually shifts away from the interests, instincts, and abilities of the individual person to the aims and interests of the institution, to the undifferentiated social whole. The evidence suggests that relying on the expansion of education for the improvement of human capital secures an adjustment toward the use of simplified (standardized) substitutes, a realization that is fatal to the development of the essential attributes of the complex human good.

The main point of chapter 5, "Markets: The Logic of Convergence," is to show through the examples of school vouchers, teacher education programs, and transnational trade of higher education how the distinction between politics and markets becomes progressively attenuated through the catalyst of expansion and the progressive division of information.

Finally, in chapter 6, "Market Failure in the Preservation of Liberty," we argue that freedom is the basis for proper analysis of the direction of cost in the socioeconomic system. Achieving a good understanding of this requires an examination of some of the major technical and social models of our era; this will include the theory of games and the social choice and contract models of Amartya Sen, John Rawls, and Jurgen Habermas. For it is in these systems of thought that we find reliance on the same logic that operates in expanding markets, namely, the separation of individual liberty from rationality (the good).

Several important results emerge from this linkage. First, the use of this logic or formula increases the capacity for unity and human cooperation, which makes for a more efficient productive and social process, and hence for greater output and trade. Second, as this book will show, the separation of individual liberty from rationality alters the central view of what constitutes the good. In other words, it changes the system of values, leading in the end to fatally distorted views of progress, of freedom, of democracy, and of human nature itself. And third, this process of separation pressures human beings to conform to nonindependence and to antirealism, that is, to a false sense of equilibrium and to a unity that eliminates from consideration the greater part of the human experience. The key idea of chapter 6 is that the benefits of market expansion conceal from us the fact that growth raises the cost of individual freedom by separating it from rationality; this places on society a steadily growing burden of cost from which it attempts to free itself by means of further expansion.

We have included the following section to show how our theory relates to some of the major political and economic ideas of the past and present.

North, Douglass. 1990. *Institutions, Institutional Change and Economic Performance.* Cambridge: Cambridge University Press.
We extend North's conception of institutions by placing more emphasis on their productive aspects. We also show that well-specified property rights need not be followed by an overall reduction in transaction costs. In the case of changes in the general level of transaction costs, it will be found that when these costs are rising, property rights may be more clearly defined and easily traded—in the universal direction.

Arrow, Kenneth. 1974. *The Limits of Organization.* New York: W. W. Norton.
Arrow's impressive book recognizes what perhaps is the core problem of civil society—how to reconcile individual and collective preferences, and the limits of human cooperation to do so. Our work retains Arrow's impossibility theorem, but it shows how the economic system succeeds in securing direction in production (the aggregation of dissimilar preferences) without a dictator, that is, without appealing to a sense of obligation beyond consent.

Hayek, F. A. 1960. *The Constitution of Liberty.* Chicago: University of Chicago Press.
We agree and are in line with Hayek's methodology in analyzing complex systems, but differ with his stand on general rules—that they advance a neutral protocol, that they maximize the public good, and that they are

cost-reducing mechanisms in society. We suggest that these rules are nonneutral transmitters of cost in the social order. We also show how market expansion ultimately leads to the same outcomes as those produced by economic planning, a significant connection that has, until now, not been seen.

Buchanan, James, and Gordon Tullock. 1962. *The Calculus of Consent.* Ann Arbor: University of Michigan Press.

All that the public choice theory has said about the failure of the political process is true and demonstrable, that self-interest gets in the way of the pursuit of the social welfare. While true, this view does not penetrate to the heart of the problem. The problem is that information is inherently unstable and asymmetric, which means that it is costly and therefore a scarce good. Even if self-interest could be set aside, scarcity is manifest in the trade-off required in rule making. Scale intensifies those trade-offs and from that shifts the structure of rules and directs these toward the universal rather than the particular. Both public and private realms will be subject to the effects of this trade-off.

Sen, Amartya. 2002. *Rationality and Freedom.* Cambridge, MA: Belknap and Harvard University Press.

Perhaps the main difference between Sen's impressive analysis of the literature and our book is that we suggest the way out of the impossibility results of social choice turns on the need not "for broadening the informational basis of such choice," as Sen has argued, but on the need for restricting the informational basis of such choice. The problem is that this restriction of information, as many will immediately see, results in higher overall costs. Sen seeks an optimistic way out of Arrow's "pessimism," but he is in a logical trap, for truly broadening the informational basis of social choice will only serve to affirm Arrow's theorem.

Becker, Gary. 1964. *Human Capital: A Theoretical and Empirical Analysis, with Special Reference to Education.* New York: Columbia University Press.

Herein lies the basic deficiency of the human capital approach: orthodox economic models assume that human capital creation can take place in expanding institutions without loss, that the good will retain the essence of its character, and that the growth of scale can only add to and improve the skills, knowledge, values, and habits of people. However, the thought that these aims are in accord is ill conceived and reveals a serious misunderstanding of the affect of institutional structures on the formation of human resources. As we show, it is impossible to satisfy simultaneously the demands of institutional (e.g., education) expansion and the development of human beings in their full inherent complexity.

Friedman, Milton. 1962. *Capitalism and Freedom.* Chicago: University of Chicago Press.
Friedman is, of course, well known for maintaining that market expansion has a net positive bearing on personal freedom, and that the possibilities of individual action are only increased by it. There is much to like about this great book, but in the light of our findings this doctrine no longer seems plausible (We sincerely wish that we are wrong about this).

Nash, John. 1950. "The Bargaining Problem." *Econometrica* 18, no. 2: 155–162.
In our book we reveal the inherent contradiction in the game-theoretical model. Our conclusion is that a theory of equilibrium consistent with the division of information is not possible.

Dewey, John. *The Collected Works of John Dewey, 1882–1953.* Edited by Jo Ann Boydston. Carbondale: Southern Illinois University Press.
What Dewey failed to recognize was the means-ends problem associated with educational production, that his end concerning high-quality, personalized educational experiences for children was logically inconsistent with the imposition of his means, a system of production tied to a technical model working against the end he sought. In Dewey's work an important irony emerges: the means of Dewey's progressive philosophy of education, when actualized in praxis (curriculum and teaching) and policy (social control) transmuted into an inconsistent end—a narrow essentialism that helped to drive the intensification of the technical model of production in education.

Habermas, Jurgen. 1998. *The Inclusion of the Other: Studies in Political Theory.* Cambridge, MA: MIT Press.
There is no small degree of irony in this analysis by Habermas either. Political control is thought to protect the very particular information that is undemocratically (ergo legitimately) sorted from choice by expanding markets. What lies waiting to be discovered is that neither the expansion of markets nor the expansion of politics appears to possess the capacity to fix value, legitimacy, or rationality in traditional notions of the demos, that is to say, if the demos represents the common people, their culture (localism), and protected spheres (rights) for individuals. But in order to expand the domain of politics or markets, rationality under any conceivable scheme of expansion will predictably be separated from philosophies of individual liberty. In this sense, it is clear that

Habermas has accurately calculated the cost of market expansion while at the same time presuming that the cost to political enlargement tends to zero.

Rawls, John. 1971. *A Theory of Justice*. Cambridge, MA: Harvard University Press.

Rawls conceived of an a priori move (the veil of ignorance) whose tenets are entirely consistent with institutional expansion, principally within politics but applicable to the economy as well. These consist of purposively depreciating particular information, divesting personal preferences from the calculus of exchange, through a set of categorical principles and procedures and the highly conscious biasing of universal, collective information. Our theory shows that nullification of particular information is a necessary condition for the evolutionary advance of universal information, especially before expanding political processes, or market forces can mediate trade-offs through an evolutionary turnover in rules and property rights. While Rawls attempts to resolve the tension between the individual and collective in an environment of scarce resources, we demonstrate how that resolution relies upon the division of information and heightens collective interests over individual ones.

De Soto, Hernando. 2000. *The Mystery of Capital: Why Capitalism Thrives in the West and Fails Everywhere Else*. New York: Basic Books.

De Soto endorses a more centralized (state) control over the resources of production. His idea is that the standardization of rules backed by the servant of the public good—the state—is the most appropriate mechanism to reorganize ownership of property and govern the socioeconomic system. The justification for this formalization (i.e., universalization) of property rights is that it will free up underutilized resources and enable people to maximize their production and accumulation of capital. The book portrays the universal rules generated by the state as benevolent impulses, as neutral entities, as nontransmitters of costs. The unquestioned assumption is "impersonal" rules make property rights more secure. What we show is that property rights, however impersonal and well defined, offer only passive resistance to expansion; they are transient standards that must, in the end, make room for more trade. De Soto's bias toward the collective (what is referred to as impersonal) allows him to easily argue the need to shift "the legitimacy of the rights of owners from the politicized context of local communities to the impersonal context of law."

Notes

1. We draw here from North's *Institutions, Institutional Change and Economic Performance* in which he analyzes the process of institutional change and how institutions determine the performance of economies.

2. In *Microeconomics* Bowles offers a comprehensive evolutionary perspective on economic behavior.
3. We thus meet Thomas Kuhn's three-element criterion, in this case, of offering a new theoretical paradigm. See Kuhn (1996: 34).
4. Given that the domain of our examination is complex social systems, our method cannot yield apodictic certainty. Still, we are certain that we can establish the plausibility of our theory of institutions through the nontrivial forces of explanation and logic.
5. See, for example Weber (1949).
6. Here it is important to cite by way of authority Kuhn, who said: "[N]o theory ever solves all the puzzles with which it is confronted at a given time . . . On the contrary, it is just the incompleteness and imperfection of the existing data-theory fit that, at any time, define many of the puzzles that characterize normal science. If any and every failure to fit were ground for theory rejection, all theories ought to be rejected at all times" (1996: 146).

CHAPTER 1

Expansion under Uncertainty

Today, there is a widespread conviction that the filtering of more market transactions through institutions raises the total output of goods and services, and that the gains from this far outweigh the losses. This belief is based on the fact that institutional expansion allows for more economies of scale, that it displaces the less-efficient ways of doing things, that it aids in the free movement of resources, that it enlarges the circle of wealth and relations of exchange. Indeed, from Adam Smith's time to our own, it has been widely believed that there are zero incremental information costs to rising scale, that is, expanding institutions are on net balance cost-saving mechanisms.

However, we have found that as the scale of trade grows, it creates a distortion in the market information system, which then transmits costs not only on alternative forms of production but on the particular ways of life with which they are intertwined. This chapter traces the distortion to the link between rising institutional scale and universal information. The argument here is that this simple relationship brings absolute losses as well as gains; it accounts for a range of effects, including: (1) change in the nature and perceptions of goods, (2) the aggregation of authority, and (3) extension of the collective action domain and abridgement of the individual action domain.

This union of information and institutional scale constitutes a powerful vehicle of transformation. Its logic compels the ways and means of production in terms of resource allocation, the specification of property rights and rules, the manner of competition, reasoning and innovation, the use of language, and conceptions of the good. As we shall show, the standardizing effect of this formula restricts the development of human capital and threatens long-term productive achievement. If we are to understand the costs to other forms of production and to autonomous relations at all levels, seeing this connection is of the essence.

The Information Priorities of Scale

Clearly small-scale institutions do not behave like large-scale institutions. There are different rules and ways of interacting at the larger level, and we experience new forces and different problems of production and exchange. The reason for this is that all things do not scale up in proportion. Or, we might say that all elements are not stressed by growth to the same degree. This problem of scale has been well worked out in areas of engineering and physics. But much less has been done in the social fields, where it deserves closer study than it has so far obtained. Indeed, many changes occur as institutions go up in size, and changes in the stock and flow of information turn out to be the most crucial, especially in regard to the long-term performance of economies.

With this in mind, it is important to recognize that a unifying goal and purpose among existing institutions is the rational increase of trade. More trade is the central thread that connects institutions of every purpose and kind. It is a preeminent goal that derives legitimacy from its identification with the common good; the main idea is that a growing volume of trade is the basis of general prosperity, that it will translate into greater wealth and well-being for individuals and society as a whole. This claim is both valid and important as those who see matters in this light are sufficiently supported by the fact that most people in most places and times have benefited greatly from rising trade. However, the story is not so simple. Placed before us are the costs of expansion—that is, the side effects and unintended consequences that are paid for socially in many forms, and are often discussed in economic literature.[1] While we are concerned with such costs in general, our focus is on a particular cost that has been largely overlooked—the information cost of expansion. Specifically, the price of generating a higher volume of trade is an impersonal drive that forces a choice between universal (lower-cost) information and particular (higher-cost) information. This choice is indispensable to the production of more trade. Indeed, it is an inescapable trade-off, and not merely an option, if expansion is going to take place and be sustained.

As a rule, what an expanding institution wants is more chances to expand. Hence the demand is high for universal information, which can add to and enhance those chances. This undoubtedly is the key to its utility and appeal, that it has the capacity to lower relative prices and raise levels of efficiency of productive operations. By its use there is less dissipation of resources needed to sustain prosperity and growth. The point here is that the selection of information is primarily driven by cost. It is expense that deters an institution from increasing the volume of particular information. As the scale of trade goes up, the competition for limited resources intensifies, which causes the institution to choose the cheaper way.

In essence, a demand for expansion is a demand for production in accordance with universal rules as opposed to particular rules, namely, policies for small numbers or arbitrary personal aims. In this sense the growth of trade is coextensive with universal information as such, that is, the degree to which universal information as a factor of production is a necessary condition to sustain institutional expansion. This, then, is the principle that ties together the arguments of this book: that the interdependence between institutional expansion and universal information is foundational. It is a necessary unity and an ongoing influence at the deepest economic level.

The Division of Information

The greater the scale the more an institution must concentrate on common characteristics—similarities—and not on things that tend to differentiate. This demand for sameness requires the use of universal information, which has two primary characteristics that join it to the logic of expansion or large-scale production: (1) its cost effectiveness, that is, its ease (lower relative cost) of handling or processing; and (2) its capacity for developing cooperation and trade on an impersonal level. Expanding institutions prefer universal information because it has the characteristic and function of lowering the cost of production; it is mostly measurable, predictable, consistent, and order generating—all attributes that tend to make communication easier, that facilitate calculation, and enable trade to move forward toward impersonal exchange.

Particular information is at variance with these features and aims. The particular entails the possibility of conflict of values, of an incompatibility between the vast variety of claims and differing purposes of diverse groups of human beings. These particularities are the dynamic concepts and categories, the mostly qualitative information whose properties are inherently variable, inconsistent, uncertain, and hard to measure; these are the sources of friction and noise within an institution, those rough edges and unsorted-out situations that tend to divide and disintegrate. The use of this information can lead to higher production costs, which, as a consequence, has an inhibiting effect on growth.

That these two classes of information push in different directions makes possible their division, which in turn paves the way for expansion. The process begins with the economizing choices of individual agents under conditions of scarcity, becomes normalized by the formation of rules, and gains momentum by the growth of scale. Its sequence stretches across time and involves a multiplicity of individual decisions to trade off some preferred values and ends for other preferred values and ends. With cost (in money or other terms) as a guide, the trade-offs decided upon become an instrument of disequilibrium. Whether unintended or the result of calculated choice, they propagate an order in which the mix of information becomes progressively abstract and uneven. At first no pattern is obvious, but as production grows, the demand for universal information rises and becomes the primary demand.

This elevation of the universal cuts across the spectrum of institutions and makes its presence strongly felt by its disposition to behave in a lawlike manner. The recurrent tendency is for the growth of scale to excite this ordering of information. Yet, there is no formalized process for the division of information; there is no broad consensus of an optimal method. In each market the division of information will be more or less systematic depending upon the play of numerous factors that relate to the institutional frame of reference and to differences in the relative scarcities of means for ends, that is, for the kind of good that is being produced.

The suggestion here is that the survival of information in an economic system is not solely a matter of cost or convenience (though cost is the dominant factor). There is a range of possibilities stretching before any institutional framework that can affect the pace and magnitude of the information trade-off. The process is sensitive to differences of context, of viewpoints, of attitudes, to time horizons, and to different commitments and aims. And there is the influence as well of differences in capital, technology, organization, and methods of coercion. The selective division of information can in fact be offset by a change in some parameter, an ad hoc decision, a breakthrough in technology, a political development, a new problem or opportunity, or a rise or fall in prices; external events and forms of human action may emerge that alter the direction and allocation of resources. The special characteristics of each market play their part in determining the extent of constancy of the division of information; all, or any, of these together can cause the information content of institutions to be divisible in varying rates and degrees.

Seen from several perspectives, this turbulent state of affairs can produce what looks like purely random behavior. But the fact that different institutional arrangements deal with this parting of information in different ways and with different degrees of effectiveness does not alter the underlying order. The reality of this trend is not discountable; it exists independent of the particular institutional setting, whether that is financial, political, or social. In terms of increasing scales, the same pattern of trading off one kind of information for another applies to complexity in all institutional settings; it persists in the face of various disturbances and continues through time on its low-cost (universal) trajectory.

The important thing to know is that the progressive rise of scale (the increasing volume of output and trade) changes the kind of information that can be effectively utilized in production. That is to say, as scale increases, the fact that resources are scarce changes the collective investment and forces a separation of the particular forms of information from the productive process. In considering a pattern of this sort, it is correct to assume that as an institution expands, the aim always is to displace the less efficient with the more efficient, to open new doors to trade, to increase the level of demand. Thus it cannot avoid the call to standardize; it cannot avoid a transformation of its productive process; and, as a result, it cannot avoid a change in the nature of its good.

All this being so, we can find no conclusion but that this imbalance in the distribution of information creates benefits and costs jointly. The benefits side is clear—it reduces certain costs and is of great assistance in increasing efficiencies of output and trade. But as we have said, this division of information, as an imperative of expansion, incrementally changes the nature and, what is equally important, the perceptions of the goods being produced. While the conventional view, with its focus on the efficient, tends to surround the effects of expansion with optimistic interpretations, our analysis is quite different. We contend that the process of institutional expansion coincides, paradoxically enough, with a certain loss of information, and that this culminates, through the resultant change in the good, in a smaller number of options, in a reduced range of open possibilities. The key problem is that much information, some of it uniquely valuable, gets excluded in the transition from one institutional scale of production to another, and that this loss of information flow is of utmost value (cost) to the production of markets and to the vitality of human exchange.

To put matters in this way is to argue that the institutions of expanding markets are dissipative systems, in the sense that they lose information to cost. It is clear that to expand as intended, the institution must expel those irregular elements and loose ends of individual experience. It must progressively displace the nonuniform inputs and confine the process of production to that which alone is constant, measurable, and capable of fitting into a rational plan. The entire trend of such an order is to head in the direction of least cost, toward a uniformity of rules, toward a condition in which the institution becomes an alliance for the ease of trade.

It is hardly irrelevant to note in this respect that the orthodox view does not anticipate that the rise in scale may adversely affect the production of the good. The pervasive assumption is that every stage of institutional growth and every consequent enhancement of output (being a response to demand) redound to the benefit of business and consumers, that this raises the standard of living for great numbers of human beings, and that the new conditions will undoubtedly provide more satisfaction than the old. The inveterate tendency is to regard any loss associated with such expansion as negligible when compared with the gains received.

Yet to adopt such a view, plausible as it may seem, is to ignore, if not to deny entirely, the presence of uncertainty in these matters. For it is by no means true that we know the full effects of institutional expansion in all of their ramifications. In any given instance we must proceed with less-than-complete information, that is, there must always be some degree of doubt as to whether the eventual results of an increase in scale are in the long-term interest of society at large.[2] Are we moving in a desirable direction? What will be the effect of our actions? May not that which is thought good in one generation be regarded as bad in the next? The fact that it is a common state of mind to conceive of economic growth as unambiguously good, to view it almost entirely as a humane proposal, is no proof that it might not lead to devitalizing distortions of the good, that it might not preclude socially productive exchange; that it might not obstruct useful developments and deprive many of what is important to them.

From all of the above it should be clear that the benefits of expansion do not necessarily outweigh the costs. The historical record supports our claim that market expansion has the potential for both positive and negative results, and there is plenty of uncertainty and grounds for disagreement. With this in mind, we now put the focus back on the cost side (the underestimated harmful effects) and bring to the fore the main mechanism that generates them. We have thus far established this mechanism as the interplay between the rising scale of production and universal information. What is in prospect here are the ways in which this linkage stimulates change in the framework of the institution and in the nature of goods it produces. The crucial issue is how such a change comes about, and what it entails in terms of the processes and factors of production. For the claim we are making is that the effects of these changes in the vast range of goods, of both subtle and radical form, can reach well beyond the specific institution through which they take place; they have implications, bright and dark, not only for the strength of the economic system, but also for the cause of individual thought and liberty.

Institutional Change

We understand institutional change to be that which contains the entire framework of institutional experience. This means nothing less than that which takes place in the form of thought and practice throughout the system, that is, in the specification of rules, regulations, contracts, property rights, etc., and in the change in norms, customs, skills, speech, drives, values, hopes, and fears.[3] All of the elements that make up the structure of human interaction, the complex network of communication, exist and function as part of one another, as a kind of circle of doing or making, as the instruments and relations of production.

In simplest terms, institutional change is the supplanting of the old model of production with a new one. It is, in effect, a change in factor prices and proportions. But what needs to be stressed, since it is little known, is that this change includes more than an adjustment in an inanimate, material thing; it also involves a change in the basic categories that govern our central concepts of the good, an altered view of utility, of what is valuable and profitable, of what is the perceived optimum pattern of behavior. In other words, worldviews are not unaffected by the changes that take place in production. Thought patterns and perceptions of the good adjust to institutional incentives and change along with the characteristics production covers. Thus, a full account of this change ought to show that it is an effort to embody a new vision of the good in both physical and nonphysical dimensions. And no analysis that ignores this fact can begin to understand that a change in the nature of the good is part of the very essence of institutional change.

What we have been suggesting is that institutional change is a reorganization of information, that it is a rational adjustment to a cost difference in information, and that this reorganization paves the way, in a progression of steps, to (1) a redistribution of scarce resources; (2) a reconstruction of the image people have of their work and activities, the basic empirical content of what is thought and felt; and (3) a reconfiguration of the model in which it is organized. The process develops through the aggregation of individual choice orderings, the millions of decisions to trade off one desire, goal, or need for another. These trade-offs alter the form and composition of the information base, which means they induce change in the provision of rules and maximizing opportunities, the direction of learning and trials, the discourse and logic—all the existing formal and informal constraints of the institution. As these constraints vary so do the prospects for production and consumption, for quality control and quantity of output, and for trade of the good.

At this point it bears repeating that the most pervasive influence affecting this shift is expansion (i.e., the rise in scale or volume of output and trade). And at the heart of expansion is the issue of the division of information (i.e., the displacement of particular by universal information). Now two things are to be especially observed here as bringing out the significance of this relationship. The first is that it has the effect of diverting resources into the least-cost means of producing the good. Each surge of growth serves to drive the distribution away from the particular, toward the universal. That is to say, it moves the system to adopt standardized rules and methods of production, low component costs and techniques that are conducive to large-scale output of a uniform product. Generally speaking, as scale goes up, production will ascend from the concrete to the general; from more to less variation; from an irregular, dynamic model to a more fixed or static model. Second, it has the further effect of altering the belief structure that supports the institution, the ways in which the states of experience are perceived and interpreted, creating a view of progress as collective and impersonal.

We may picture the union of rising institutional scale and universal information as a process that promotes and affirms growth as an end. Its chief purpose is to capture more gains from trade. To that end, it tries to dissolve all conflict and turmoil by removing them from the structure of normal thought and practice. The trend is toward the smooth and harmonious, toward a frictionless system in which differences are, as far as possible, eliminated, and the influences of independent judgment and personal aims are reduced and pressed into a single, uniform pattern. The principal thrust of this movement is to furnish the maximizing framework with rules that conform to universal interests, those that work to standardize and raise the level of prediction and control. In other words, it installs rules that increase the prospects of expansion and a higher rate of return. But while this process may translate into a greater supply of goods and services, it has by now become impossible to think of it as harmless.

In the unfolding of this order, the particular appears as a constantly diminishing sphere of private action, as a receding area of self-expression, as fewer divergent paths to pursue, as a weaker defense of variety, as smaller local life. The logic of this order requires particular information to be regarded as the root of discord and chaos, as forming irrational exceptions to the rules intending greater output of production and trade. These trends raise important questions about the designation of what is good and worthy of production, about the effects of particular inputs becoming scarcer factors of production. They lead us to ask, specifically, how the movement toward the universal transmits costs, how this mechanism modifies production probabilities, and what, due to the loss of information, is prevented from being produced and exchanged? In other words, what is the value of the excluded information?

Technical Model of Production

We have up to this point argued that the economizing constraints of expansion tend to increase the flow of information in one direction and decrease it in another. And that it is this division or trade-off of information that alters categories of thought no less than the physical aspects of goods. As this subject is considered further, it will be apparent that the interactions of rising scale and the division of information facilitate the imposition of universal laws and policies (regularities), and—more important—through such impositions the scope and content, and thus the potential utility, of many goods are greatly diminished.

How all this comes about has been suggested earlier. It is that the growth of scale creates within itself a momentum toward a technical model of production. We can think of this gravitation toward the technical model as the path of least cost, or a process of substitution: universal in place of particular information, abstract and general forms as opposed to concrete and specific forms, more unity and less variety; it is the rise of impersonal factors and relations instead of personal distinctions; it is the physical and sense bound over things that cannot be sensuously comprehended; it is numbers in place of morals. In its strong or extreme form, the technical approach embodies its own vision of reality: one of efficient means and universal ends, of belief in the unbreakable link between cause and effect, of a symmetrical set of rules and wholly explicable laws, whose categories are the categories of abstraction, of mathematical reasoning and language in terms of causal uniformities.[4] It is a view in which all real statements about the world must be reducible to generalization and capable of calculation.

In its developing form, the technical model is a summarizer and a collector of similarities. Its aim and purpose is to unify measures of the good, to codify a common understanding of good work and commercial propriety, and to remove barriers to consolidation and control. This move toward universal measures and standards allows for stable, controllable expansion. The same measurements, the same rules and laws, the same terminology and viewpoint, the same "fair" conditions lead to a convergence of means and ends and to a wider sphere of trade. As the institution expands, it reacts to the competition for scarce resources by arranging itself in opposition to the unique and particular. This opens the way to a more streamlined structure of production that advances on the grounds of its ability to (1) sustain accumulation and handle large volumes of information, (2) integrate units of production, (3) lower the costs of decision making, (4) decrease the unpredictability of events, and (5) create a system of reliable expectations. The model derives its legitimacy from the growth of scale and the higher returns to capital that it tends to generate. Expansion of output and trade is the prime mover toward the technical model. And the repeated satisfactions of moving production in this direction reinforce the previous decisions and provide decision makers with incentives to stay on the course.

But it is important to emphasize in this connection that the shift toward the technical model is a matter of degree and will vary with institutions. The absolute size and rate of this change often depends on multiple factors, the origin of which may lie inside or outside a given system. Every institution has its own history and traditions, its own mode of belief, its own direction in which to obtain answers, its own illusions and legitimate operations that may quicken or delay the pace of this change. Thus there is, as a rule, no simultaneous or equal shift in productive practices. Each institution creates a different kind of good and each must deal with different relative scarcities of resources to do so. Nevertheless, in whatever form, and in whatever activities they engage, we assume the pattern to hold. That is, as institutions expand, the general trend will be to formalize production in the technical direction.

The significance of this shift will be clearer once we spell out its implications. As might be anticipated, the more technical the approach the more the institution must turn qualitative distinctions into quantitative ones; the more it must deal with instances of the type, not the individual; and the more it must simplify its productive structure and in the process become increasingly irrelevant to the production of certain (complex) kinds of goods. It is this last point, in fact, that is central to our thesis. We have found that the information imbalance associated with expansion leads to a growing disjuncture between the mode of production and the reality (subject matter) to which it is applied. In more basic terms, the simplified means that arise from the growth of scale are unsuitable for the production of complex goods.

Goods, of course, come in diverse forms and vary in their complexity across time. And for many highly complex goods it is the case that the individual human being is the primary factor of production. These would include goods such as health care, education, the arts, law, religion, and so forth. The relationships of all such goods, or we may use the term "systems," produce nonlinear types of behavior; in every instance, extensive variation (noise) dominates the component parts of the data. Bear in mind that it is the kind of information, more than the volume, which is the key to their complexity. Consider the information that is discontinuous, that cannot yield precise definitions, that has no exact boundaries to measure, that is unpredictable—all of it is part of the nature of complex phenomena, and all of it applies to the field of human relations. A complex good is an unstable world, one that thrives mainly on individualized information, on rival ends and purposes, on improvisations and peculiarities, on the crooked lines of human thought and action.

Nothing tends to be more appealing than free self-expression, spontaneous or ad hoc events, artistic creativity, novelty and change, but these are not often compatible with a capacity for precise planning and control, with some fixed pattern or imposed blueprint of a logical structure. Arguing that the idea of distinction itself is not natural to the technical model; that it must, from the very nature of its interests, reduce the good to its common elements; marshal the data into a uniform, planned order; bring greater certainty of results by creating conditions in which production will unfold exactly the same way each time; we may now draw the conclusion, as common sense suggests, that there is no development in it of a capacity for production of the basic attributes and constitution of complex goods.

It is hard to overstate the significance of this problem of means and ends. For we see each phase of institutional expansion as leading to another turn of the technical screw, to a perpetual tightening of production, and thus to a decrease in the number and kinds of characteristics that production covers. The point is not merely theoretical. For the technical model sets up prescriptions that make it impossible to adequately produce or describe the dynamic process of complex social reality. Indeed, the greater the complexity of the good, the more susceptible it is to the distortions (simplifications) of the mechanistic framework.

We should at once make clear that the efficiency of the technical model is not in question. What is in question is its sufficiency as a source of information. Its narrow and precisely defined boundaries omit too much; they cannot adequately deal with the social phenomena with which much of production is concerned. The social web is too intricate and complex, the facts, things, events too many for the logic of the formal scheme. Indeed, the very strength of the model is because of its exclusion of all but a very narrow set of recurrent similarities, chosen samples, and also because of noting only the common characteristics of human experience. As we have said, the technical model binds production to universal information. But this does not mean that there is no infusion of particular information. It means, rather, that it is not being augmented, that it is being subordinated and excluded from the productive agenda. It means that as scale rises, particular information becomes a dissolving influence, a factor that fades into the collective scene, bearing less and less fruit within the institution. All of which, again, suggests the linkage between expansion and the division of information.

What this pattern serves to bring out is that the drive to expand inclines the institution to select and use more controllable forms of information. As it does this it pressures the institutional framework to subtract details; to create a simpler production structure; and to relegate individual will, values, and beliefs to less-significant positions. Expansion inclines the institution to magnify the ideas of uniformity and of continuing progress toward harmonizing conflicting interests. In a sense, it compels the institution to become a protest against exception, an opponent of distinction, and to lay insufficient stress on the importance of the human component in production.

Rules of Production

Much of the literature on institutions separates rules from production, institutions from markets. This separation, however, cannot be maintained in the light of the division of information. Under expansion, the rules become progressively biased in favor of the collective. As scale increases, the rules raise the price of the individual as a factor of production. Therefore, it is not mere speculation to argue that scale (growth) automatically imposes costs on markets. Markets must lose information as they expand because the rules underpinning them must divide on the basis of the cost of information. This, indeed, is why expansion leads to a more dominant role for institutions in the economy.

This joining of the rules to production calls into question several assumptions about institutional development: (1) that universal rules maximize the public good, that they advance a neutral protocol, and that they are on net balance cost-reducing mechanisms in the economy;[5] (2) that expanding markets can exist independent of a larger state, or, that the scope of state actions grows simply because it represents a clamoring of special interests;[6] and (3) that the movement toward the universal has no negative bearing on personal freedom, that the possibilities of individual action are not limited by this move.

Suffice it here to say that we find no compelling grounds for these claims; they do not seem to match with the way things really are. Yet, what these assumptions describe could conceivably be true; they could be true if resources were not limited and if information were free with respect to the institutional construction of rules. But the problem, of course, is that information is not a free good; it has an inherent cost that asserts itself in rules. Hence, it begins to look as if neutral institutions (rules) cannot be drawn up. Indeed, if they are conveyors of incomplete information, that is to say, if they are not free from the reality of scarcity, and if they have a bias, we must, by necessity, accept the fact that institutions are sources and transmitters of costs. And if this is true, we must accept that these costs define and transform production probabilities and that preferences absorb these costs somewhere in the economic system.

Now when we speak of preferences we usually mean first choices. But for the present, we can stretch the term to also include values, beliefs, desires, and the social relations that inevitably accompany them; here they are not merely attributes of consumption but essential aspects and potential forms of production. In many ways they represent the impulse to create.

With this in mind, it is instructive to note that from an economic point of view preferences are indistinguishable; they have no inherent value or cost until they run up against price (in a market) or rules (in an institution). The rules transmit a cost onto these preferences; cost becomes activated by the interaction of a source (rules) and an absorber (preferences). This means that at any given time the cost of a preference is the degree of dissonance between it and the source with which it interacts. Or, we can put it this way: a preference that lines up with the rules absorbs fewer costs than one that conflicts with the rules. Thus it is clear that preferences, which themselves are always changing, have varying degrees of cost. They are, in a way, forces to control in institutions.

If the above account of the matter is correct, it suggests that particular preferences (values, etc.), and the forms of production they represent are, to a large extent, scale dependent. The main reason for this is that scale alters the information structure of rules. Recall that as the scale of production and trade grows, the contest for scarce resources biases the trade-offs of information and establishes a universal direction in production. The trend, which no expanding institution can evade, is to increasingly standardize the rules of production, that is, to specify the property rights, laws, policies, and norms and customs around the collective. What matters is the ability of rules to generate higher profits; that they become the tools with which to maintain the flow of investment and trade; that they lower risk and uncertainty, ease distributive conflicts, and coordinate exchange across sectors. Indeed, as rules change and become more uniform and impersonal (i.e., apply to more cases), they work to alter the prices of inputs. The effect is to lower the overall production costs on the side of the collective, and at the same time to raise the costs elsewhere—on the side of the individual.

This point is all important for understanding that rules, specifically property rights, however well defined or universal, do not function to lower costs in any absolute sense in the social system. Instead, as scale grows, they shift the burden of cost from one source of information onto another. In other words, they redistribute cost or uncertainty in the economy: from one set of preferences onto another, from the universal onto the particular, from the collective onto the individual. Now if we proceed on the assumption that this is the role that expanding institutions play, then we have the possibility that the universalizing trend that parallels expansion may in fact yield a higher balance of costs in the social system.

To explore the prospect of rising costs, it is essential to see that there is no finality or permanence to rules in an expanding system. Rules go through a cycle in which trade grows outside the purview of the existing rule structure. This leads to problems of internal discord and chaos, and to a progressive loss of control, as the rules no longer seem to operate successfully and begin to lose legitimacy. The arena of institutional rules must enlarge to embrace the new trade, but this requires a reformulation of the rules—substituting more universal information for particular information. As we have seen, the rules must become more universal before they can animate plans for further expansion.

The cost problem associated with institutional expansion is that the old rule set, which once was seen as universal information, now becomes seen as particular information. This occurs because each sequence of expansion involves a disruption of the rules and a transmission of cost on previous information—on rules of an earlier phase. These costs alter the matrix of rational choice, pressuring actors to see the old rule set as obsolete and as something to abandon (defect); eventually almost everyone defects and accepts the new order of rules. That becomes the rational choice in the system: the choice matrix reorganizes around the larger sphere of trade and the rule set(s) that support that trade. The crucial thing from our perspective is that the loss of information increases as universals transform into particulars; costs rise overall as yesterday's universals become today's particulars.

Expansion, as may now be seen, is not a straight road to more secure rules or property rights; it imposes costs on existing property rights and relations (Hallowell 1943; Demsetz 1967; Sax 1983; and Barzel 1989). Whereas an owner of property may once have been able to dispose of it in any way that he wished, he now becomes bound up, (constrained) by more universal rules that weaken his old (preexisting) property rights. He cannot sell or trade his property (fire a worker, sell his land) just because he wants to. Indeed, rights become more, not less, rooted in the polity (the collective) as trade expands. The property rights of the individual become less under his control. He becomes more accountable to and dependent on the collective. The efficiency of production and the assessment of property rights needed to support that production are constantly shifting away from the valuations of individuals toward the valuation of the social whole. This shift is being driven not primarily by power and politics but by expansion and the information cost of rule making itself, by the reallocation of scarce resources associated with the making of rules.

Given the material and ideological advantages of expansion, it is hardly surprising that few connect it with the idea of loss or even inconvenience. On the contrary, the growth of scale provokes confidence in the idea of the institution as a system of nondenial; it becomes identified with the common good, that is, with the avenue to various forms of human happiness—to higher status, economic strength, social freedom, and so forth. The rules of expansion wear the appearance of unlimited opportunity; they are not seen as blocking any doors, as being a restraint on freedom of choice. On the face of it, the forfeit of independent thought and action does not seem to be required. Indeed, all the facts seem to favor the conviction that one may retain the freedom of rational self-direction, and one may continue to hold on to all values and ideals as strictly and as passionately as ever.

But this is neither true nor even plausible. For the plain reality is that over time the logic of expansion alters the content and meaning of these values and beliefs. They attach themselves to a different conceptual base. The gains derived from expansion anchor conceptions of rationality (the common good) to rules that promise greater expansion—rules that do not engage the irrational self-interest of particular preferences. In other words, as the scale of trade grows, what fulfills the claims of rationality shifts toward the universal. And out of this shift comes the view that to be fully rational in thought and behavior is to cling to and identify oneself with the true nature of human progress—namely, with the path and structure of expansion. As this change in categories and vision takes place, the means of self-expression is more and more in the wider whole; self-fulfillment becomes social fulfillment; and, in the end, the collective vision becomes the personal vision.

From this it is natural, and almost inevitable, that growing numbers of human beings would come to view government (the state) as the most rational means to expansionist ends. This view entails the belief that there is no higher or better mechanism by which to establish rules of competition, adjudicate rival claims, weld diverse elements together, and enlarge and protect the frontiers of trade. It is clear, as the discussion in the next chapter will show, that developments in this direction have now gone very far. For the state, as the authority of reason, has assumed regulatory control over progressively more aspects of life. Indeed, the public in general sees no sense in curbing or curtailing the authority of the state; instead the tendency is to prop up the enlarged realm and role of the state within the economy as the most effectual means to public power and collective self-direction.

All that is necessary here is to recognize that the growth of institutional scale requires the replacement of particular by universal information. And that the systemic effects of this trade-off center on the loss of personal liberty: it removes more of the human component from the realm of production; it breeds less fear of dependence on the state; and it narrows the range of options and choices open to all. An economy whose costs exceed its benefits may nevertheless continue to expand.

Notes

1. There is a vast literature on the question of social costs, externalities, and spill-over effects. See, for example, Coase (1960).
2. For an in-depth discussion of the presence of uncertainty in the economy see Knight (1921), Schmidt (1996), and Alchian (1950).
3. See North (1990, 2005). See also Eggertsson (2001: 76–104).
4. See, for example, the classic works by Whitehead (1938) and Popper (2002).
5. For a discussion on the function and possible neutrality of general rules, see Hayek (1960).
6. The special interest argument is central to the theory of public choice. See Buchanan and Tullock (1962).

CHAPTER 2

The State: An Information Theory

The search for the causes of government growth, and in particular the question of why there must be further extensions of the government's decision-making power (despite the record of repressive systems this has led to down through the ages), brings us to what perhaps has been scarcely recognized at all, namely, that the market and the state (government) function to reinforce each other's growth through the division of information. From the point of view of the state, the order of this process can be broken down as follows: (1) the state divides or narrows the information base available to social choice through the use and development of rules that conform to universal interests; (2) these rules increase probabilities of production by lowering costs in one direction and decrease probabilities of production by raising costs in another; and (3) the demand for the services of the state goes up on both sides of the market—on the cost-saving (universal) side and on the cost-raising (particular) side of production.

As we attempt to explain this trend we should not forget that there is a need for universal rules that promote the increase of trade irrespective of the source of those rules—whether they arise from government, business cartels, or the market itself. As we well know, each of these areas produces general rules; but it is clear that the state, more than other forms of organization, has the strength and legitimacy to create and enforce rules that apply to every agent and transaction within a given sphere of trade. As an overarching institution, it can effectuate economies of scale that other entities with stronger attachments to the particular cannot match. Like the firm, the state can economize on the information costs of production by applying the same set of information to many cases. With its complex network of dependencies, this form of authority has the capacity to unify measures and standardize property rights across economic zones and markets; it cuts across all loyalties and aims to bring about no autonomous ends.

The point is that the universality of rules translates into opportunities for increasing the sum of output and investment, and there is little doubt that such rules induce the growth of trade. As the gains from growth pile up, they procure legitimacy for the rules and heighten the demand for the system that makes and enforces them. This, in turn, enlarges the capacity of the state to standardize the rules of competition that function to arrest the flow of particular information. The agencies of the state do not conserve particular (i.e., individual or private) information, since the costs imposed by these rules drain it away.

The thing we must stress is that the rules of expansion transmit costs to particulars, and that these costs—whether low or high, short-term or long-term—change the objective situation. They make their presence felt in a decline of discovery in the sphere of the particular, in changes that occur in the nature of goods, and in the cessation of production—in the multiplicity of mutual exchanges that do not take place. All of this is in keeping with the spread of universal rules, which by nature are not conducive to the survival or increase of particular ideals and preferences or to the prospective ways of life connected with them. The function of such rules is to limit prerogatives and to define particulars out of existence.

What stands out is that by creating rules that forward the interests of the universal (collective), the state provides for its own continuance and expansion. For as the rules purge the higher-cost information from the realm of production, individuals and groups increasingly turn to the government to obtain from it what they want and need. More people must appeal to the state and enlist its power to preserve the desires and values of local and personal life. In time, and by virtue of the origin of these rules, people come to accept something that opposes their own individual interests. They come more and more to believe that what matters is the many, not the one, and that only by affirming the centralized activities of the state is it possible to realize values, maintain order, and increase the sum of production and trade.

The logic set out here implies that the state constrains the flow and price of information, and that this is the principal means by which the state expands. By creating more rules that conform to collective interests, the state serves to widen the cost difference between universal and particular information. As described earlier, this adds pressure to the system of decision making, in which the changing cost of information (preferences) induces a series of trade-offs that in turn transform the information base of the economy as a whole. It creates a distortion in the information field that sets a least-cost direction to production, shifting it to an impersonal (collective) plane.

This shift in the flow and use of information becomes the basis for a change in the relationship between authority and production. The reason for this change, which by now should be fairly clear, is that the state and universal information are mutually dependent. The state, which embodies the collective, functions, as a matter of routine, to create and process universal information. Its bureaucratic structure is singularly suited to manage this information from a distance; indeed, it feeds on and draws strength from large volumes of it. Thus it follows that the economy that has a growing proportion of universal information, that is, whose rules extend to cover the ever-expanding network of trade, will, in time, shift more of the command over the resources of production to the agencies of the state. This can only have the effect of entrusting more power to the state and deepening its bonds to production. It endows the state with the capacity to organize and direct investment and to gain control of future development.

Rather than the authority of the government showing signs of being a collapsing order, we see exactly the reverse: an expanding scope of state intervention at all levels of society, a growing volume of government purchases and production, and an increase in the aggregate demand for the basic services of the state. The examples that follow will help convey the idea that this change in the attributes of rules accelerates the forces of centralization and raises the importance of the state as a producer of the good. With the build-up of universal rules and the gains in order, efficiency, and real output that tend to follow, the state increasingly has the last word on what stays and what goes, on what is worthy and unworthy of production. Eventually, with the progressive rise of institutional scale, the state becomes synonymous with production, a common means to achieve diverse ends.

This view of the state may seem foreign to those used to seeing a sharp distinction drawn between the logic of markets and the logic of politics. Here, and in other sections of this book, we use the established phrase "politics and markets" without holding to the usual sharp distinction that is made between the two concepts. Our working assumption is that politics and markets are not autonomous or separate domains. Indeed, we argue that political, economic, and cultural institutions interact across markets and determine their efficiency and the range of choice in production and exchange. In order to understand our work, one first must recognize that it is cutting a pathway between economics and the state separate from the one opened by public choice theory. In essence, we are offering an alternative to public choice with respect to the economic origin of state behavior and its consequence. The two theories need not falsify one another. They can coexist because neither claims to be a comprehensive theory of the state. Each observes the state through a discrete analytic lens and each focuses on a different terrain.

We break with public choice because we approach the state through a different theoretical construct. Whereas public choice enters the state through the logic of the rational actor seeking to maximize economic self-interest, our theory follows the logic of cost (scarcity), specifically the varying cost of utilizing different kinds of information in the making and enforcing of rules. This means that it can not only carry the weight of more robust human motivation (an altruist would need to face up to the problem of cost), but that it can also see a continuity between the rule making of the state and that which takes place in markets—in both spheres the principle of maximization is subject to an information (cost) constraint that we identify as the incremental trade-off of particular for universal information. This allows us to view the state as an institution (or set of institutions), and to exclude the public choice view that separates politics (the state) and markets based on the distinction between decisions involving primarily private and public goods. In our theory, differentiation of product is not fundamentally important. The state responds like other institutions to the stresses and constraints of scale and scarcity.

Both theories posit an information loss that occurs as the state seeks to make rules. But each locates the origin of this loss differently. We see the origin of the loss as embedded in scarcity (cost).[1] Public choice identifies the loss as residing in the discontinuity between individual and collective rationality. It holds that the enterprise of the state fails because the public good that it is called upon to produce (the product) is incompatible with the economic interests of the individuals who make governmental decisions. Any public choice arising from individual, economically self-interested participation, therefore, represents a bias, a loss of information, which manifests itself as an underproduction of the public interest.

One faction of public choice looks upon this inefficiency as a maladjustment, a problem potentially resolvable through the discovery of a superordinate set of constitutional rules that secure consensus.[2] What this endeavor implies is that information is abundant, but for self-interest. Nudging this logic forward, it means that in the absence of self-interest (1) the rules could be written without bias, that they could retain neutrality among competing conceptions of the good; and (2) that it could solve the problem of the identification of fair and cognizable public interest. This, in turn, leads to the possibility that competing values, such as justice and efficiency, can be united under the umbrella of a neutral constitutional framework, that there would be no incompatibility or conflict between ultimate values in such a system.[3]

In chapter 5 we undertake an extended critique of this normative effort. Suffice it to say here that we do not believe the problem is fundamentally one of self-interest. The problem is that information is inherently unstable and asymmetric, which means that it is a costly and therefore scarce good. Even "if men were angels," the problem of scarcity would manifest itself in the information trade-off required in rule making. Scale intensifies those trade-offs and from that shifts the structure of rules and directs these toward the universal rather than the particular. Both public and private realms are subject to the effects of this trade-off.

Taken as a whole, our work projects a very different view of the state and its role in production than the one portrayed by public choice theory. Public choice finds government failure just about everywhere it looks. It sees a state ensnarled in rent seeking, chaotic social choice, and the elevation of individual interest over the collective. We do not deny the importance and relevance of this research, but we believe it represents an incomplete picture of what is taking place. Behind the day-to-day hubbub of pork-barrel politics and logrolling lurks the constraint of cost. This constraint, we argue, gives rise to progressive uniformity in the structure of rules; and this proves to be the basis for the following.

- Least cost redirection of markets: The division of information enables social choice by redistributing costs—lowering costs in the direction of the universal and increasing them on the particular. This redistribution of cost allows institutions (such as the state) to secure direction by altering the returns on preferences and the production possibilities they represent. Preferences that align with more universal rules see increasing returns whereas rising costs mute voices in favor of particular information. This means that the division of information weakens the grip of Arrow's impossibility theorem on the polity, permitting directional social choice to occur under the aegis of assent and without invoking a dictator. In essence, the calculation of self-interest, the preference set, and the ideological construction of the social good are all being reshaped as multiple votes take place over time under the incrementally changing cost constraints associated with institutional expansion.

- Increasing prevalence of centralized forms of production: The division of information favors a technical model of production. In markets, this form of production gives rise to the large (corporate) firm, and in mature markets, to the tendency toward oligopoly. In politics, it manifests itself in a more centralized state, one whose jurisdictional reach encompasses a larger sphere of trade. The reason for this change in production is that the division of information confers economies of scale on planned production. National building and electrical codes, for example, enable firms to utilize the same construction information (plan) again and again, thereby substantially lowering marginal construction costs relative to that which would pertain in an environment of different local rules. Governments likewise expand on the proposition that political centralization will enable the society to capture the gains of trade made possible by more universal rules. The political principle of subsidiarity (local government) gets sacrificed for more centralized control over an expanding zone of trade. In essence, the demand for growth requires an institutional trade-off of information— local control (the particular) for centralization (the universal).

- Convergence of public and private ends and means of production: The division of information integrates the market and the state. Both expand on the substitution of universal for particular information, and both tend to become functionally integrated by that information. We demonstrate this proposition in chapter 5 by showing how a central policy recommendation of public choice theory (vouchers and privatization of public education) is undercut by the information convergence that takes place between markets and the state. Contrary to the expectation of voucher advocates, the differences between the two sectors are narrowing rather than widening. Ironically, much of the standardization uniting the two sectors has its informational origin in the market (standardized tests, accreditation, college and university admission's requirements). This is to be expected because the distinction between markets and politics becomes attenuated through the interaction of scale and information.

- Shift of economic and social valuation away from the individual toward the collective: The division of information shifts the reference point for judging value in the institution. The position of the individual at the center of economic transaction diminishes as the rules disengage from local culture, norms, and mores. As an instrument of growth, it becomes rational for the institution to narrow the range of values and to elevate the rules beyond the reach of particular preferences by selecting information universal to an expanding domain of trade. Efficiency, therefore, comes increasingly to be identified with the collective. Goods become labeled "public" or "private" not in terms of their economic characteristics, but in terms of their conformity to universal rules. Keep in mind that this relationship of the individual to the collective will look very different depending upon the unit of analysis. When trade grows outside the purview of the institution, the existing rules absorb cost, lose legitimacy, and become seen as a source of inefficiency. From this perspective, growth appears to sponsor individualism because it frees individuals from the constraints of the old rules. But growth eventually brings greater, not less, centralization, for the new rules must become more universal in order to sustain and nurture economic expansion. As such, they widen the cost difference between information in the institution, and shift the burden of cost from the universal onto the particular, from the collective onto the individual. This means that the fundamental political trade-off in economic expansion is not the one public choice puts forward. Public choice presents us with "politics without romance" (to use Buchanan's phrase) but sees the market as providing a refuge for the human spirit. Ours is a more somber appraisal based on the disobedience of scarcity. It suggests that the primary choice lies not between the market and the state, but between growth and freedom.

The examples developed below will explore the characteristics of this process. When taken together they lend support to our contention that the logic of expansion renders government control over decision making more necessary, that it offers no permanent restriction on the scope of political intervention, and that it places a high cost on the desire to go one's own way, to be apart from the collective will and pattern of social development.[4]

The Delocalization of Measures

For centuries the problem was this: too many different standards of weights and measures. The trade of nations suffered from a lack of a unifying framework, a single language of measurement that every country of the world would use. The solution came in 1960. That was the pivotal year when the ruling powers got together as the eleventh General Conference on Weights and Measures, and officially established the modernized metric system as *Le Système Internationale de Poids et Mesures*. For convenience everyone called it the SI. As Andro Linklater noted, that was the point at which "the government of every industrialized country in the world, including the United States, [had] signed the Treaty of the Meter. All their weights and measures were defined in relation to the meter and the kilogram. Most had gone farther and adopted the SI as their official system" (2002: 246).

The sweeping advance of the SI as the global language of measurement is a striking example of the division of information that occurs under expansion. As we said before in this book, markets committed to expansion undertake to direct the distribution of resources away from (higher-cost) particular information toward (lower-cost) universal information. In practice this appears as the pursuit of uniformity and commonality in the creation of rules, those that conform to broader interests and are conducive to production and control on a large scale. For this reason the logic that upholds expansion also limits the possibility of preserving particular information; it sets the structure of rules against the noncommon and variable elements, against the unruly tendencies of local custom and control.

So it was in France some 200 years ago when the metric standard was born. On the eve of the revolution, credible reasons were not lacking for the reform of the system of weights and measures. The growth of mass production, of long-distance trade, of overseas empires, and of the bureaucracies that served all these meant that a new social pattern had begun to emerge. The problem was that the way people measured things differed from place to place. The great variety of local methods of measurement did not correspond to the emerging macro order.[5] Market expansion had created a disjunction between the rules of the local (particular) economies and the rules of the nationwide (universal) economy. This disjunction opened the door to considerable instability in exchange relations: it aggravated the permanent human situation by providing opportunities for exploitation of trade and ownership, and fraud, corruption, and injustice were widespread (jobs were plentiful for lawyers then). General uncertainty grew in the miscommunication between these two orders. The whole state of affairs served to weaken government oversight and control and formed a barrier to further growth.[6]

In the interest of increasing the number of people who cooperate in producing and trading things, in the interest of maximizing profit and restoring the public order, in the interest of the Enlightened State and progressive thinkers everywhere, the National Assembly of France directed the Academy of Sciences to devise an invariable standard for all measures and weights. In 1790, a commission of scientists appointed by the academy proposed the creation of an objective system of measurement based on the decimal scale and the uniform properties of nature.[7] In 1791, the legislature accepted the commission's idea that the base of the new system was to be the length of one ten-millionth of a quarter meridian—the distance between the North Pole and the equator. This distance would be called a *metre*, which is derived from the Greek *metron*, a measure (Donovan 1970: 40). In 1795, the revolutionary assembly legalized the use of the metric system. Working through the turmoil of the revolution and its succession of governments, the academy refined and gave shape to the new metric standard. In 1799, the definitive metric system was presented to the Counsel of the Ancients in the symbolic form of a platinum (meter) bar and was housed in the archives of the republic (Alder 1995: 58). In that year, the metric system became the official standard of weights and measures of France. However, the greater part of society was opposed to the new system.

To arrest the growing discontent, the government decided to legalize the use of the old measures alongside the new ones. This led to extreme uncertainty and, in time, to repeal of the policy.

The new decimalized system was part of a wider revolutionary movement of unifying reforms of institutions. Government officials and intellectuals proclaimed its establishment to be an act of liberation and justice, an embrace of rationality, a rejection of the old regime, consistent with the ideals of equality of citizenship and equality before the law. It was presented to the people as natural, more precise, logical, and belonging to no particular culture or nation (Kula 1986). The assumption was that all this would make it palatable to the population as a whole. And yet, as it turned out, views of the new system in daily life were divided, with the bureaucrats and the scientific elite largely in favor of the reform and the common man strongly opposed to it. In essence it was the cost difference of interacting with the new set of rules that provoked these different views.

The common citizen suffered the cost of complying with the new metric code in at least four ways. First, there was the day-to-day expenditure of time and money in having to learn to calculate in metric terms and then having to convert the customary measures into their metric equivalents. This task proved daunting even for the most educated of persons. Second, the shift to the abstract standard involved the loss of many of the meaningful correspondences to local practices and traditions and to the natural phenomena of the local setting. As Witold Kula (1986: 251) stated: "Moreover, traditional metrological systems had fairly often been—as we have noted elsewhere—functional; they stood for some social reality: they were bound up with man, his work and the fruits of it." In other words, the introduction of the new standard involved the loss of the practical benefits of the local measures, which often conveyed more accurate and more meaningful information than the abstract metric system.[8] Third, the population had to internalize the new metric language. Thought patterns, conceptions of quantity and quality, and overall life views had to be redirected. Minds had to shift from thinking in terms of the old dimensions and categories to the new ten-based ones.[9] And fourth, metrological unity meant loss of local latitude in determining the direction of markets and public affairs. With the introduction of the metric standard, local areas of life became more visible and legible to, and hence more controllable by, government authorities. Bear in mind that local measures were in effect a local language, a code that could be impenetrable to outsiders. They acted as protection, as a kind of insulation, from external competition and control. But visibility meant predictability, which meant loss of power for the local peasantry.[10]

These costs added up to a widespread dislike of the metric system. And while there was a certain amount of effort to comply with the reform, most people refused to go along with the new system. Open criticism of it became routine. Nevertheless, the government sensed no disutility from adopting the metric standard. From the state's point of view the new system was for the public good. It increased the state's capacity to standardize the competitive economy, to better resolve distributional conflicts, and to provide broader grounds for consensus and material prosperity. Besides that, it was clear that the simplified system of weights and measures facilitated the flow of goods across borders, made record keeping and police work easier, and extended the state's ability to extract revenues at the local level.[11] The crucial point was that standard units of measurement made possible central monitoring by giving the state more direct access to its citizens and by removing limits on what was considered legitimate state action. This aided the state's ability to penetrate to the local level, to exercise greater influence over the direction of markets, and to override the autonomy of independent decisions.[12] Hence, the government had no logical use for the local (nongovernmental) measures; they became expendable.

It would take about 50 years for the pressures of state building and economic expansion to wear down the opposition and help swing the pendulum of public opinion in the metric direction. By 1840, the logic of measuring things in metric units had been hammered into the heads of most people in France and the empire. They had come to accept (even if reluctantly) the metric reality. It was then that the French government repealed the dual systems option and reimposed the metric system of weights and measures upon the people. The metric system became the only legal system of weights and measures for use in France.

What happened in France was to become common. Over the course of the next two centuries, similar results would follow metrication in almost every nation on earth. Though each nation would have its own motives and its own cultural style, on the whole they seemed destined to follow the same stages toward metrication: the drive to expand (i.e., economic, political, and technical growth) would, in due course, lead to a craving for uniformity in the institutions of social and commercial life; this would provide the government with the impetus to issue a law or a directive to change to the metric system. Next would come a relatively long period of transition in which the public would resist the high price of adapting to the new environment; followed finally by an act of the state that would make the metric system obligatory, with stiff penalties for noncompliance.

By the turn of the twentieth century, a total of 41 countries had either officially converted to or were in the process of converting to the metric system

(Donovan 1970: 46). From that point on, awareness of the benefits of standardized measures became very widespread. There was ample evidence that metrication created closer ties among regions and nations; that it raised levels of efficiency, reliability, and interchangeability; and that it was well suited to scientific research, commerce, and the modus operandi of government.

Well set in motion by the growth of international trade, by political expansion, and by advances in science and technology, the metrication of nations proceeded at an accelerated pace after World War II. Political forces were convinced of the necessary triumph of the metric system.[13] It seemed no country wanted to miss the opportunity to join the global metric campaign. Power and profits were at stake.

Today, the victory of the metric system appears to be final.[14] About 95 percent of the world's population now uses the SI units.[15] The United States is the only industrialized nation where the SI metric system of weights and measures has not been fully adopted. Yet the extent of its metric use has greatly increased over the last several decades. In recognition of economic and political realities, the United States has decided that it cannot afford to disengage; it too must move forward toward full metric conversion.[16]

The metric system has proved to be of great satisfaction to the world. It is quite easy to see that its benefits are real. However, the benefits have not altered the fact that time after time the mass of ordinary people has resisted its introduction, above all because it has come at the cost of the destruction of traditional norms and customs and a reduction in the range of independent choice.[17] All of which explains why in country after country the standardization of measures has needed the power of the state to enforce its adoption.[18] And it is worth mentioning that in every case, given the intention to expand, government insistence on the right to impose the metric standard has been justifiable.

The success of the metric system has consisted precisely in its emergence as the global, technical language of commerce and control. In this role it has worked to stabilize expansion, allowing for a convergence of means and ends, for more efficient productive operations, and for higher returns overall. And as part of this process, it has created a more legible economic and social space, which has had the effect of altering the distribution of authority in the economy as a whole. Nobody disputes the fact that it has enabled governments to extend their authority into more spheres of production and trade.

The worldwide metric momentum testifies to the truth of the division of information. It seems to leave no doubt that what matters to an expanding environment is not the particular, but the universal; not difference, but similarity. It is not the claims of the individual that count, but the claims of the collective; what matters is not more freedom, but more control from above.

International Financial Institutions: The International Monetary Fund

Government leaders, political theorists, and economists created international financial institutions (IFIs) after the costly chaos of World War II. In many ways, IFIs are market mechanisms constructed upon the a priori principle of humankind's "unsocial sociability."[19] As the Kantian political theory goes, global order requires such cost-reducing mechanisms in order to constrain the human appetite for banal self-interest or irrational extensions of individual liberty. IFIs are a set of universal rules that carry the potential for a cosmopolitan civic society, in which individuals and individual nation-states rationally trade off their liberty-seeking preferences for cooperation, order, risk attenuation, and an ideal of human progress.

In theory, a global order aligned with the rational principles and ideals of human progress would tend to alleviate the cost of maintaining a warlike posture and help to prevent war itself. Post–World War II elites and idealists thought that enlightened, operational rationality at all levels of human existence (global to local) would deliver humanity from "heartless competitive vanity [and] the insatiable desire to possess and to rule!" (Kant 1784). Near-perfect collectivity or equilibrium being the answer to risk and security, IFIs and other international bodies emerged to bring about increasing degrees of order. It is, however, little recognized that IFIs in their 60-year history have, in fact, been cost-generating entities chiefly through the mechanism of the division of information, by trading off the local and particular for the global and universal, and by trading liberty for growth. In this section, we will examine the International Monetary Fund (IMF) as a further example of the direction of information during state expansion.

After the Great Depression and World War II, and under the auspices of the new United Nations, the IMF was created in 1944–1945 by 45 nations as an overarching institution to help shape the world economy through a framework of coordination and cooperation. Its essential mission was to prevent global economic depressions and stabilize currency exchange. The basic logic behind the IMF "was a need for collective action at the global level for economic stability, just as the United Nations had been founded on the belief that there was a need for collective action at the global level for political stability" (Stiglitz 2003: 12). Within the considerable influence of John Maynard Keynes (an original IMF adviser) and other economists of the day was the ardent belief that political controls through government could help assuage market imperfections; that linking markets to enlightened, growth-inducing political policy would create more reliable and stable economies, which in turn would craft a maturing stage of global equilibrium. Hence the IMF in its original incarnation had as its aims the following principal responsibilities.[20]

- Promoting international cooperation
- Facilitating the expansion and balanced growth of international trade
- Promoting exchange stability (fixed but adjustable exchange-rate parities)
- Assisting in the establishment of a multilateral system of payments
- Making its resources available—under rules—to member governments experiencing balance of payments difficulties

Today, the IMF has a membership of 184 countries and a surveillance regime over 115 countries, of which 92 voluntarily publish their country's economic data, and loans extending (as of 2005) US$90 billion to 82 countries. As a *public* institution (receiving its revenues from member countries' taxpayers) the focus of its policy has gradually shifted to include areas of microeconomics, such as working with developing countries. The reasons behind the shift included newfound market orientation designed to liberalize governmental structures otherwise seen as impeding market performance. The IMF shift also revealed the complexities of cost structures generated by a new market.

Some have alleged that the conscious purge of Keynesian principles, for example, the avid belief that the institution of government should inform, guide, and regulate market institutions, from IMF doctrine is a contravention of its original mission.[21] It is more plausible, however, that the formula of growth and development never subrogated the role of government (or politics). Rather the IMF, as an international source of rules, largely substituted itself—through the formal rules of conditionality—for the individual nation-state and its policymaking apparatuses as the governing political body in the management of a domestic market's economic policy. In this respect, Keynesianism is alive and well.

We should also keep in mind the axiom that the institution of government (politics) is itself a market and both politics and economics expand together; there is no differentiation in the informational direction. Thus, the original Bretton Woods (1945) emphasis on Keynesian economics coexisting with the guiding hand of government was not abandoned or traded off in the Reagan-Thatcher era of the 1980s as Joseph Stiglitz and others believe. The shift toward microeconomics directed at postcolonial countries and their development (which is what the World Bank was designed to do) allowed the IMF to enlarge its zone of influence and become a political body as well as an economic one. This convergence provided the rational power to alter the direction of an individual nation-state's government policies vis-à-vis its economy. Through the processes and rules of growth and expansion, Keynesian political power was preserved and (mostly) transferred from the participating nation-state and lodged within the IMF bureaucracy.

The question over whether partial transfer of sovereignty into the IMF regime is sustained after the terms of the agreement are satisfied and the loan is repaid is an interesting but ultimately not relevant one here. The institution of the IMF, through its rule-making authority over monetary policy, trade, and the allocation of resources, is in the business of lowering the costs on countries that wish to take part in the enlarged trading environment and raising the costs on those who do not. In other words, the IMF is part of that greater movement and evolution toward the universalization of rules over production. Its intrusion may or may not have staying power, but the fact that it possesses such authority (and legitimacy) is an indication of a shift in the locus of decision making—upward and to the center. Merely being a member carries a set of expectations to collaborate with both the IMF and other members to achieve stable and orderly growth.[22]

Relative to growth and expansion, there are two major activities of the IMF that make it important as an example for this chapter: (1) surveillance and (2) conditionality. Among the IMF's original tasks was prevention of a global depression, which requires reliable internal economic information of member countries. In this respect, IMF surveillance over member countries entails both the acquisition of members' exchange rate policies as well as adoption of rules to guide members with respect to those policies. Each member is under an obligation to "provide the Fund with the information necessary for such surveillance, and, when requested by the Fund, shall consult with it on the member's exchange rate policies."[23] Put into practice, the primary aim of surveillance has been to monitor the economic policies of members, which ultimately affects exchange rates and the monetary system (Mussa 1997).

The fund carries out its surveillance by consulting with each member's principal government officials, with the IMF staff generating reports for the 24-member executive board and preparing semiannual reports compiled in the *World Economic Outlook*. Surveillance, then, is the IMF's ability to monitor a nation-state's economic policies, for example, exchange, growth, and trade. In case a nation-state encounters difficulties, the IMF makes economic assistance (advice and money) available on terms of contract (rules). "Conditionality" is the term used for the trade-off of a certain measure of a country's decision-making sovereignty for the money and rules that come to govern economic policy direction.

In the late 1970s the IMF began to shift its focus toward oil-importing developing economies. This shift has had significant consequences in many postcolonial states, particularly during the 1980s and 1990s. The conscious (some might say ideological) charge into microeconomics has had the effect of extending the domain of IMF influence into the economic affairs of developing sovereign nation-states. Often the cost for not accepting IMF assistance results in having to borrow from other creditors at higher rates of interest, further constraining policy options.

The Case of Tanzania

Sub-Saharan Africa once had several sources of political control. Among these were Anglo-European colonial powers such as Great Britain, Portugal, France, Germany, Belgium, and others. During the 1950s and 1960s, many of these colonial powers formally divested their political systems from various African nation-states, though largely retaining loose economic interests in their former colonies. Tanzania became independent in 1961–1962, when the British government resigned its venture. Western European divestiture initially created a vacuum of political control over the resources of Africa. During this period, individual nation-states had to struggle to form governments and construct or reconstruct domestic institutions. Overall, African political independence did not survive its infancy, partly due to severe fiscal mismanagement by its new leaders and partly due to the forces of globalization (Ayittey 2005). In the global competition over markets, it was not long before forms of colonialism reemerged in the pretext of Western-dominated IFIs (Havnevik 1993).

There are, as we have argued, a logic and rationality to the political expansion of the state, including the IFIs. Expansion entails a mechanism (the division of information) and a *telos* (growth), both of which are attempts to address issues of scarcity and risk. However, the central cost in this process is the one raised against liberty, witnessed in this brief case study concerning Tanzania.

The repeated collapse of legitimacy in the existing social order within Tanzania from 1960 to 2005 led to more centralized authority and new, scope-expanding universal rules. These rules captured the factors of production in ways that wrested sovereignty away from bearers of particular information—in this case, as time played out, an entire nation-state—over time, housing sovereignty within regulators of the enlarged sphere of trade (e.g., the IMF).

The postcolonial socialist president Julius Nyerere, whose time in power lasted from 1964 to 1985, emphasized a familial, interdependent sort of society where local preferences of *ujamma* (self-reliance) superseded—at least philosophically—the externalities of the then competing world powers (United States and Western Europe vs. the Soviet Union and Warsaw-pact countries).[24] Nyerere rhetorically embedded Tanzania's economy with communal thought where bonds of community and kinship received heightened preference over mere commercial exchange.[25] Yet there was no shortage of self-interest underlining Nyerere's government.

After British rule, state-centered Tanzanian socialism formed the common good around the collective, imposing a cost on local communities, including the 100-plus different tribes, in an effort to unify all Tanzanian markets around the new rules. All groups that had previously benefited from the colonial regime were required to conform to the legitimacy and direction of the new market. In other words, as is consistent with our theory of the state, Nyerere's government emerged as the only legitimate source of rules in the new Tanzanian society. So as not to impede expansion, individual resistance was eliminated either through subsidies or through coercive measures such as imprisonment. For example, rather than work within the indigenous tribal structures, which for centuries operated efficient private markets and reliable democratic forms of local government, Nyerere engaged in a "villigization" program, forcing some 13 million peasants and tribe members to relocate into 8,000 cooperative, government villages. The central government planned, confiscated property, and exercised control over all means of industrial and agricultural production. In addition to loss of human liberty, an ecological disaster soon emerged across the countryside from deforestation, overgrazing, and miscultivation of crops (Ayittey 2005). Social-ecological complexity was set aside for ideological commitments.

A series of events occurred during the 1970s that ultimately threatened Nyerere's socialist project and Tanzanian sovereignty. Among the main events were (1) the first OPEC oil crisis in 1973–1974, (2) the end of the coffee production boom in 1978 (Tanzania is a coffee-exporting country), (3) Tanzanian intervention in the Ugandan crisis in 1978, and (4) the second OPEC crisis of 1979 (Holtom 2005). Owing to the political philosophy of self-reliance, when Tanzania ran into foreign-exchange problems in the early 1970s the government initially secured IMF loans without terms of conditionality. Later, in 1975, during a period of increased oil prices that caused foreign exchange shortages, Tanzania secured IMF loans through "weak" conditionality (i.e., the government received "special drawing rights" on the fund without the usual strength of IMF rules) (Stein 1992). And then again in 1980, after Tanzania had intervened in the Ugandan crisis, it appealed to the IMF for assistance. On this occasion, the IMF offered nearly US$300 million in exchange for restrictions "over imports, foreign exchange and price controls, devaluation of the national currency, and an end to the growth of the sizable public sector" (Vreeland 2003: 27).

Nyerere initially rejected the austerity measures and later negotiated a much softer set of conditions: a three-year loan agreement beginning in 1980 in which Tanzania would later devalue its currency and put a ceiling on government borrowing. When the Nyerere government exceeded the agreed level of borrowing, the IMF suspended loan disbursements and imposed new, even more severe, conditions for the remainder of the loan money. These conditions consisted of currency devaluation, deficit reduction, wage controls, removal of gas and oil subsidies, increased interest rates, increased producer prices, and removal of import controls (Stein 1992: 65). But in order to not trade off their particular economic and political preferences, Nyerere and his government rejected the IMF's "technocratic" conditionality and appealed to national pride to get by. As a result foreign investment percentage relative to Tanzanian GDP dropped from 11.8 percent in 1982 to 8.9 percent in 1983, triggering an internal debate within the government over the direction of policy.

Yet by 1985, when Nyerere stepped down and a new reformist president emerged, Tanzania had already adopted many of the economic policy reforms originally advocated by the IMF. For reasons of politics and economics, policy orientation had already shifted away from shielding local preferences and toward avid participation in the new universal rules. Even without *direct* IMF coercion, principles and incentives of market liberalization had begun to take hold and progressively replaced principles of Tanzanian (Nyererean) socialism; this was specifically achieved through a domestic Structural Adjustment Program. Still, retributive internal political divisions caused by Nyerere and others in his party had prevented further market reforms and had persuaded the new government of Ali Hassan Mwinyi to invite IMF intervention to help advance Mwinyi's growth package (Kiondo 1992: 21–42). In 1986, when official Tanzanian economic preferences had fully aligned with those of the IMF, Mwinyi and the IMF signed an 18-month rules-for-money conditionality agreement, which sent a positive signal to growth-minded foreign creditors.

Ultimately, the new universal rules of the IMF allowed Tanzania to lower its economic costs by agreeing to participate in the expanding global framework and its informational direction, but they also raised costs against the particular political framework of Nyererean socialism and its emphasis on self-determination (local autonomy). The lesson here is that growth and expansion and their accompanying turnover in rules, over time, help to alter the categories of thought that lead to rational action (defined in the collective direction). The lower-cost direction of information leads to greater centralization, which in turn leads to a progressive convergence between public and private spheres.

The objective result is a global, cosmopolitan unification of market activity. This in part explains why the agenda of nation-states is often found consistent with superordinate institutions such as the IMF. In other words, states are willing to trade off even their *cultural* distinctions—in Tanzania, the distinctive of ujamma—that permeate society in order to secure gains from the expanding zone of trade created by multistate entities. Once incentives are aligned in this market direction, resistance is often viewed as too costly; it becomes subvention of individual sovereignty by other means.

The European Union: Police, Justice, Security, and Customs

What is clear from this example of political enlargement and institutional integration is that the trade-off for a European superstate is the progressive diminishment of local authority in decision making. Over time, the particular informational preferences (rules) of sovereign states are traded off by treaty for increasing returns to scale: dynamic gains from trade, increases in market expansion, political and legal consolidation, a program of enhanced security, the socialization of risk, the virtual elimination of military conflict among member states, and an allegedly expanding zone of liberty. The universal information imposed by the precondition of membership trumps individual state sovereignty to fashion ideals, preferences, and modes of production dissimilar to collective ones.

The progressive expansion of the European Community (EC; 1957) into the European Union (EU; 1992, with 25 countries by 2004) brings with it a commensurate expansion within all of its political and market institutions. Expansion necessitates the eventual harmonization of differences, the inevitable centralization of decision making as well as the development of a common set of universal ideals, principles, and rules. When all 25 member states ratify the treaty establishing the European Constitution, this will consolidate and replace many of the preexisting treaties now in force within the EU. Yet if we know anything of twentieth-century political history, we know that many, if not most, of the rationales for expanded state authority within institutions such as police work, justice systems, and customs regulation developed from arguments premised on benefits of enlargement: gains from trade, enhancing security, socializing risk, and advancing peoples' freedom.

Owing to the belief in growth and development and their presumed connection to collective freedom, the original EC emerged by treaty (the Treaty of Rome) in 1957, with a preamble and set of purposes that began the transition from individual nation-states to a federal community (Articles 2 and 3).[26] The proposed draft of the EU Constitution (2005) reflects a firm belief in the immense compatibility between growth, development, and (positive) liberty. Its preamble concerning governing authority, values, and objectives indicates that (1) formerly exogenous authorities in the EC structure will become endogenous in the new EU framework; (2) common, pluralistic, and humanistic values entail few if any trade-offs—that is, there is no inherent incompatibility among them; and (3) the objectives of growth and expansion endemic to a superstate will extend *more* liberty to member states and their citizens, even while adhering to the superior legal authority that is the Union. In other words, the EU Constitution as it is presently written appears to deny that scale and scarcity enforce a division of information between universal and particular information, which migrates the information base away from the individual state and toward the collective Union, thus escalating the locus of decision making.[27]

As for the relations between the Union and individual member states, Articles 1–5 will, if implemented, further require that each entity be "sincere" in their respect for and cooperation with the other, authorizing the rights of member states to retain sovereignty as long as that sovereignty is exercised consistently (or does not conflict) with the Union and the EU Constitution, refraining "from any measure which would jeopardize the attainment of the Union's objectives" (*European Union Constitution,* Articles 1–5). On matters of law, the EU Constitution adopted by the institutions of the Union will supercede the respective domestic law of member states (Articles 1–6).

The consequences of this shift toward the collective—in the present case, transnational confederation—are many. Perhaps chief among these is the collapse of the principle of state sovereignty inherent to the Westphalian model of nation-states.[28] Individual nation-states have been disempowered by (1) a loss of state capacities for control, (2) a growing legitimation deficit in decision making, and (3) the increasing inability to provide legitimate and effective steering and organizational services (Habermas 2003: 88–89). In other words, the transitions from ethno-nationalism to Euro-federalism to Euro-cosmopolitanism progressively subvert political particularities, including local democratic autonomy. Whereas Euro-federalists use existing transnational treaties as a means to advance the completion of an EU Constitution, Euro-cosmopolitans see the EU and its constitution as a "point of departure for the development of a transnational network of regimes that together could pursue a world domestic policy, even in the absence of a world government" (96).

However, the EU Constitution has not yet (as of publication) been ratified by all of the 25 member states. Thus it remains a potentiality, although one that is likely to be realized sooner rather than later. Until it is ratified, however, other treaties exist that have the force of law. We turn now to these and witness how the institutions of customs (security) and law enforcement (police and the Court of Justice) operate within the expanded trading zone of Europe.

Customs and Security

Like police work and justice systems, the institution of customs is expanding within the EU. Union enlargement, of course, requires a reduction in border friction. In the EU scheme, previous nationalistic barriers to trade and travel of goods, services, and people within internal borders are lowered or altogether lifted (advancing trade) while barriers along external borders are raised (assuring security and socializing risk). The new customs strategy emerging from the European Commission, Council, and Parliament is one predicated on three themes: (1) to provide a common framework whose rules are transparent, stable, and appropriate for EU trade; (2) to provide member states with the necessary resources to support the framework; and (3) ultimately to protect society from unfair trading, and to secure EU interests. In this, demand for the services of the EU goes up on the cost-saving side (producing and coordinating universal rules) and on the cost-rising side of production (by condensing and sorting the particular rules from member states).

In 2001, the Commission proposed five action areas for customs union: (1) simplifying and rationalizing legislation; (2) improving customs controls (standards and implementation); (3) providing good service to the business community; (4) improving training; and (5) improving international cooperation. In 1995 the Schengen Convention came into force, abolishing member states' internal borders and creating a single external European border, as well as enshrining a single set of rules regarding visas, asylum rights, and external border checks in order to facilitate the free movement of persons. To strike a balance between freedom and security, a set of "compensatory" measures were also introduced, including an information system— the Schengen Information System (SIS) and its sequel SIS2—so as to provide rights of surveillance and exchange of data on people's identities and faster protocols for transborder extradition. Among the older member states, only Ireland and the United Kingdom have opted out or modified the terms of the Schengen Convention, with the Council permitting the United Kingdom in 1999 to adopt such protocols as police and legal cooperation in criminal matters (e.g., drug trafficking) and the SIS.

Concerning security and crisis management, the Common Foreign and Security Policy (CFSP) was established in the 1993 Treaty on the European Union and later updated by the Amsterdam Treaty of 1999. The CFSP enlarges Union interests and tethers these to the principle of the United Nations Charter.

Its program design is to smoothen cooperation, which ultimately commits member states to adopting certain policies and courses of action on security matters and crises consistent with EU policy. Expanding EU capacity comes at rising cost against local determination.

Police and Justice

Unlike other EU institutions, police cooperation and consolidation has not accelerated at the same pace. The reason is twofold. First, systems of law are deeply rooted in culture, and culturally dependent institutions tend to evolve more slowly than do institutions with less connectedness to culture (one major locus of particular information). The French peoples' initial rejection of the EU Constitution in 2005, with 55 percent casting a "no" vote, exemplifies the temporary power of cultural preferences rooted in national identity and sovereignty.[29] Second, systems of law and police work—like systems of measurement and scales—signal particular information in ways that connote sovereign identity (consider the British acre and the French hectare). Indeed, police work goes to the heart of what constitutes a sovereign state.

Yet, to paraphrase J. S. Mill, police work today is clearly becoming more cosmopolitan.[30] Traditionally, the term "police" was associated with the Greek term *polis* (city): a metro-polis agency was a metropolitan or city police department, a civil force that was entrusted with maintaining law and order in a locality. In this regard, police work traditionally responded to the particular needs and preferences of a locality such as a city, county, or, in some instances, an individual state; in more recent forms, it has been under the control of a local political body. In Europe, police agencies that were once coupled to a locality (and its information) are, in fact, becoming more cosmopolitan. And, by responding to the universals of central planning, they are consequently being decoupled from particular information. The term "cosmopolitan" comes from *cosmo-polis,* meaning a universal polity free from national limitations or attachments, belonging to all parts of the world and not restricted to any one country or its inhabitants.[31] Scaling up police departments along cosmopolitan lines may yield efficiencies of scale, but it also necessarily alters organizational structures, depletes information, and adjusts the orbit of legitimacy closer to mandarins and further away from the demos.

The initial national intransigence in Europe is being resolved over time through a sequential turnover in the rules and their concomitant schedule of rights. Since the implementation of the Schengen Agreement of 1990, the Europol Convention of 1995, the Vienna Action Plan of 1998, and the

1999 Treaty of Amsterdam, police cooperation within Europe is beginning to demonstrate trends of expansion and consolidation. The institutional framework for harmonized, united, and transborder police work that flattens the metrics of information is being constructed in the following ways:

- A common definition of the nature of police work
- A universal strategic approach to internal and transborder police functions
- The development of binding instruments of authority adopted by the European Council
- The improvement of empirical research on police and customs cooperation
- The creation of centralized, interoperable information databases and communication systems
- Police consolidation and dissemination of best practices concerning investigative techniques, forensic science, approaches to terrorism, rules of procedure
- The establishment of Europol in 1995 (through the Europol Convention and whose office is located at The Hague) whose tasks are to facilitate the exchange of information between member states; provide Europol liaisons to member states; obtain, collate, and analyze information for member states; aid investigations in member states; and prevent and combat terrorism, drug, vehicle, and human trafficking
- The incremental advancement of Europol authority through the Europol Information System (EIS), which centralizes organized crime and citizens' personal and nonpersonal information for member states
- The formation of an EU Police Chiefs Task Force, which meets biannually to improve communication, practices, and increase the mutual assistance among member states' law enforcement authorities with Europol
- The creation of the European Police College, including the establishment of the Internet-based European Police Learning Network (EPLN), with a legal personality that would provide a central learning institution for the training of police officials and their leaders

Removing the geographic barriers for the trading of information helps member states to standardize theories and practices of police work. In Europe, the theoretical impetus behind police expansion is freedom- and security-centered. The argument is that expansion fosters improved cooperation, which, in turn, allows for the free movement of persons within and among member states and increases the likelihood of preventing and resolving crossborder crime, including terrorism, fraud, money laundering, and currency counterfeiting. In other words, the expansion and standardization of rules governing police work allows for greater freedoms and security for EU citizens.

The EU is presently fashioning its institution of law enforcement along a similar model originally employed by the United States during the 1930s. The Wikersham Commission (1932) undertook the first national assessment of law enforcement in the United States. The commission was originally charted by President Hoover in 1929 on premises of trying to allay heightened public fear of crime, including the bloody mafia wars in Chicago, police abuse of citizens, and issues surrounding cross-state jurisdiction. One of its central recommendations was the standardization and professionalization of law enforcement departments across the United States. To help accomplish this aim, the Federal Bureau of Investigation (FBI), in 1935, instituted a national academy—the FBI National Academy—for the training of local, state, national, and international law enforcement personnel, particularly mid-level command staff and chiefs of police. The course of study includes law, behavioral and forensic sciences, leadership development, specialized training and issues of communication during ten rigorous weeks. The civil rights movement of the 1950s and 1960s accelerated federal intervention and control of "national" law enforcement problems.

In the intervening 70 years, the FBI National Academy has graduated over 38,000 municipal, county, and state police officials, including 2,500 international graduates. Its graduates demonstrate the informational impact and influence of the National Academy in the leadership roles played. Of the 22,851 graduates (as of 2005) serving in law enforcement agencies, over 5,300 graduates serve as chiefs of police, 560 are sheriffs, 107 are directors of state police agencies, and 276 are heads of their respective agencies. Centralized training of command-level police officials in the United States has been one sure way of flattening metrics across existing jurisdictional boundaries. A local chief of police gains certain informational advantages from having graduated from the FBI National Academy. Likewise, this gain is reciprocated by the FBI having an operational ally at the local level, someone who is going to understand and abide by the universal rules of law enforcement production.

Another example of a universal metric is the FBI's National Crime and Information Center (NCIC), which centralizes and regulates federal and state criminal information. The NCIC system is similar to Europol's new EIS. While obvious trading advantages exist, it is important to keep in mind that a flat, standardized information system of any institution is usually a precursor to new rules for central authority in decision making and financing of operations. The state must match rules to scale. As in Europe, the more recent rationale in the United States for police expansion is an escalation of mass concern or fear often requiring the socialization of risk that institutional expansion can deliver. This imposes a cost on negative freedom (see chapter 6) through an eventual turnover of rules; local concerns merge with national ones, requiring hierarchical solutions to problems of scale. A call for a hierarchical authority system by national government potentially rids the United States of the inhibiting barriers of federalism (states rights) and certain statutory restrictions on federal authority, for example, from the Posse Comitatus Act of 1878.

Demonstrating an ever-increasing vesture of power within the European Parliament (732 members from member states, weighted by population), the European Council (87 members), and the European Commission (20 members), Title VI of the Amsterdam Treaty of 1999 also gave the Court of Justice of the EC an expanded role within EU affairs, though member states still retain sovereignty on some key legal issues, such as maintaining law and order and safeguarding internal security. Indeed, the Court of Justice since 1990 has had judicial review responsibility (1) when a national court of final appeal requires a decision by the Court of Justice in order for the national court to render judgment on a question concerning the interpretation of EU rules or on the validity and interpretation of acts by the EC institutions that are based on it and, similarly, (2) when the Council, Commission, or member state asks the court to rule on a question regarding the interpretation of a new law or of acts adopted on the basis of the law.

The Amsterdam Treaty requires member states to formally acknowledge and accept the jurisdiction of the EU Court of Justice, and to identify which of their respective national courts of final review are charged with requesting an opinion or ruling concerning EU rules from the Court of Justice . While the Court of Justice is the supreme judicial organ of the EU, it is important to note that the EU Council remains the principal actor in the bureaucratic implementation of EU rules.

What this example reveals is that there lies within political expansion—which is to say, growth away from the local and particular to the superstate and universal—a hidden but very real cost to democratic choices by local communities over which information to use in decision making. Here we have very briefly examined an increasingly integrated set of markets across Europe (police, justice, customs, and security), which, as they expand and achieve a hierarchical and standardized profile, impose a cost against local mores, customs, and cultural ways of forming justice systems and regulating all-important police functions.

More so than perhaps any other market, police functions of the state are the single largest challenge to individual liberty. When departments of police and justice are separated from local authority and decision making, they arguably become less democratically responsive or less accountable, not more, to the individual (or to a local set of individuals). Local information so rooted and set in culture, sometimes centuries old, and nearest to the people, is formally depleted from the location that arguably needs it the most: the cop in the local precinct, the local judge, and other local community officials charged with developing and enforcing law. It is the logic of this informational trade-off that lowers information costs in the direction of the superstate (the universal), bringing about expanded central control and authority as well as generating narrower disparities in preferences, choices, and values between that authority and the people, who are further removed from the decision-making apparatuses of the central government.

We have seen in the examples of the metric system, international financial institutions, and police apparatuses of the EU how state expansion works in concert with diverse markets to divide information. While these institutional examples and many more assure us of this economic reality, perhaps it is within the institution of education that the division of information and its effects may be most readily observable. The human good of education, in its inherent complexity, requires particular information for its full production. What are the consequences, then, when that particular information under the press of expansion gets discarded from the economy of exchange? We explore this question and its consequences in the next three chapters.

Notes

1. To gain perspective on the cost problem, consider that rule making constitutes a massive capital commitment. Examine any organization and look at the cost of administration (the rule-making arm of the organization) and one will find that a substantial portion of total expenditure (up to 40–50 percent in education) devoted to rule making—that is, the gathering, processing, and human energy required for handling and manipulating information that goes into rules and their enforcement.
2. See, especially, Buchanan (2003).
3. The logic of this view suggests that the state becomes the source of relief for its own self-interested activity.
4. We will argue later that under the logic of expansion freedom is increasingly regarded as a triumph of collective effort, as compatible with authority, and as being created and enhanced through the growth and interactions of social institutions. Such logic militates against autonomous life and individuality; it narrows the area of nonencroachment and creates conditions in which the idea of an inviolable zone of independence becomes an index of irrationality.

5. In his book *Revolution in Measurement: Western European Weights and Measures Since the Age of Science,* Ronald Zupko (1990: 113) found that "on the eve of the Revolution in the last quarter of the eighteenth century, France had more than 1000 units of measurement accepted as standards in Paris and the provinces, with approximately 250,000 local variations."

6. In *Seeing Like a State: How Certain Schemes to Improve the Human Condition Have Failed,* James Scott explained: "Because local standards of measurement were tied to practical needs, because they reflected particular cropping patterns and agricultural technology, because they varied with climate and ecology, because they were 'an attribute of power and an instrument of asserting class privilege,' and because they were 'at the center of bitter class struggle,' they represented a mind-boggling problem for statecraft" (1998: 29).

7. It is useful to recall that the idea of a decimalized system was not new at this time. The scientific community had long recognized its methodological possibilities and envisioned a metrological standardization based on a decimal scale. In 1670 Gabriel Mouton, the vicar of St. Paul's Church in Lyon, had proposed a decimal system of weights and measures having a fundamental unit based on the quadrant of one minute of a great circle of the earth. Mouton was perhaps the reformer most responsible for moving metrological research forward along decimal lines. See for example Donovan (1970) and Zupko (1990).

8. The way people adjust in an effort to contend with the variable conditions and details of their environment often reveals the practical limits of using a generic or universal measure. Examples of this abound. Linklater in *Measuring America* (2002: 239) discusses how the metric system forced people to separate the measure from the activity: "The traditional measures had variety because they related to different activities. Cloth was measured by the ell or the *aune* because it was natural to hold it and stretch out the arm to full length. A journey was measured by the yard or the *toise* because the road was walked. Land was measured by the acre or the *arpent* because that represented work." Consider also this interesting example provided by Scott in *Seeing Like a State* (1998: 25): "In the part of Malaysia with which I am most familiar, if one were to ask 'How far is it to the next village?' a likely response would be 'Three rice-cookings.' The answer assumes that the questioner is interested in how much time it will take to get there, not how many miles away it is. In varied terrain, of course, distance in miles is an utterly unreliable guide to travel time, especially when the traveler is on foot or riding a bicycle."

9. The book to read is *Measures and Men* by the Polish historian Witold Kula (1986: 288), who highlighted this aspect of the French program of metrication. He said: "Through this innovation, moreover, the whole nation was made to acquire common ways of thinking, to share the same perceptions of space, dimensions, and weights, and to grasp—albeit with the greatest difficulty—the principles of decimal division."

10. In support of this point, Scott (1998: 54) said: "Illegibility, then, has been and remains a reliable resource for political autonomy."

11. It was government bureaucracy that readily embraced the metric system. "As Napoleon himself had been forced to admit, the simplicity of calculating in decimals suited bookkeepers—and prefects, and bureaucrats, and government officials of every kind." Quoted in Linklater, *Measuring America* (2002: 241).

12. It is widely known that the power to regulate commerce is the key to expanding the scope of authority.

13. Scott (1998: 30) pointed to these incentives: "No effective central monitoring or controlled comparisons were possible without standard, fixed units of measurement."

14. Most of the old units of measurement have disappeared over time. But the triumph of the SI has not meant the complete elimination of traditional ways of measurement. In almost every country that has officially adopted the metric system, there remain vestiges of the old ways of measuring. Even in France, the birthplace of the metric system, traditional, nonmetric units are still in use in shops, restaurants, schools, and industry, most of which are correlated to the metric standard.

15. This is according to the National Institute of Standards and Technology, Gaithersburg, MD. http://www.nist.gov/metric.

16. The metric system was actually made legal in the United States in 1866. But for the most part its use remained on paper for nearly a century. Then after World War II, the metric system began to take hold in the United States. The Omnibus Trade and Competitiveness Act of 1988 amended the Metric Conversion Act of 1975 to make the metric system the "preferred system of weights and measures for United States trade and commerce." In 1991, Executive Order 12770 directed all executive departments and federal agencies to make the transition to the use of metric units in all business-related activities. Today all inch-pound measures are defined and calibrated to the SI metric system. Official conversion to the universal measure appears inevitable.

17. "Detractors saw nationalized counting and measuring as a hegemonic attempt to link centralized authority to mathematical abstraction, leveling qualitative difference under quantitative uniformity while running roughshod over the real interests of highly differentiated communities and markets," wrote M. Norton Wise (1995: 97).

18. "Around the world the metric system had always been introduced from the top rather than in response to popular demand," observed Linklater in *Measuring America* (2002: 248).

19. See Immanuel Kant's, "Idea for a Universal History from a Cosmopolitan Point of View" (1784).

20. See Article 1 of the Articles of Agreement.

21. See, for example, Stiglitz (2003: 16).

22. Under Article 1, section 1, each member shall: "(i) endeavor to direct its economic and financial policies toward the objective of fostering orderly economic growth with reasonable price stability, with due regard to its circumstances; (ii) seek to promote stability by fostering orderly underlying economic and financial

conditions and a monetary system that does not tend to produce erratic disruptions; (iii) avoid manipulating exchange rates or the international monetary system in order to prevent effective balance of payments adjustment or to gain an unfair competitive advantage over other members; and follow exchange policies compatible with the undertakings under this Section."

23. See section 3 of Article 1.

24. For further commentary on these philosophical commitments, see Nyerere's Arusha Declaration of 1967 in *Freedom and Development* (1974).

25. For background to such economies, see Polanyi (1944).

26. The EU Community: "[Article 2] The Community shall have as its task, by establishing a common market and an economic and monetary union and by implementing common policies or activities referred to in Articles 3 and 4, to promote throughout the Community a harmonious, balanced and sustainable development of economic activities, a high level of employment and of social protection, equality between men and women, sustainable and non-inflationary growth, a high degree of competitiveness and convergence of economic performance, a high level of protection and improvement of the quality of environment, the raising of the standard of living and quality of life, and economic and social cohesion and solidarity among Member States. [Article 3] [T]he activities of the community shall include [an abbreviated list]: (b) a common commercial policy; (c) an internal market characterized by the abolition, as between Member States, of obstacles to the free movement of goods, persons, services, and capital; (e) a common policy in the sphere of agriculture and fisheries; (f) a common policy in the sphere of transport; (g) a system ensuring that competition in the internal market is not distorted; (h) the approximation of the laws of Member States to the extent required for the functioning of the common market; (k) the strengthening of economic and social cohesion; (o) encouragement for the establishment and development of trans-European networks; (u) [common] measures in the spheres of energy, civil protection and tourism."

27. Consider, for example, articles one through four from the EU Constitution: "[Article 1-1] 1. Reflecting the will of the citizens and States of Europe to build a common future, this Constitution establishes the European Union, on which the Member States confer competences to attain objectives they have in common. The Union shall coordinate the policies by which the Member States aim to achieve these objectives, and shall exercise on a Community basis the competences they confer on it. 2. The Union shall be open to all European States which respect its values and are committed to promoting them together. [Article 1-2] The Union is founded on the values of respect for human dignity, freedom, democracy, equality, the rule of law and respect for human rights, including the rights of persons belonging to minorities. These values are common to Member States in a society in which pluralism, non-discrimination, tolerance, justice, solidarity and equality between men and women prevail. [Article 1-3] [an abbreviated list] 1. The Union's aim is to promote peace, its values and the well-being of its peoples. 2. The Union shall offer its citizens an area of freedom, security and

justice without internal frontiers, and an internal market where competition is free and undistorted. 3. The Union shall work for the sustainable development of Europe based on the balanced economic growth and price stability, a highly competitive social market economy, aiming at full employment and social progress, and a high level of protection and improvement of the quality of the environment. It shall promote scientific and technological advance. It shall combat social exclusion and discrimination, and shall promote social justice and protection . . . solidarity between generations and protection of the rights of the child. . . . It shall respect its rich cultural and linguistic diversity, and shall ensure that Europe's cultural heritage is safeguarded and enhanced. 5. The Union shall pursue its objectives by appropriate means commensurate with the competences which are conferred upon it in the Constitution. [Article 1-4] 1. The free movement of persons, services, goods and capital, and freedom of establishment shall be guaranteed within and by the Union, in accordance with the Constitution. 2. Within the scope of the Constitution, and without prejudice to any of its specific provisions, any discrimination on grounds of nationality shall be prohibited."

28. Though it should be noted that strong and weak versions of the Westphalian model exist. See, for example, Strik (2005).

29. Though it ought to be pointed out that by the occasion of the French vote in May 2005, Austria, Germany, Greece, Hungary, Italy, Lithuania, Slovakia, Slovenia, and Spain had ratified the constitution.

30. Mill originally suggested that capital was becoming more cosmopolitan.

31. See the *Oxford English Dictionary* (1989). See also Toulmin (1990).

CHAPTER 3

Establishing Direction in Education Production

The highly conscious endeavor to expand the educational institution is what accounts for the fundamental character of modern education. Central to this expansion is the precept that the amount of schooling one obtains should approximate the amount of knowledge one acquires. In other words, as individuals climb higher up the ladder of formal education, they should gain higher or commensurate levels of knowledge and skill. The goal of advancing the public good is embedded in this principle; thus its proper administration has, from the outset, been a special concern within the educational institution. The general consideration is that the public good obtains in the long-term symmetrical operation of this formula:

Educational Attainment = Knowledge and Skill

Preserving this symmetry, however, is problematic because the information costs of producing these ends are different. The production of educational attainment primarily utilizes universal (lower-cost) information, whereas the production of knowledge and skills primarily utilizes particular (higher-cost) information. As we have already shown, the requirements of expansion force the institution to trade off higher-cost for lower-cost information in production; in other words, while it preserves the universals (attainment), it denies the particulars (knowledge and skills) full access to the productive agenda.

This means that scale undermines any prospect of creating a balance between educational attainment and the acquisition of commensurate knowledge and skill, because as the institution expands it makes an increasing capital investment in communication channels organized around the production of attainment. At some point the magnitude of this investment makes the direction of production appear unalterable. Path dependence becomes locked-in. The weight of the institution's accumulated capital (information base) tilts the balance of production conclusively toward attainment and away from knowledge and skill. The various lines of production and associated services and activity converge and organize around the goal of increasing attainment.

The dilemma of preserving this symmetry is resolved by lowering the information costs of producing knowledge and skills. That is, as the institution advances toward a more technical model of production, it achieves greater cooperation and efficiency by standardizing rules and unifying measures of production. This changes the information content of knowledge and skills, which transforms them into a less-complex good. Relative to attainment, the good of knowledge and skills becomes the adjustable factor under expansion. The losses resulting from this change in the good affect most students in the system, but we can hardly doubt that they get especially concentrated on the people who are most dependent upon institutionally provided services and who generally lack market power.

The Importance of Scale

Every view we may take of the institution of education will serve to show that each phase of educational expansion gives the production of attainment more power and influence. This system fixes attainment in the mind and makes it the governing principle of action. It is a system that relies on the expansion of trade to combine scales of individual utility into a scale of ends—a common good as it were—objectively valid for the institution as a whole. This means that it relies upon expansion, particularly on the growth of gains created by it, to align and coordinate the productive efforts of millions of interactive human beings.

As individuals, groups, and various production units attempt to make themselves better off, their selection of information on the basis of cost sets the long-run direction of educational production. Self-interest recommends increased investment in the production of attainment, for which the demand is greatest and the rewards more certain, and reduced investment in production of upgraded knowledge and skill where demand and certainty of payoffs are relatively low. It is this pursuit of profitable opportunities that results in a preference to utilize information compatible with planning in education production. This is the kind of information (universal) that is most conducive to maximizing the production of attainment: measurable, predictable, uniform, and linear. It is the type of information that can model regularity, yield a high degree of certainty, and can, and often is, described in quantitative terms.[1]

When compared to the cost of information that is variable and not fully predictable, the cost of this planned (universal) information is minimal. As is well known, less variance in information lowers the cost of transacting. Hence the value of information used in planning consists mainly in the opportunities it provides for cooperative outcomes, gains from trade, and efficiency in production. Expenditures of resources on methods that enhance the production of attainment more readily satisfy cost-benefit assessments. The balance sheet will show a profit to attainment, so that as the system expands there appears to be less and less risk and uncertainty in allocating resources to produce more of it. All of this information goes full circle and feeds back into the system of decision making.

Production, therefore, constantly changes with scale. As the institution increases in scale (quantity of production and trade), it builds up an information base—that is, property rights, incentives, rules, customs, and skills—with the kind of information that enhances the production of attainment. This information base reinforces the direction of production by providing a framework for future learning and investment decisions. That, in turn, sets the stage for another iteration. These incremental additions to the network of communication bring new forms of behavior and create connections and commitments that were not there before. Tastes change, even basic views of education change, as the institution increases in scale.

It is this dimension of increasing scale that allows the institution to transcend what otherwise would become intractable social choice impossibilities surrounding the establishment of direction in production. Scale adds time to this choice matrix. It affords a multiplicity of voting cycles under incrementally changing conditions in which the preference set, the calculus of self-interest, and the ideological construction of the social good themselves are being influenced by the volume of trade, which, as it grows, heightens the demand for less-costly (more certain) information in production.

The path of institutional expansion, however, is not linear. Reform movements sporadically arise that attempt to realign what is being learned with the level of schooling attained. And there always are some voices present within the institution's various production units calling for renewed attention to issues fundamental to the quality of learning. But when scarcity inevitably imposes itself, the tendency is to economize on information in the name of efficiency.

The price of this production system is a fundamental change in the nature (quality) of the good being produced. This change is the essence of the distortion that makes the institution appear to be more productive. It starts out claiming to produce one type of good but ends up producing a partial rendering—a facsimile—of that good. It alters its demand curve by changing the characteristics of its product. The output of attainment increases, but the education good itself does not remain the same.

It is against this backdrop of growing scale that we now separate the part from the whole, and examine in more detail each of the components of this production process. We first delineate two kinds of information (planning and exchange) required for the maximum production of the education good, and then describe how the various production function studies conducted over the past 40 years reveal the inadequacy of relying on planned (universal) information for the production of knowledge and skill. We then introduce the problem of scarcity, and analyze how the cost of information factors into production decisions: specifically, how, under conditions of increasing scale, high-cost exchange (particular) information, vital to the production of knowledge and skill, gets pushed off the production agenda in favor of more planned (low-cost) information. The chapter concludes by showing how this evolving direction of production (path dependence) aggregates the preferences of millions of participants around the expansion of attainment.

Planning and Exchange

All decisions concerning production are necessarily a function of information and how that information is processed. To obtain the most effective production of the education good requires the input of both low- and high-cost sets of information. The former involves terms of specification, efficiency, universal parameters, measurement, certainty, standardization, and so forth. These categories in education can be lumped together under the broader category of planning. The latter employs terms more fluid than these, and which make up the less-ordered realm of exchange. In this realm we can expect to find a collection of opinions, value judgments, moral principles, that is, the specific beliefs, feelings, and volitions of an individual life. This kind of information is inherently qualitative, subjective, variable, uncertain, hard to measure, and so forth.

The contrast we are drawing is not that between two opposed but two complementary strands of information. Indeed, it is the coming together and the interdependence of planning and exchange that makes up the broad spectrum of education production. At the heart of this process is the interplay between the forces of stability and instability, objectivity and subjectivity, linearity and nonlinearity. It is where combinations of order and disorder meet and create the possibility of growth and development in some direction. Their active union includes what is done in education and the way in which it is done.

At its core, planning is a reduction—a dividing and subdividing of information to make the production of education orderly and more efficient. It is a set of procedures, practices, and goals, without which the immense institutional matrix of education could not be made to function. Planning may be thought of as being a deliberate set of decisions about the allocation of resources involved in production, or as being the selection and arrangement of means—of subject matter, of methods, of books and supplies, of the entire social setting of the school. It is the act of determining the environment that will interact with the individual to create a meaningful learning experience. Planning, in other words, is the rationalization and regulation of the production of knowledge and skills; it is the logical ordering, the a priori pattern, of the educational experience.

Planning does not seek to maximize the use of widely dispersed and constantly changing information. Part of its purpose is to seek the removal of such uncertain (costly) information. This means that what planning establishes can never suffice to constitute an adequate notion of education production. That is to say, because its information content is necessarily partial, it is not expected that planning is sufficient in itself to induce maximum production of the education good. The order-generating information of planning must be combined with the rich and varied information of exchange, or nothing much by way of progress toward raising the educational experience to the highest level can be accomplished.

Exchange is the phenomenon of interaction between the environment and human experience. It is the personal side of education production, the interaction of an individual with natural and man-made things and other persons. It is everything that is liable to convey the human effort to know, to be, and to do something. This involves certain amounts of vagueness, ambiguity, speculation, as well as precision and hard facts, all of which combine in the pursuit of a vast variety of ends, often unrelated and contradictory ends. Exchange is the energy of learning, where the knower may add to that which is known, where final production of the good takes place.

John Dewey offered a most articulate description of exchange; here, from *Experience and Education* (1938), he deserves to be quoted at length:

> An experience is always what it is because of a transaction taking place between an individual and what, at the time, constitutes his environment, whether the latter consists of persons with whom he is talking about some

topic or event, the subject talked about being also a part of the situation; or the toys with which he is playing; the book he is reading (in which his environing conditions at the time may be England or ancient Greece or an imaginary region); or the materials of an experiment he is performing. The environment, in other words, is whatever conditions interact with personal needs, desires, purposes, and capacities to create the experience which is had. Even when a person builds a castle in the air he is interacting with the objects which he constructs in fantasy.

(43–44)

With exchange, then, we are plainly dealing not with terminology of an exact science but with an organic, mostly qualitative process of states of mind, character, habits, judgment, acts of choice, observation, passion— something that no precise formula or mathematical treatment could convey. The data of exchange are the context of time and space, the sum of conditions and antecedents that cumulatively determine learning; they are those transforming moments of insight and inward comprehension in which the individual human being (the cause and effect of production) is uniquely different from all others.

This exchange of knowledge and skills is so closely interwoven with the subjective experience of the individual that we perhaps shall never know all the causal factors and complex links that operate. It seems that too many situations and too many causes upon which the events of exchange turn remain inaccessible. They involve a vast number of interrelations that cannot be sorted out and predicted, and thus they are incapable of being wholly represented by numbers. The point is that the exchange process remains an area of production where vastly more is not known than is known.

It is clear that exchange and planning impart very different dynamics into production of the education good. Exchange starts with the information of the individual, and is driven by variations in points of view and differences in opinion as to the value of the good being produced. Its concepts and categories refuse to bow to the language and structure of efficiency and mathematical certainty. On the other hand, planning seeks to operate on a quantitative basis. Planning proceeds on the assumption that we can know in advance what is going to be learned at particular times and places. As a rule, it adheres to some fixed pattern between educational inputs and outputs, and it treats only the measurable aspects of the education good as real. Planning has to do with social ends, exchange with individual ends.

These are the salient differences that underlie the need for their interaction in education production. Planning and exchange must work closely together in order to create conditions in which the fullest use of information in production of the education good can take place. That there should be some planning in education production is quite clear; otherwise education becomes an aimless, even chaotic, act of improvisation. But there is an equal, perhaps even greater, risk for planning to push exchange out of production, because planning offers efficiency gains not realizable through exchange.

This lure of efficiency was a significant factor in the construction of the modern institution of education a century ago under municipal reform (Callahan 1962; Eaton 1990; Ravitch 2000; Horn 2002). Education then, as today, promised that under an expanding system greater efficiency could be realized in production without a significant loss in quality. This promise generally holds for the production of attainment, but fails in the production of knowledge and skill because a condition essential for minimizing the quality-efficiency trade-off is not present.

Efficiency gains accrue to this planned production because the same set of information can be utilized repeatedly to produce many copies of the good. Quality loss is avoided to the extent that the set of planned information controls variation in the input factors while simultaneously incorporating the desired attributes from inputs into the final product.

Information costs inevitably place an upper limit on the efficiency of a production system. A production process may approach absolute efficiency (or think that it has), but it never can be reached because real-world manifestations of input attributes, which vary from unit to unit, affect the quality characteristics of a given product. Improvements in quality at some point in production require adding information whose cost impinges on efficiency.[2]

The magnitude of this trade off between efficiency and information may be reducible when the causes of variation in the inputs are known. If, for example, the distribution of variation is known to approximate that of a normal curve, sampling can substitute for inspection of each and every input throughout the production process. Likewise, when variation in the hardness of steel is understood scientifically, producers can order in steel by the number with some assurance that variation is being held within a specified tolerance. This knowledge of variation makes it possible to lower the volume of information utilized in production without losing too much quality of information (Arrow 1974). Each input case, in other words, can be treated similarly to the next.

The information utilized in the production of attainment conforms to the requirements of planning because it is, or can be made, quantitative without much loss in quality. By abstracting the individuality of the student into a singular quantity, labeled a full-time equivalent student or average daily attendant, and then combining that with other quantifiable inputs such as numbers of classrooms and textbooks, scientific management of education proceeds to create a planned production function that yields significant improvements in school production.

But those net gains cannot be realized where exchange information is vital to the maximum production of the good such as in the case of knowledge and skill. The individuality of the student intrudes on efforts to establish a planned production function, because that variation interacts with each of the other variables included in such a function. For one individual, X dollars may effectuate some specified increase in test score while for another it may require X+ dollars to achieve a similar magnitude of increase. Smaller class size may improve learning for some students but not for others. It is not that these input factors do not make a difference; they do. But that difference varies from student to student. Each student's individuality is part of the production process that necessitates the incorporation of qualitative information derived from exchange—with teachers, classroom and school climates, other students, physical objects such as textbooks—to optimally produce knowledge and skill. This individuality of the student cannot be abstracted out of production without adverse consequences, for therein reside the gifts and talents unique to each student—the very human capital that the institution contracts, indeed, has an indispensable obligation, to cultivate. Here efficiency (a quantitative reduction of information) is always bought at the cost of less quality (a qualitative reduction of valuable information).

Education as a Technical Model

Scholars have long recognized that if there is any hope of reducing inequality in education, it lies in a better understanding of the production process. Thus, over the past four decades there has been a substantial body of research seeking to improve the relationship between educational inputs and learning outcomes. Hundreds of studies have tried to identify a single overarching formula for the optimum production of the education good.[3] But all such efforts have ended in failure.

The reason for this failure stems from a basic belief that unites all orthodox production function studies of modern times, namely, the belief in the possibility of the optimum education as the product of a technical procedure. This is a method of solution by systematic analysis and precise measurement. It is a process that seeks to establish a system of causal or statistical laws on the basis of what most often or invariably does occur. Studies that use this procedure are committed, on principle, to formulating the education good as a fixed-objective activity; they must specify a time frame, order priorities, and, so far as possible, establish with certainty the relationship among the factors of production. The aim is to construct a model that can yield accurate predictions about, or deliberately control, the behavior of educational events, one that can be tested by purely logical or mathematical means.

The production function (technical) model is attracted by a notion that a high degree of precision or certainty is attainable. The clear assumption is that if the plan has been correctly established, then a conclusive pattern or solution must be discoverable. It is part of this same line of approach to assume that preferences are known and unchanging, that there is universal acceptance of educational goals, that we know the full range of choices and options before us, that there are no time constraints, that all the relevant information is fully available; and thus the only unsolved problems are technical: how to select and organize the best means to attain the given educational ends.

However, there seems to exist very little justification for the use of this procedure. Its assumptions are not credible since they bear no resemblance to the real world of uncertainty and change that we find in education. Insufficient resources, in fact, dominate the problems in the production of education: incomplete information about our options and the means to achieve them, and our need to choose, to sacrifice some ultimate values to others. What we are dealing with is a situation in which a multiplicity of ends must compete for a limited quantity of means. Numerous individuals are attempting to work out different educational goals and purposes, yet they are not in command of the same resources and opportunities for doing so. Thus choices must be made, and losses accepted in the pursuit of some preferred educational ends.

Which educational goals should be chosen, who will do the choosing, what are the valid criteria for such choices, and many more questions of this kind are not purely technical. They are not merely problems about the best method to secure a given end, nor are they mere questions of fact, of logical or deductive reasoning, but are more properly, and in the broadest sense, economic. These pertain to the economic field because so much of it deals with the social process, with communicating information, with reconciling contending human interests and desires, and with making the most effective use of the resources we have, which in its very essence involves value judgments and real human choices.

Many economic phenomena can, in principle, be reduced to rational calculation of given quantities of goods. But this is far from being the case in education, where its operations extend well beyond the bounds of the technical system. To think of the production of education is to bring human volition and potential infinite variables into play. This includes what people want, admire, select, reject; it involves the interpretation of signals, the evaluation of advantages and disadvantages, the invention of problems and new solutions, the adaptation to past experience, and the risk of misfortune. The very forces that shape the production of the education good rest on the uncertainty and unpredictability of human thought and action. The process is one of trial and error; it is a procedure of discovery in the development of human beings, the features of which may perhaps never be traced in detail.

The main point is that this whirlpool of diverse information is vital to the production of the education good. Indeed, maximum production of the good will not take place without the utilization of the rich and varied information derived from exchange—which, once more, is the interaction of individuals with other persons and things. The mistake of the technical method is to assume that complete production of the education good can take place prior to the exchange. But clearly this is not the case—learning does not occur without the active participation of the learner.

To adopt the categorical planning of the technical model is to take away the most crucial part of education production—independent human action—and treat that production as if it consists only of quantities of goods and services. We should not forget that where human intentions and acts of choice play no part, it is imperative to drop the context of what education is desirable and to whom. For no serious questions about educational ends or values can arise, only empirical questions about the most efficient means to the goal.

By its failure to establish an all-inclusive production function, the orthodox model has made it quite clear that disorder tends to turn up in the production of education. This body of research has gone a long way to show that the complex pattern of human exchange, with all of its uncertainty of variation, is an intrinsic factor of education production, which, in its turn, carries with it several implications.

Consider that for most information goods the cost of reproduction is much less than the cost of production, software being the classic example where once the information is put together it is not scarce. Its marginal costs are minor. Kenneth Arrow has pointed out that whether production is for one unit or one million units, the same piece of information can be used repeatedly and indefinitely multiplied without diminishment, which leads to fixed costs.[4]

However, marginal costs look different in a domain where the individual is seen as a factor of production, and where we cannot control for the variability of the individual. Such is the case with education, and with other information systems that share these properties, that inputs vary from unit to unit, and can change in multiple ways throughout the productive process. In other words, input prices vary with each unit of production, because the amount and kind of information required for production is different for each person. In essence, education approaches something of an infinite production set (or a nonproduction function), where each student's learning is in many respects a special case, an individual order.

Given the high information content and uncontrollable variation of the inputs, we do not know if it is less expensive to reproduce the education good than to produce it in the first place. These costs are uncertain, and, in theory, can range from zero to infinity depending on the context and the abilities and needs of the persons involved in the exchange. Economies of scale may be possible, but only if individual exchange is diminished as a factor of production. Fixed costs do not exist where the producer and the product are one and the same—and human.

In the light of the foregoing, it is clear that the technical approach to education production is inadequate to its task. Its failure lies in the fact that it disregards too much of the unique information of the individual—the essential factor on which the maximum production of the education good depends. This is not to deny that the system may make genuine gains in order and efficiency and in predictive power by detaching individual exchange from production; but in doing so it sacrifices its capacity to amass the information needed to narrow the gap between its production of knowledge and skills and that of education attainment. However, none of this has restrained education's production process from being drawn toward the strict planning of the technical procedure.

Trading Off Information

The impelling forces of greater institutional scale have increased the volume of demands on education. These demands include the fundamental aspirations, ideals, and the deepest needs of human beings: personal rights, civil liberties, moral and religious obligations, conceptions of education, and so forth. They are what people long for and live by—their principles and values, preferences and desires; they may embody what is common or separate, trivial or important, good or evil, permanent or transient. All of these demands, be they public or private, represent information of varying costs within the institution, information that needs to be managed and directed in production, information that must compete for resources under conditions of inherent scarcity.

When goals or values clash, questions of choice inevitably arise. Should public security in a given situation be promoted at the expense of individual liberty, or cooperation at the expense of competition, or quantity at the expense of quality, or expediency or loyalty at the expense of truth? When such dilemmas arise, it is incumbent upon the decision makers to adjust claims and engage in trade-offs—values, principles, and desires must yield to each other at varying rates in specific circumstances.

But how do we choose between competing possibilities? What are the standards that guide education decision makers in choosing between alternative uses of scarce resources? The actual decision to trade off one value against another depends to a remarkably large degree on the context; it may be influenced by local customs, ideologies, perceptions of reality, transaction costs, political considerations, or a host of other formal and informal constraints at work in a particular environment. Often there are no hard and fast rules when it comes to making such trade-offs. A given trade-off may be highly valuable in one case, somewhat valuable in another, and absolutely damaging in still another case. The relative weights of costs and benefits vary from situation to situation.

For example, in a certain instance it may be more important to sacrifice some improvement to the school library in order to fund the marching band, or forego hiring more teachers for hiring more administrators, or give up learning foreign languages for learning to drive, or sacrifice artistic studies for technical studies. When contemplating complex trade-offs, the question at any point is usually one of degree: how much of one desired goal should we demand at the cost of getting less of another (Sowell 1980). These decisions may differ from place to place, even as they occur within the perimeter of the same institution. They are all changeable and incrementally preferable depending upon the situation at hand.

In essence, each one of these decisions is a trade-off of information; each is a factor in the system that drives productive activity; each, with and without intention, functions to supply information to the production of the education good. Here again we must stress the point that in many cases there is no single standard or litmus test for determining the choices between competing options. Each is a unique event, in which one ambition, rule, or value may at any given time outrank another. In other words, there is no bottom line or marginal cost rubric that applies to all transactions— cost comparisons are contextually bound. Thus the process seems ad hoc and patternless. However, when we survey the whole field of these trade-offs over time, they form this clear and consistent pattern: two types of information are being incrementally traded off for one another according to their respective costs. In a word, low-cost (universal) information is being selected, while high-cost (particular) information is being set aside.

To understand the reasons for this trade-off, we need only reflect a moment on what makes information more or less costly in the productive system. Information is less costly (in financial or other terms) to the degree that it (1) successfully connects cause and effect; (2) yields a sense of certainty; (3) exhibits clear utility; (4) complements profitable activities; (5) uses relatively fewer resources to ascertain its costs and benefits; (6) increases legibility, verification, and enforcement; and (7) is comparatively easy to acquire, process, reproduce, and transmit. This kind of information tends to be technical in nature. That is, its properties tend to be quantifiable and are least subject to change; its costs and benefits can be estimated with a fair degree of precision; and its categories are logically compatible with planning and the production of education attainment.

By contrast, it is the dynamic terms—variable, indefinite, and nonlinear—that capture the essence of the higher-cost sources of information. This is the kind of information that is most applicable to the field of human activity, its qualities stir up and facilitate interactions between persons, and its varying strains play an indispensable role in making possible the exchange of knowledge and skills. This correspondence to the flow of human activity means that its costs and benefits are hard to pin down. They generally are not capable of demonstration by common mathematical techniques. They tend to consist of the nonquantifiable categories—those that create noise and uncertainty in the system. Thus, the resources needed to ascertain particular information's costs and benefits are, on the whole, greater than those of the technical (universal) categories of information.

This filtering of information through the sieve of cost proves to be a rational means of establishing what is good for education (or where the rewards are highest) and how to achieve this. Indeed, the cost metric induces a parting of the ways: it serves to separate the relevant from the irrelevant, the worthwhile from the worthless, the permitted from the forbidden, and the expensive from the cheap. Cost (assessed in money or other terms) is the decisive distinction between the two sets of information. However, no clear boundary marks this division. In practice the line between the two is often blurred, for any given trade-off may involve a mixture of both high- and low-cost types of information—with some nearer to, and some farther from, the line that divides them.

That we cannot precisely bisect this information, however, does not mean that a split is not taking place. The division of information—the displacement of high-cost information by low-cost information—is a pattern that arises over the long term. It is an ordering of information that emerges from the vast array of demands and preferences that are constantly being traded off against each other. What is involved here is a redirection of productive resources into the least-cost means of achieving the good.

This selection of low-cost factors of production over high-cost factors is assuredly the most significant aspect of the division of information. What makes it crucial is that it determines the form and content of the network of communication—the framework of rules, incentives, codes of conduct, rights, beliefs, and customs of the institution, all of which function as the productive structure, all of which become more technical in reason as the roster of low-cost information builds up in the system.

This circulation of technical information creates an environment that lends itself to the production of attainment, one whose elements can claim greater precision, verifiability, and an increased capacity for rational control. Such a model is intent on bringing all production before the bar of efficiency. Its aim is to lower operating costs, to diminish disorder, and to allow for a minimum of change. In time, the work of the entire framework becomes adjusted to a narrow, instrumental conception of the good—to production designed for the large scale. This education, understood in the light of technical reasoning, leaves little or no space for individualized (high-cost) forms of information; it becomes a rigid and depersonalized entity, with no integral connection to the uniqueness of the individual. This is what the division of information comes to: an environment of mere objective phenomena, which over time grows less and less favorable, even hostile, to the production and exchange of knowledge and skills.

Path Dependence

All of the foregoing effects intensify and become more prevalent with the expansion of the institution. With the increase in scale, more and more of the thought and practice of the institution—its stock of rules, incentives, traditions, and beliefs—absorb the logic and reasoning of technical (universal) information. And as this information gains a secure foothold, it moves the productive system to adopt more measurable and more predictable processes, edging it closer to the cost-saving regularity of the static model, growing the conditions in which there is greater capacity to organize around the production of attainment. Here the reality of path dependence is in sight.

Path dependence is, above all, the ways in which human beings deal with one another. It is a development based on the assent of millions of interacting people, a direction long and generally observed, the cumulative consequence of our whole thinking about education. In other words, it is what becomes normative in such notions as progress, the good, quality, moral duty, and so forth. This involves an inner and an outer conformity to the demands of a specific form of organizational life, a persistent tendency to believe in and pursue a particular course of action.[5]

The ascendancy of this course of action depends on the internal necessities of this process: the selection of information, the adaptation to future events; the competition over resources, the learning of new skills; the growth of returns, and the aggregation of individual preferences. Each does its part to produce the full interwoven fabric of path dependence, that is, to shape the structure of human action, to define the opportunity set of individuals, to build a body of knowledge, and to create an environment congenial to a particular form of production. But this is not the whole of path dependence, to be sure, for it is itself an obscure name for the uncountable totality of events that include the most immediate experience of human beings.

One enters into a union with this institutional path not so much by means of its laws as with belief in the order of thought, language, feeling, and volition that are being created. The orthodoxy that emerges is the work of years of conflict, strife, and consent; and it owes much of its form to putting into practice again and again those ends, beliefs, and policies that tend to pay off in the system. All of this, in turn, paves the way for specialization of function, for one form of production winning out over others, for the forces of feedback to indicate to the institution as a whole that the effort to increase the level of educational attainment is a dividend-paying investment.

With its lower costs and higher net gains, the production of attainment carries the force of being the most richly rewarded work in the system; it is the act that advances profit making most visibly and most significantly. Hence attainment is the goal toward which the institution most amply and most willingly responds—pouring its capital and energy into activities that enhance its growth. The gains realized from this effort tend to breed new and more intense effort in the same direction, after which the entire cycle begins again. Once it starts, this process of replication acquires the property of perpetual expansion, which, in the very exercise of its activity, proceeds to clear the way for a single standard of evaluation to emerge.

This involves more than a brief or isolated change in assessment procedures. In fact it involves a radical change of the entire base and rationale of decision making. In essence, it is a shift from a more generalized notion of cost (or value), one that for the most part is contingent on context, to a notion of cost that is primarily dependent on measures of attainment. The shift takes place over the long term as the institution submits to the attraction of expansion, for in so doing it has the strong incentive to resolve more of its concepts and questions of choice by the trial of attainment.

The change that this involves means that attainment becomes the controlling reference point, the fixed or axiomatic standard, in terms of which all expressions claiming to be profitable can be certified as genuine. It becomes the benchmark that lurks in the background of almost every kind of decision; it constrains future choices, defining success and failure, and dictating the terms of institutional production. Considering the strength of the incentives, it is not difficult to see why this should happen. For, the use of attainment as a decision-supporting metric satisfies the demand for an objective way to estimate the marginal change in welfare that results from a policy or regulatory decision. In other words, attainment proves to be a dependable instrument by which to derive cost-benefit profiles; it serves as a systemic method by which to judge the comparative advantages of different uses of resources. The point here is that by using this standard the costs of decision making go down, which may be where its chief advantage lies.

We must conceive of this process as creating a state of affairs in which the avowed object is to get more people to pursue higher levels of schooling. Under the circumstances, every effort is made to assimilate everyone's primary needs to those that are capable of being met by more education. It stands to reason, then, that any source of information that does not meet the requirements of being verifiably relevant to this end is regarded as no more than ancillary to the productive agenda of the organization. Such information makes communication difficult, and thus it tends to be judged as problematic (expensive), needing some special explanation or justification for investing in its selection. Indeed, if any information obstructs the pattern of maximizing attainment, or if it is in some way found to be incompatible with arrangements required by this ideal, it must be excluded from the process of production. All deviation from the path of attainment can prove costly.

From this point on there is a readiness to adjust to conventions and submit to the direction that gives meaning, value, and legitimacy to all that we do in education. There is a willingness to move in line with and confirm the perceived optimum pattern of behavior. In this environment all structures of thought become vertical, and all the individual goals and ends become bound to one another in steadfast pursuit of more attainment. The rise of this single standard of evaluation signals the emergence of path dependence—the integrative force that creates deep layers of belief in the benefits of increasing education attainment.

Path dependence blends together the elements of scale, time, and competition to create an institutional landscape in which the balance of preferences shifts toward attainment. It is through competition for the resources of production that individuals discover where the returns exceed the costs; they discover that more profit is to be gained in a particular way; they discover the fact that there simply is not enough to go around. This forces all productive units to adapt to probabilities and to use scarce resources more efficiently, which, as the quantity of trade grows, results in systemic trade-offs: attainment in place of knowledge and skills, planning instead of exchange, quality given up for efficiency, and the individual sacrificed for the collective. In time, this competitive process creates a unity and coherence of views about what is best and most rewarding; and it is because of it that the structure of rules and property rights become organized around the production of attainment.

This highlights an important point, and what perhaps is the main merit of this process, namely, that coercion may be kept to a minimum. The system succeeds in securing direction in production without appealing to a sense of obligation beyond consent. Such a force draws on time and its stages of growth and on the accumulation of precedents to eliminate the motives for the pursuit of ends that may not conform to what seems to constitute the productive forms of education. Its pattern of expansion offers unity, security, and sufficient strength to divert demand into the direction of attainment while preserving the impression of free choice. Indeed, it does not call for the abdication of choice or liberty; rather it demands rationality and sublimation of choices and options to the exigencies of its productive process.

In this framework, where moving up the education ladder presses upon every mind, the agenda mechanism need not affirm a preferred conception of the good. It does not have to take sides. Competing conceptions of the good fade into the background, and all possible alternatives to the work of increasing attainment are seen as diversions of energy toward less-valuable interests and occupations. Students, teachers, managers, and public officials alike—all adhere to the line and priority of attainment, their common quality being a devotion to an order the value of which is not open to question. It is a system in which the direction has been set for them, and chosen by them, and all exercise their choice to function in an organized way to raise the production of attainment. It is the total triumph of this vision and course of action that makes possible the aggregation of dissimilar preferences without complete authority or compulsory power.

The inference to which we are brought is that path dependence represents a massive capital commitment on the part of the institution. This commitment rests on a specific vision of progress and the construction of a vast network of communication whose web of interconnections leads us to assent to the demands and promises of greater educational attainment. And if to this consideration we add that it provides beneficial effects on a progressive scale, and that it rests on the principle of consent, it will easily be seen that it is not a readily reversible process.

Notes

1. Habermas (1988: 96) provided the following explanation of the usefulness of measurable data: "Methodologically speaking, measurements fulfill two functions. Data that have been measured have the advantage of making possible a reliable simplification of controversies about the accuracy of existence claims; measurement operations that can in principle be repeated guarantee the intersubjectivity of experience. Measurements are also of interest in the construction of categories. Data that have been measured have the advantage of being precisely defined through operations; the measurement standards permit subtle distinctions and thus more precise descriptions than are possible in everyday language, even though the operational definitions themselves remain dependent on ordinary-language explanations."
2. For a clear and concise explanation of variation and how different production processes attempt to handle it, see Wheeler (1993).
3. Attempts by a generation of scholars to identify the mix of resources that constitute the educational production function have not yielded robust results. Only a miniscule portion of the total variation in school achievement can be directly connected to the allocation of specific resources. Even the once-promising research on effective schools has lost much of its luster as scholars deconstruct "effective leadership" and "focused mission" and discover that these constructs are either tautologically related to school performance or exceedingly difficult to transport to schools outside the sample population. Had this research succeeded—or if it does sometime in the future—it could greatly improve efficiency in allocating scarce resources because a system of property rights could be attached to resource exchanges. If we knew what mix of resources caused learning in students, we could devise an allocation system that results in far greater equality of achievement and attainment than is presently being realized. See Hanushek (1989). See also Monk (1996) and Card and Krueger (1996).
4. For Arrow's explanation of the way in which an information theory of value could be developed see Chichilnisky (1999).
5. For a thorough description of the concept of path dependence, see David (2001).

CHAPTER 4

The Individual and the Collective in Education

Every major reform effort in education over the past 100 years has proceeded on the belief that expanding access to education would increase social welfare. The belief rests on the assumption that the efficiencies of scale will enable the institution to better meet the needs of more students, that growth will unify the diversity of interests, that it will balance the claims of the individual and those of the collective.

However, expansion prevents the realization of these goals. The growth of scale requires the division (trade-off) of information, which is inconsistent with equilibrium. The interaction of scale and information must favor the collective over the individual. This means that within the institution collective valuations increasingly replace the valuations of the individual. The effect is to downgrade or lower the estimate of the individual's purposive character and role in production and resource allocation.

In this chapter, we describe the part certain reforms have played in facilitating this movement. The explanation of this shift toward the collective in production identifies (1) how the educational philosophy of progressivism evolved into essentialism, (2) how the locus of decision making moves from local to centralized control, and (3) how the filtering of educational production and trade through the institution violates the central precepts of human capital (market) theory. First, we show that one of the principal architects of twentieth-century education, John Dewey, failed to understand the mean-ends problem associated with educational production, that his end concerning high quality, personalized educational experiences for children was logically inconsistent with the imposition of his means, a system of production tied to a technical model working against the end Dewey sought. Second, we show how the expansion of access to higher levels of attainment required a closing of this means-ends problem through standardization (essentialism) and more centralized control over the terms of educational trade. Third, we show how human capital theory fails to take into account the dissipation of information about human talent development that occurs under institutional expansion.

Dewey and the Means-Ends Problem

The last 100 years of American education have been a tribute to one of its chief architects, John Dewey. For better or worse, Dewey's role and contribution to the institution of education cannot be underestimated. He helped to provide the theoretical impetus for expansion while failing to understand that the subsequent effects upon information would prevent the achievement of his high-quality, high-cost educational ends for individual children. This miscalculation would later produce patterns of inequality and student marginalization that continue to plague us today. In Dewey we have a premier example of the misapplication of a means to a given end. But an important irony also emerges—the means of Dewey's Progressive philosophy of education, when actualized in praxis (curriculum and teaching) and policy (social control) transmuted into an inconsistent end: a narrow essentialism that helped to drive the intensification of the technical model of production in education.[1]

A key to understanding Dewey is located within his mature epistemology. Remaining under the influence of Hegelian synthesizing, Dewey in his Gifford Lectures (*The Quest for Certainty,* 1929) rejected earlier epistemologies because, he argued, they require that a preference be granted to the object under or within one's view; that an independent objective reality was difficult to control and must be subjectified and bounded under the domain of human control. Subject and object are in effect isolated from each other; all prior epistemologies (e.g., idealism, realism, and skepticism) sought to separate out or dichotomize the knower from the known, theory from practice, particular from universal, individual from collective, and knowledge from making and doing (action). "Knowing" in realism (warranted true belief), antirealism, and skepticism all seem to require granting, in Dewey's terms, "regal aloofness"— making the object in view "king"—"to any beholding mind that may gaze upon it" (1929: 17–20). These earlier epistemologies were inherited from a prior age and quest for certainty, but restrict human ingenuity.

Given Dewey's theory of action, these old epistemologies could not be allowed to hold sway any longer; they all interfere with heightening the human knower (and collective species) requisite for collective problem solving (all philosophy for Dewey was problem solving); they artificially separate theory from practice, thought from action; and they construct barriers that prevent the individual from being fully integrated into the collective. Dewey's solution was to vest (qualified) certainty into science (its methods, procedures, etc.) and reduce nearly everything else to mere belief; in science we can be certain, everything else is a reduction and probabilistic. Here, a substitutionary move is achieved: "traditional" ontology is replaced with the new tools and procedures of science. Dewey tried to meld theory to practice, the individual to the collective, and the particular to the universal in order to achieve a social equilibrium based upon just (like) relations among people. In this sense, Dewey is an important forebear of game theorists and political philosophers such as John Nash and John Rawls who tried to achieve similar sets of conditions.

Thus Dewey, a preeminent proponent of the technical model, was schizophrenic in his view, wanting on the one hand to retain high-cost (high-quality) aims of education for children and, on the other hand, wedding these to low-cost means of production. In essence there are three senses of Dewey: one deeply interested in the high-quality teacher/school exchange with the individual child; another concerned with the productive individual (their interests, talents, and desires) being absorbed into the social interests of the collective; and a third with the ingenuity to provide a technical means by which the individual is in fact absorbed into the collective. Even within its historical context (e.g., heightened humanism and robust momentum of the social sciences), the logic of Dewey's means and ends were conceptually incoherent; his means, the absorption of the individual into the collective by technical means, necessarily won out over his ends, the high-cost individualized educational exchange.

Dewey, whose thought was colored by the values of individualism, believed that the advantages of knowledge could be secured by providing a maximum degree of liberty. As Dewey saw it, learning requires the development of self-directed, creative beings, students possessing maximum freedom of choice in a dynamic environment producing maximum opportunities for individual and social growth. In his conception of education, the school was to provide high-interest (high-cost) opportunities in the curriculum for children and adolescents. But Dewey's emphasis upon the development of individual growth gave way to an even more important and larger goal: social advancement. Dewey suggested that social democracy is the final object of all curricula, of all the factors of education production (1973b: 454–467). Social progress depended upon the work of the schools; Dewey's central reform was to align the work of the school "along common lines, in a common spirit, and with reference to common aims" (1973a: 459). In other words, the progressive conception of schooling was one of a natural social unit where productive exchange had a unified, standardized aim of activity. It is not far from this point that individuality (privately held interests and preferences) must be subsumed or assimilated into collectivity (group-held interests and preferences), which is to say that costs are transmitted onto particular information.

Dewey's morphic account is in contrast to Adam Smith's view of markets (and later, that of human capital theory) wherein the social realm and the public good are by-products of individual rationality. Dewey sought a solution by the wedding of means and ends through social science methodology, a process that seeks to establish a system of causal relations, and solve educational problems, principally on the basis of changes in the rules of procedure within the technical model of production: "The other alternative [in the production of education] is systematic utilization of scientific method as the pattern and ideal of intelligent exploration and exploitation of the potentiality inherent in experience" (1938: 86). For Dewey, questions about the right education and the life people should lead were capable of empirical treatment. He believed that if all the relevant factors were allowed for, and when these were aligned in the appropriate social sequence, a single path to human fulfillment could be realized through a scientific (re)organization of human life.[2] Dewey believed that the antitheses between "individualism and socialism, capitalism and communism" were mere platitudes and suggested that the central issue was really between "chaos and order, chance and control: the haphazard use and the planned use of scientific techniques" (1973a: 396).

What Dewey ultimately failed to realize is the reductio of his incongruent positions: that the expansion of education as an institution primes demand for a low-cost methodology (in delivery and assessment) and goals relative to the good; it ultimately must attenuate libertarian individuality. Dewey thought that "human growth" could become the standard of measurement (the end). But under increasing scale, the division of information forces growth to be measured in low-cost, usually quantifiable ways (e.g., test scores). Growth can never mean the development of the "whole" person for two reasons: (1) the technical model superimposes ontologically narrow and rationally restrictive meanings of "person," and (2) the information cost is simply too high to assess all the nuances of individual human growth. The result is that Deweyan ends (high-cost quality exchanges) are forced to cohere with, and are therefore assimilated by, Deweyan means (a technical realignment of production).

In rejecting this conclusion, Dewey and the Progressives lost the debate for establishing control over the very questions they had explored so profoundly. The answers to the big questions of social policy—what should be taught, to whom, and by whom—were captured by the Essentialists who courted education through the lure of technique, delivering a means for standardizing teaching-learning, making possible mass education, and, with it, an expansion of attainment. Quantifiable measures of intelligence

(IQ scores) substituted for "human growth" potential, curricular tracking for individual choice. As the institution expanded, a whole range of education ends that Dewey espoused—citizenship, moral development, ingenuity and creativity, aesthetic appreciation, as well as much of the traditional K-12 curriculum, namely, music, performing and fine arts, ancient and modern languages—became vulnerable to the educationist's knife because it was methodologically difficult to measure their sanctifying benefits.

Ironically, Dewey's quest promoted science (technical methods) as a universalizing method, a logic of information, creating an implicit air of certainty;[3] but its philosophic vulnerability rested upon an as-yet-unrealized inductive promise; it has not (principally because it cannot) provided certainty within or about the human realm. It is restricted from doing so by its own tenets, resulting in an important paradox: while giving the appearance of providing a method for achieving certainty about human action, it does so while at the same time reducing everything—all such knowledge claims, including its own—to an a priori probability. Technical methods may address the *what* of education, but not the *why;* they may identify the *conditions* of the classroom, but cannot deal with *values;* they can speak about the *sensory systems* of the human being, but are less qualified to discuss the inner sanctums of the *human mind,* its products (ideas, ideals, and preferences); they can produce *facts* for policy makers and managers, but are less capable of evaluating educational *aims,* future consequences, ethics, and decisions.

The technical model engages a large volume but narrow range of information. It can succeed in bringing together means-ends relations, but must do so through a division of information that separates out particular from universal information. It is this process that has made essentialism the dominant philosophy of education. It enables reformers to address the big questions of policy by shifting the frame of reference for judging value within the institution from the individual toward the collective, identifying the public good with the collective and labeling the values held by individuals as private interests, even though in an economic sense the realization of these individual preferences procures broader (highly important) benefits to society. In essence, it shifts the meaning of public-private from an economic to a social construct—one that makes the public good coextensive with the division of information taking place within the institution.

The Trend toward Central Control

Over the past century, governance in education shifted from local to more centralized control—from the neighborhood school to the unified school district, from the local district to a partnership of state and federal governments.

These shifts in the primary unit of educational governance should be viewed as a turnover in property rights resulting from the interactive effects of expansion and the division of information. The demand for expansion of the institution requires a trade off of information—local control (the particular) for centralization (the universal).

The withering away of local control occurs because institutional expansion—the granting of increased access to higher levels of attainment—carries with it a requirement for more universal (standardized) rules of production that must be made by an authority, a governing unit, which has influence over the enlarged zone of trade. This process of change in the structure of property rights proceeds in two phases: (1) a destructive one in which accessions to demands for expansion undercut the legitimacy of the existing order of rules, and result in recognizable institutional failure; and (2) a reconstitution of rules and the governing unit that issues them.

The fundamental choice that underlies institutional expansion is not between freedom and bigger government, but between freedom and economic growth. This choice imposes itself because the efficiency (even existence) of markets depends upon the presence of a secure system of property rights. The fact that most people may have an antipathy to the kind of external control government represents is no bar to political centralization. They also want the benefits that economic growth can bring.

The process begins with a build up of demand for more schooling—triggered by changes in technology, the exhaustion of opportunities available under the existing institutional framework, and the encroachment of external markets. In the case of the shift from the school to the school district, it was the macro changes of industrialization and urbanization, and their impact on occupational structure that gave rise to demands for schooling beyond grammar school.[4] The neighborhood school, and its rural counterpart, the one-room schoolhouse, could no longer function as the primary governing unit when entry into the labor market required secondary education for an ever-growing proportion of students. The institution required a system organized around the provision of both elementary and high school education. It, therefore, eliminated tens of thousands of local governing boards through the device of district consolidation. By mid-century there were fewer than 20,000 school districts operating in the United States, where there had once been more than 200,000. Yet, the primacy of the school district did not hold. During the second half of the century, the school district itself lost influence to state and national governments as demands for college education increased in response to the rise of the service (knowledge) sector of the economy and the press of global economic competition on the workforce. Once again the unit of governance needed to be enlarged (centralized), and once again the public traded off the principle of subsidiarity (limited government) for the benefits of growth. This shift in control from the district to the state/federal government occurred because it enabled the institution to increase attainment from elementary-secondary schooling to higher education. Control expressed itself in statewide master plans integrating the curriculum across these sectors, the specification of matriculation from one level of schooling to the next (standards and testing), and guarantees of some form of postsecondary education to almost all students who stayed in the system (civil rights). District governing boards still existed, but they legislated within a framework of institutional rules that severely attenuated their control over resource allocation. State and federal governments became the primary units in setting the terms of trade and production, a remarkable turn of events given the credo of localism that once imbued the institution.

These shifts in the primary unit of governance entail a changeover in property rights that is discontinuous, prolonged, and conflicted. Conflict arises because of the interactive effects of scale on the formation of property rights. Relative to the rules of localism, the centralized governing unit constructs a framework of property rights that strengthens production on a more technical basis: unifying measures of ends and standardizing (the means of) resource allocation across the enlarged governing unit. In so doing, it purges, or weakens, rights particular to what were once autonomous, local communities. The diversity of ends and means that once existed comes to be seen within the new framework as an impediment to growth, as a barrier to higher levels of educational attainment, as an expression of special interest, as something to get rid of. Slogans such as "let's keep politics out of education" and "no child left behind" impute local rights as the principal barrier to progress, and invest rationality in more centralized control.

This conflict helps explain why reform of the old governing unit does not work. The new rules constitute an externality on the existing framework of property rights; they weaken the ability of holders of property rights within the jurisdiction of the primary governing unit to allocate resources efficiently. The more the system tries to reform itself, the more loss of control over production it generates. This loss manifests itself politically as chaotic, circular, social choices, and a system beset by special interests. The primary governing unit, under the pressure of reform, loses its ability to set goals and allocate resources rationally. The primary consequence is a loss of production—a persistent shortfall in the production of knowledge and skill relative to that of attainment. Eventually, the governing unit is declared an institutional failure and replaced by a more centralized one capable of developing a coherent system of property rights across the new, larger sphere of trade.[5]

Generally speaking, this turnover in rights is a prolonged process, because a large market must arise capable of absorbing many smaller, autonomous ones. This means that sufficient economic and political capital needs to be invested to establish a market roughly coterminus in size with what will become the new governing unit. In the nineteenth century, for example, it took a long time for the seeds of secondary education to sprout. The movement away from a property right framework built around neighborhood governance gained momentum in the 1870s, but it still took until roughly the 1910s for trade in secondary education to reach a size where municipal and rural educational reformers could restructure rights around the district as the primary governing unit.

Sidebar 4.1 Andrew Carnegie and Central Control

At the beginning of the twentieth century, at the outset of the era of the modern educational system, Andrew Carnegie (1835–1919) encapsulated particularly well the argument for state control of education. Carnegie at first thought that any young person could achieve economic success in America through hard work and enterprise. In his writings and speeches, Carnegie repeatedly asserted his confidence that every individual, regardless of origin, had an equal chance to achieve material and social success in an open and free society. He often pointed to himself as an example of this possibility by noting that he had grown up in poverty but emerged as one of the wealthiest individuals in the country.

His position on this matter gradually changed, however, as he examined more carefully the growing importance of large-scale corporations within the economy. The bureaucratization of the economy, as manifested by the rise of large corporations, increasingly placed a premium on education for obtaining a job within these organizations and for moving up the corporate hierarchy. The new economic environment created by industrialization was making education vital to the sorting process of the labor market. Convinced that opportunity was disappearing in America, Carnegie eventually agreed that some form of state intervention was necessary to assure each individual an equal opportunity to compete for jobs.

Andrew Carnegie is an especially good example because his argument for government intervention in education forcefully stated the most common line of reasoning on this matter. Carnegie and other advocates for state control of education successfully argued that education produced benefits that spilled over to all members of society. They argued, for example, that decisions about whether to go to school should not be left to the individual (or the family unit) but rather should be determined collectively.

This collectivist vision held sway. Education came to be identified with national progress, nation building, economic prosperity, and manifold other social benefits. Throughout the twentieth century, education was widely seen as an instrument of socialization capable of changing moral values and individual behavior, as well as instilling utility skills needed in the labor force. Advancement within the professions and the bureaucratically structured corporate entities increasingly depended upon one's educational achievements. Another view widely and strongly held was that secure, objective instruments of the state (e.g., public policy, law) would allow individuals to obtain jobs in the labor market, based on merit and the knowledge and skills they acquired in school. State intervention in education was necessary to offset the socioeconomic inequalities of class privilege and family background. Proponents such as Carnegie argued that the state, presumed a just arbiter between individual-collective issues, should intervene between the institutions of the family and the labor market in order to make the sorting process fair and provide each child with an opportunity to succeed.

The arguments for state control over schooling were strong, yet the fulfillment of such a policy was remote without the establishment of an integrated ladder of educational attainment—one that linked primary, elementary, secondary, and higher education into a unified system. Many educators, civic and business leaders, such as Carnegie, as well as ordinary citizens, called attention to the need for a coherent, unified system of schooling to fulfill the vital function of career preparation. For many people throughout the century, a unified system of education offered some hope in restoring and maintaining a society based on equality of opportunity.

Carnegie and others recognized that because not all the rungs on the educational ladder were meant for everyone, the state became the logical instrument of unification that facilitated access and expansion. Subverting individual and family-unit decision making was not seen as a cost against society; the visible benefits of social improvement through state intervention in education tended to conceal it.[6]

Resistance within the primary governing unit also prolongs matters. Big-city school districts were able to blunt federal influence in the 1960s by subvention of federal funds, coopting mandated citizen advisory councils, and pushing federal projects off to the periphery of their instructional delivery systems. For a time it appeared that they had the upper hand. But that changed as the emerging market became more robust and its rule system more dense. District control over the primary inputs to education production—budget, personnel, curriculum, and student policy—became increasingly circumscribed by court rulings, state and federal legislation, and a plethora of rules supporting trade within the emerging market. In this environment, where property rights were being made less secure, district officials created loosely coupled organizational structures, reinvented machine politics, hired legal counsel, and established special departments to regularize relations with state and federal governments. These adjustments bought time, but they did little to solve the problem of control loss that beset production. By the mid-1980s it was painfully obvious that not only was the district, as the primary governing unit, no longer delivering coherent, consistent educational services, but that it had also lost the capacity for doing so.

Just as had occurred following the decline of the rural one-room schoolhouse, recognition of institutional failure of the district provoked consideration of various alternative frameworks—site-based management, parental choice, and professional autonomy (Katz 1975). But these discussions, for the most part, failed to recognize that the driver of institutional change was a changeover in the relative importance of markets—from one organized around elementary-secondary education to one encompassing universal access to higher education. The origin of the failure of the district was not rent-seeking bureaucrats or self-interested board members.[7] It was the cost being imposed on that governance system (and its framework of property rights) by the growth of a market outside the reach of local governance. That market thrived because federal and state governments continuously strengthened its framework of property rights during the latter half of the twentieth century. Civil rights, for example, weakened the governance of local school districts in areas such as curriculum, personnel, and student policy, but it also opened the higher education market to a vast number of people who ordinarily did not participate in the education process (by century's end, more women than men received college degrees). Universal rules, such as these, gained value because they allowed expansion (growth) to continue; they increased the capacity of the institution for developing social cooperation; they became seen as the source of stability, the means toward realization of the common good, whereas the particular (local control) absorbed cost and lost legitimacy.

Centralization functions to set the agenda for the direction of production around the larger market. It enables the institution to make a discontinuous break with its past: to purge itself of the costs of local rights, and fully integrate production and trade within the more global market. In so doing, it offers the promise of greater allocational efficiency by changing uncertainty into ascertainable risk, to borrow North's term (1991: 105 106). It makes the exchangeable property right (the flow of education goods and services, degrees, and credentials) more secure by specifying the good to be exchanged and the rules of competition. For the consumer, it offers a relatively low-cost channel of information from which the individual can roughly gauge the probability of success in climbing higher up the education ladder. For the supplier, it offers a set of specifiable criteria for optimizing the allocation of scarce resources.

This change in the property rights structure (the rules), and the movement toward greater centralization have important implications for the production of the education good. These include (1) the institution's realignment of the production of knowledge and skills with attainment, and (2) a shift in command over resources of production away from the individual and toward the collective.

Alignment in an expanding system requires that the informational properties of attainment and knowledge-skill be brought together. This requirement exists because rules lose information to scale. As they seek to apply to more cases in a larger market, rules discard the properties of particular information and retain the attributes that allow for standardization and quantification (measurement). Thus as educational governance centralizes, the institution moves further toward a technical model of production. It aligns knowledge and skill to attainment by simplification.

Competition among subunits in the delivery system intensifies this process of alignment throughout the institution. It narrows each of the subunits' range of rational choice relative to the centralized rules of production. It induces each unit to lower its production costs by jettisoning particular (high-cost, exchange) information. The rewards of competition—in a centralized system of rules—go to standardization. Even expected differences in organizational domain evaporate in the face of this principle: public and private research universities have become nearly indistinguishable in their organizational characteristics due to competition over federal research monies. The diversity of individual preferences is traded off for the preferences of central priorities, as expressed in the rules.

As an instrument of growth, it is perfectly rational for the institution to narrow the scale of values to facilitate the arrangement of centralized priorities. Decision makers must seek to elevate the rules beyond the reach of changeable particular preferences by selecting information universal to an expanding domain of economic trade. Alignment of knowledge and skill to attainment rests on a policy of diminishing disorder and inefficiency by the exclusion of elements that are capable of causing them. As the rules become more universal, the particulars become seen as the source of inefficiency. Goods become labeled public or private not on the basis of their economic characteristics, but in terms of their conformity to institutional rules. Many aspects of moral education, for example, which may transmit important positive externalities to society, lose admission to the production agenda and are labeled private interests, simply because they instill controversy. Even qualities of citizenship are subject to this litmus test.

This conscription of the idea of the public good mitigates the awareness of information loss to production. The division of information that takes place under centralization not only changes the nature of the good being produced in fundamental ways, but also alters the criteria for judging value. Legitimacy congregates around the universals, not the particulars. Attention is drawn to the increases in output and efficiency that accompany realignment, not to the transactions that no longer take place.

In this context, the preservation of individual options gives way to the imposition of the preferred options of the formal hierarchy. The diversity of individual preferences is traded off for the preferences of centralized priorities. Political subsidiarity is sacrificed for growth.

What has generally been seen as a movement of individualism in school reform was actually an incremental process of shifting control to higher levels of governance, favoring central control over local control. Major reform movements during the twentieth century including Progressivism, municipal reform, and the civil rights movement, were part of a process of a transfer of power to higher decision-making units. As one property rights structure was unraveling and another was being created, costs were being transmitted from higher to lower units of governance within the system. The individualism of the 1960s and 1970s, for example, reflected the costs of superordinate rules being absorbed by local property right holders. Individualism flourished because the framework of rights supporting control over resources at the district level was being made less secure. In the midst of the chaos at the district level, authority over production of the education good, and command over the resources of production, was shifting away from the individual (local control) toward more centralized control.

This movement toward centralization creates a greater disproportion in cost between universal and particular information and in the forms of production they represent. The cost difference increases the probability of production on the side of the universal (collective) and lowers probabilities of production on the side of the particular (individual). The rules that promote expansion become the standard of evaluation, or criterion of rationality, for good practice. All information that cannot be demonstrated to expand the system is seen as particular or private information. For example, most of the principles of good practice espoused by the "managers of virtue" would today be seen as representing particular, local interests, and therefore not part of the public good.[8] Their virtues become self-indulgent vices in an expanded system. Their belief that knowledge makes for more virtuous students (and therefore better citizens) buckles under the press of defining virtue.

The realignment of production that accompanies centralization alters the prices, and relative importance, of the factors of production. As the institution adopts a more technical model of production, it diminishes the value of exchange information and elevates the role of planning. The individual loses status as a primary agent of production. The qualities of individuality represent cost to a planned model of production. Rationality lodges itself in the rules of production. The forces of the polity grow ever more important to production because rule changes reconfigure costs and opportunities throughout the institution. Rule managers, and the chief executive officers who realign production to the rule environment, gain status as the primary agents of production. Central authority becomes more closely identified with the evolving configuration of production, whereas the individual becomes a standardized unit of production.

Sidebar 4.2   GI Bill

Expanding the system of higher education under federal control, inducing a liberal turnover in property rights, is readily seen in the example of the postwar GI Bills. A central postwar concern of the Roosevelt administration was how to repatriate 15 million service members who would return from World War II. Like many of Franklin D. Roosevelt's New Deal programs, the focus was on keeping men (especially young men) employed and off the streets. By 1942, the American Council on Education (ACE) was doing preliminary work to propose veteran's educational benefits for returning service members. Due in part to the grim memory of the veterans' bonus march of the early 1930s and a dour forecast of a postwar depression, the Congress drafted the Servicemen's Readjustment Act of 1944 (or, simply, the GI Bill).

The GI Bill made its way through Congress in large part because of lobbying efforts by the American Legion, a powerful nongovernmental organization. Henry Colmery, a former national commander of the American Legion, wrote the original draft of the bill in January 1944. Days after Colmery wrote the bill, it was introduced into the House of Representatives and the Senate. Colmery stated that the purpose of the bill would be to provide aid to develop opportunities and reach the goals that service members otherwise could have had had the war not interrupted their lives. The bill itself provided a modest compensation for unemployment, grants for higher education and vocational training, and extended loans for home purchases. Consistent with the theme of promoting educational opportunity for servicemen, the news media tycoon William Randolph Hearst was notably instrumental in generating public support for the bill through his multiple news-service outlets.

The GI Bill of 1944 created six important benefits for returning service personnel: education and training; loans for homes, farms, and businesses; unemployment compensation; job-finding assistance; veterans' hospitals; and military review of dishonorable discharges. The Veterans Administration (VA) administering the GI Bill provided up to 48 months of full-time education depending upon the length of a veteran's service. Additionally, the VA also provided up to $500 per year in tuition, books, and fees. These benefits were adjusted upward in future years. At a total cost of $14.5 billion, approximately half of the 15 million veterans participated in the educational and training benefits of the GI Bill. Naturally, the impact of the GI Bill on higher education was dramatic. In 1947 alone, veterans accounted for nearly half of all college enrollments, with almost 2.3 million participating in the academy. The postwar flood of people into college caused the institution of higher education to rapidly expand. From 1950 to 1970, total college enrollment increased from 2,659,000 (6.2 percent of total population) to 8,581,000 (11.0 percent). Educational attainment of the white-collar American laborer during this postwar period increased markedly, nudging the criterion for labor market entry from a high-school diploma (1940s) to some amount of college education (1950s) to a college diploma (1960s). Following the success of the first GI Bill of 1944, successive GI bills emerged for the Korean (1952) and Vietnam (1966) war veterans, and for the veterans of more recent conflicts.

A Difficulty in the Concept of Human Capital

As an extension of the neoclassical model, human capital theory sets before us two ends that are at variance; namely, institutional expansion and the individualized development of complex human beings. It is a mistake that is shared by other theories that operate within the orthodox framework. In fact, no part of the format or tradition of neoclassical economic thought has recognized that these aims collide and are irreconcilable. Such models assume that human capital creation can take place in an expanding institution without loss, that the good will retain the essence of its character, and that the growth of scale can only add to and improve the skills, knowledge, values, and habits of people. However, the thought that these aims are in accord is ill conceived and reveals a serious misunderstanding of the effect of institutional structures on the formation of human resources. For, as we have shown, it is impossible to satisfy simultaneously the demands of institutional expansion and the development of human beings in their full inherent complexity.

The reason for this is apparent the moment we realize that an expanding institution alters the flow of information in a manner that changes high effective complexity into general characteristics; when we see that the growth of scale continually pulls the data toward uniformity; that it ties production to a standardized reference system and makes a gradual unification out of personal needs and aims, out of the diversity of individual life. What is being argued here is that institutional expansion is purchased at the price of information, that is, the complex, dynamical properties of information, the loss of which is incompatible with the varied dimensions and wide scope of human experience. Where such information is lacking, the pattern of belief and practice tend to draw in and narrow (including the sense of reality, conceptions of the good, and opportunities for developing distinct capacities).

The crucial issue is that this depletion of variation furthers the cause of standardization—the act of bringing into line and making the rules and inputs of production more uniform and consistent. Such steps increase the possibility of order and prediction, which in turn tend to lower costs and quicken the pace of production. Here the empirical evidence is quite clear. By removing differences (by standardizing), systems are, as a general rule, able to realize greater degrees of efficiency and gains in the stream of output and trade. But consider, on the other hand, the very success of these homogenizing actions as leading to systems in which the balance is not on the side of wider freedom, in which a sustaining sense of faith in the rules and benefits of expansion is generated at the same time as a reduction in the realm of free choice and in the value of the individual person.

No one should doubt that these trends are with us. For they conform only too well to the general pattern of human experience. But the point we want to bring out here is that they can hardly be anticipated on the basis of the prevailing orthodoxy. As is well known, the human capital (neoclassical) model separates the matter of the development of persons from the question of the specification of rules over the means of production. That is to say, the theory does not integrate institutions into its model. It rests on the assumption that the institution has neutral properties, and that it does not alter the cost of transacting; in other words, that its rules operate without bias, distortion, or costs in raising the level of human skills. With such a view it should come as no surprise to find no trace of real opposition to the institution or to its increase in human capital thought. What we find instead is quite the reverse. The accepted premise is that the institution is a progressive force, and that its growth always is sufficient to bring to pass the good desired and endeavored for.

The substance of this approach shows up most plainly in human capital's devotion to the cause of expanding the system of education. Indeed, to attach the greatest possible importance to the expansion of formal education and to affirm its abilities to add to the quality of the human agent—this is the hallmark of human capital theory. The assumption here is that schooling is the most pertinent factor in improving the distribution of individual skills and knowledge in the market, that it enhances productive efficiency through the general upgrading of skills needed in jobs. From which comes the view that as access to education expands, there will be more opportunities for individuals to develop their distinct needs and talents. As the neoclassical model sees it, such an expansion does not in any way offend against the good. The belief is that it offers a stable growth path for the stock of human assets, promising to satisfy the wide set of preference orderings and to improve the ability of the population to produce (Mincer 1958; Schultz 1961; Denison 1962; and Becker 1964).

On the face of it this view seems plausible enough. But it can be safely rejected on the grounds that expansion has a precisely opposite influence on the production of education. With the rise of scale, education's rules of production become less able to satisfy the broad information requirements of complex reality. They become an ineffective source of individualized information and are less able, therefore, to meet the diverse needs and interests of the public at large. So too, and for the same reasons, the logic of expansion constrains the way of thinking within the institution. It alters the meaning and perception of the good, that is, the notion of progress, of failure, of growth, of the human being, of freedom, and so forth. It sets in motion a process in which the starting point for education continually shifts away from the interests, instincts, and abilities of the individual person to the aims and interests of the institution, to the undifferentiated social whole. The greater the scale involved, the clearer this pattern becomes.

These are the reactions of a system forced to deal with the reality of scarce resources. It is a system forced to continue to lower the cost (the uncertainty) of reproduction as it expands. Recall that this takes place in stages as people make trade-offs and substitutions and channel the flow of resources to their most profitable uses. It takes place in the creation of the rules and regulations and the norms and customs of the institution. The thing to remember is that all these are acts producing separations of information. Indeed, what is going on inside all of this activity, at a level much harder to observe, is the perpetual yielding of higher-cost (particular) information to lower-cost (universal) information. For, in order to sustain expansion, the entire network of communication must be involved in moving production in a universal direction. In other words, it must be elevating the rules beyond the reach of diverse individual or local preferences, in effect ruling out the use of particular information in production. The departure of this information becomes progressively more acceptable as its costs rise and interfere more with the growth of trade and with education's ability to expand. And so in fact it turns out that both the incentives of scale and the constraints of scarcity demand that it becomes a scarcer factor of production.

Take the quality of the good produced; take the central view of what constitutes that good; take the values and desires of the actors in the system—all of these things are being constrained and conditioned by the informationpriorities of expansion. That this should be the case is not the least bit contrary to common sense. As more and more private or particularized information drops out of the productive picture, education achieves a condition of fewer qualitative distinctions; it achieves a state of greater coherence with more stability and control over the data, and certainly this means it achieves levels of lesser complexity.

The trouble, of course, is that the essential quality (and the key to the health of the good) lies in its complexity. This is the nonlinear side of the good. It is the expression of independence that works its way through intelligence, emotion, imagination, acts of will—all the essential aspects and distinct individualities that make up human personality and the education good. The loss of such complexity thus goes hand in hand with loss of the intricacies of human exchange. It involves the sacrifice of self-expression and the liberty to achieve personal ends. And it may be justly argued that from this decrease in the range of options we get a fragmentation in the production of human goods; we get a deprivation of capability in terms of initiative, creativity, versatility, emotion, depth of insight, and so forth, the very elements and relations on which the full production of the education good, that is, the full realization of human potentialities, depends.

The point we want to establish is that these are the effects of a suboptimal distribution of information, and that the drive to expand is what ushers it all in. It distorts the flow of information in such a way as to reduce the number of would-be transactions and with it the chances of creating richer experiences of education. To grasp why this should take place we need only see that against the pressures of expansion the complex (the particular) has to give way, it must make room for a simpler, more efficient social process and model of production. Hence the constant tendency is to integrate, to position persons evenly, to link the causal chain, and to compress the good into a uniform mold, one that is more predictable and less expensive to reproduce.[9] All in all, as the system moves through time, these actions work well to simplify the complex bonds of human interaction; they lower the price of inputs and help drive the process of growth.

We do not wish to deny that the motive to expand education (in length, number, function) rests on a genuine desire to serve the deepest needs and interests of the people. Yet, as we know, the intention does not carry as much weight as the reality. And the reality, if we can bear it, is that the progressive rise of education achieves the opposite of its intention; it sacrifices more than it adds. Consider the testimony of some of its substitutions: in place of the particular, the universal; in place of more options, fewer options in the production set; instead of emphasis on the primacy of individual reason in the choice of ends, constant stress on the primacy of collective reason in the choice of ends; in place of stress on combining the unlike in cohesive social action, there is now the habit of uniting the likes, a unity of what is common and commensurable; in place of questions of value, questions of fact; in place of adjusting knowledge and skills to fit the diversity of individual talents and needs, we now have knowledge and skills adjusted to fit the attainment of the whole. Above all, we now have emphasis on expansion, on units produced, on efficiency, on growth itself as the mark and measure of value and reason.

What this sequence shows, as does all experience, is that social aggregation takes place not through a broadening of information, but through a narrowing of it.[10] It shows that education proceeds on the course toward a less-complex, less-personal order, and that the whole endeavor to expand, with its inducements to remove particular information, clears the ground for the reconstruction of people's views of the good, the basic beliefs and values that govern production. If we are to judge a system of this sort aright, it is necessary to realize that this shift involves a migration both of thought and action away from the individual and toward the collective, the larger whole—the group, race, state, culture, nation, etc. It is a move that is in line with and sustained by the drive to direct from the center, to standardize, and to align the system of creation with the side of material gain. These forces predominate in determining the direction of growth. Together they act to take the rules of production out of a (higher-cost) personal frame and set them on a (lower-cost) collective base.

It is sufficient to say that the successive measures taken with regard to the expansion of education lead to a system that operates increasingly in the rationality of the collective rather than in that of the individual. And it is for this reason, if for no other, that the conscious idea of the individual as a unique process of production ceases to be operative. This is the way the institution advances. The trend is toward a set pattern, a system in which individualism has no continuing force; in which the demand for a social return to production continues to mount; in which individual endeavors are normal, rational, and significant only in the path of the all-inclusive whole. More and more, the trade-offs decided upon within the expanding framework create an order in which the person has value only insofar as he is a consumer of the good and a sustainer of the rise of the sanctioned order. Whether in domestic markets or international markets, the view is the same. For, what is the individual person but an imprecise, uncertain, multidimensional center of cost, a detached set of qualities and quantities, a complex irreproducible that has an all but endless capacity to obstruct the growth of trade. Hence, for practical reasons, the rules of expansion can offer no lasting protection or privilege to the many normal but less-efficient claims of the private life.

The flaw in the human capital scheme is that it extends the idealized assumptions of neoclassical thought into the realm of real life. In so doing, it discounts the costs of the structure of property rights that underlie a real-world market. This results in analysis that continually rediscovers the need for the growth of trade to create more options, to realize values, and to enhance the conditions for personal growth and achievement. From this it is easy to move to the belief that expanding the size of markets can right almost every wrong, and that it is in the satisfaction of the requirements of expansion that all progress—moral, social, political—depends.

The errors in this line of thought are many. For, as we have seen, any such conception of expansion runs up against an order of rules and norms that demand the restraint of complexity in all its forms; these distort the information system of a market and raise the price of the individual as a factor of production. This is tantamount to saying that the rules of institutional expansion make the system as a whole poorer in terms of the kinds of exchanges that do not take place because of these rising prices. However strong the desire to rely on the growth of markets (e.g., education) for the improvement of human capital, it should by now be clear that such expansion will secure an adjustment toward the use of simplified (standardized) substitutes, and that this realization is fatal to the development of the essential attributes of the complex human good. We pay for the expansion of education with the loss of the capacity to produce the good in its full inherent complexity.

Notes

1. Evidence of this reduction is perhaps most revealed by this sentiment from Dewey in 1932: "In spite, then, of all the record of the past, the great scientific revolution is still to come. It will ensue when men collectively and cooperatively organize their knowledge for application to achieve and make secure social values; when they systematically use scientific procedures for the control of human relationships and the direction of social effects of our vast technological machinery. Great as have been the social changes of the last century, they are not to be compared with those which will emerge when our faith in scientific method is made manifest in social works. We are living in a period of depression. The intellectual function of trouble is to lead men to think. The depression is a small price to pay if it induces us to think about the cause of the disorder, confusion, and insecurity which are the outstanding traits of our social life. If we do not go back to their cause, namely our half-way and accidental use of science, mankind will pass through depressions, for they are a graphic record of our unplanned social life. The story of the achievement of science in physical control is evidence of the possibility of control in social affairs. It is our human intelligence and human courage which are on trial; it is incredible that men who have brought the technique of physical discovery, invention, and use to such a pitch of perfection will abdicate in the face of the infinitely more important human problem [of social development]" (1931–1932: 62–63).

2. An example of Dewey's view: "Where there is technique [or scientific method] there is the possibility of administering forces and conditions in the region where technique applies. Our lack of control in the sphere of human relations, national, domestic, international, requires no emphasis of notice. It is proof that we have not begun to operate scientifically in such matters. . . . It is that by the use of all available resources of knowledge and experts an attempt is being made at organized social planning and control. Were we to forget for the moment the special Russian political setting, we should see here an effort to use co-ordinated knowledge and technical skill to direct economic resources toward social order and stability" (1973a: 395).

3. Dewey's positivism was unequivocal: "Here lies the heart of our present social problem. Science has hardly been used to modify men's fundamental acts and attitudes in social matters. It has been used to extend enormously the scope and power of interests and values which anteceded its rise. Here is the contradiction in our civilization. The potentiality of science as the most powerful instrument of control which has ever existed puts to mankind its one outstanding present

knowledge. . . . We no longer regard plagues, famine, and disease as visitations of necessary 'natural law' or of a power beyond nature. By preventative means of medicine and public hygiene as well as by various remedial measures we have in idea, if not in fact, placed technique in the stead of magic and chance . . . the physical and mathematical technique upon which a planned control of social results depends has made in the meantime incalculable progress. The conclusion is inevitable. The outer arena of life has been transformed by science. The effectively working mind and character of man have hardly been touched" (1973a: 393–394).

4. For historical interpretations of these changes and their impact on public education in the United States, see Cremin (1962), Tyack (1974), and Peterson (1985).

5. Elwood P. Cubberly at Stanford University was one of the most influential voices in the early twentieth century calling for the deconstruction of the one-room rural school system. His 1914 book *State and County Educational Reorganization* helped set the agenda for school district consolidation. The report of the National Commission on Excellence in Education, *A Nation at Risk: The Imperative for Educational Reform; A Report to the Nation and the Secretary of Education*, played a similar pivotal role in shifting control from the school district to a partnership between the state and federal government.

6. See Carnegie (1886), Perkinson (1995), and McCloskey (1964).

7. The public choice critique of public schools assigned deficiencies to self-interested behavior on the part of the custodians of the public good. The pioneering theoretical work by William Niskanen, Jr. (1971) was especially influential.

8. David Tyack and Elizabeth Hansot (1982) coined the phrase in their highly influential book, *Managers of Virtue: Public School Leadership in America, 1820–1980.*

9. The tendency toward uniformity and the central control of education was already well under way by the 1920s. Many people saw the dangers of this trend and resisted it on libertarian principles. Perhaps the era's most eloquent and prophetic spokesperson against the move toward standardization was the Princeton professor of theology, J. Gresham Machen. In 1926 he testified before the House and Senate Committees on the proposed department of education, in which he argued as follows: "I have tried to observe, in the sphere of education, the results of the present tendency toward standardization, and I think those results are lamentable. I think we are having today a very marked intellectual as well as moral decline through the gradual extension of this principle of standardization in education. People are ready to admit to some extent that there is a sort of moral decline, but what is not always observed is that there is a terrible intellectual decline, and that intellectual decline comes through the development of this principle of unification and standardization to which I object; for I think that in the sphere of education uniformity always means not something uniformly high but something uniformly low."

10. See chapter 6 in this book for a more detailed discussion of how the division of information impacts the social ordering of preferences.

CHAPTER 5

Markets: The Logic of Convergence

Markets and politics are converging. This understanding is different from the way we know about institutional development from neoclassical assumptions. These assumptions tend to draw a sharp distinction between the logic of markets and politics in decision making, and suggest that markets and politics can, in principle, remain separate within the expanding economy.

This process of convergence is a transmitter of costs; it undermines the viability of alternative forms of production and exchange; it expresses the changing capacity of individuals to achieve their values and ends; it becomes formulated in terms of the social whole, shifting sovereignty away from the individual toward the collective. The good is increasingly conceived in social terms. In essence, it represents a restriction on the flow of information in the production of complex human capital.

Our chief interest at this point is to show through the examples of school vouchers, teacher education programs, and through the transnational trade of higher education that this distinction between politics and markets becomes progressively attenuated through the interaction of scale and information.

Public-Private Convergence and the
Case of Voucher-Receiving Schools

The admirable theoretical goal of libertarian agency for parents and students has increasingly occupied the attention of economists, political scientists, and educational theorists (Brighouse 2000; Chubb and Moe 1990; Friedman 1955). In contrast to many well-grounded arguments on behalf of vouchers for independent education, the reality of the matter is that independent schools receiving the vouchers will often voluntarily trade off their own preferences (higher-cost particular information) for the universal or standardized information driving the greater trading environment. Catholic schools, Protestant schools, Muslim schools, other religious and nonsectarian independent schools operating within a Western-style framework of education will predictably move deeper into the orbiting pull of universal information where greater organizational gains can be achieved, informational costs may be lowered, and fewer trading disadvantages and penalties encountered.

Lower-cost systems of assessment oriented around educational attainment— preferred by accrediting agencies, as these tend to facilitate institutional expansion—are one evident trend in the convergence between public and private, imposing a vicelike lock (and cost) upon an independent school's traditional (or nontraditional) curricular and cocurricular emphases. As central control over information constrains local preferences, it will become increasingly difficult to operate outside the parameters of the collective and its managers; public and private spheres of educational trade are converging and becoming indistinguishable.

Perhaps the chief contribution of this section is methodological. The idea here is that theorists using an organizational unit of analysis cannot fully explain the information costs associated with remaining outside the legitimacy and rationality of the collective good, the standardized trading environment sanctioned by a state or market trading body. In order to secure a clearer picture of the effects of institutional expansion, we believe that the unit of analysis should shift from the organizational level, where power, politics, and locus of decision making exist as key variables, to a (wider) institutional level where the framework of rules, rights, incentives, and agenda possess their own momentum and operate largely independent of position and personality (North 1990, 2005). An institutional framework of analysis will better explain and approximate the determinative and derivative variables driving the voluntary and implicitly coerced choices of persons and organizations that influence the trade-off of particular information for universal information.

If our theory of institutions is correct, as research begins to accumulate around private-independent education and the voucher movement, researchers may begin to recognize a two-part information pattern. First, they will begin to see private schools disregard their particular preferences and move closer toward universal standards where gains are capitalized. We have seen this information pattern already reaching maturity in urban public school districts within the United States (e.g., Los Angeles, California), where students are treated as lower-cost units of production, perpetuating "life-long" student consumerism, but never fully bridging education in directions that lead to responsible individual autonomy (Brighouse 2000) and complex human development.

Second, researchers will increasingly find in the coming decades a unification of ends and means oriented toward mere educational attainment (i.e., attainment in asymmetrical relation to knowledge and skills development), with managers of universal information extending rule sets and standards ever further across public-private boundaries. Examples of this will show in independent schools that will incrementally adopt modes, methods, and missions oriented around attainment, including textbooks, standards-based curricula, quantitative testing and assessment procedures, lower-cost pedagogical exchanges between students and faculty, and growing similarities between management theories, particularly a transition from managers of virtue to managers of demand.

There has been a tendency to lean on the assumption that the information operating within the institutional framework of education is costless; that there is no substitute for a more open and competitive environment; that such competition ensures a more distinct demarcation between the individual and collective, the organization and the institutional environment; that rules can be fashioned in such a way as to be neutral in cost between the collective and individual interests. In its perception of advancing the good, the optimistic belief in the productive capacities and differentiated variances of information flowing through the existing educational framework in western societies has been eclipsed by the reality that the framework itself is incapable of sustaining or securing these widely held assumptions. The framework of Western education is impersonally sorting variance and viable choice.

Even within the private sector, schools will be subject to progressive simplifications within the framework, directing scarce resources away from the location of higher-cost particular information and toward collective interests, ultimately altering action as well as categories of thought. Individuals and individual organizations tend to respond to the incentives within the greater institution and, if our theory is correct, receiving state-funded vouchers will only accelerate public-private convergence. As long as its capital commitment is directed toward attainment, as long as the constraints of the existing institutional framework are intact, whether receiving a voucher or not, private-independent schools are today only marginally private.

The principle of convergence, or undifferentiated universalism, occurs on two levels: (1) between the public and private realms, and (2) between means and ends. The means of public-private convergence tend to standardize forms of production as they increasingly adapt their processes to the expansion of educational attainment, the common end. The catalyst in this convergence is expansion and the progressive division of information that accompanies it.[1]

Expansion of the institution biases the trade-offs of information in the form of the specification of rules over the public and private means of production to maximally move the system toward the end—the collective "ought" of more people climbing the ladder of attainment. The public and private means as represented within knowledge and skills development are the adjustable factors; through institutional constraints, high-in-cost individualized knowledge and skills development give way to the path-dependent pattern of attainment or credentialism (ends).

As educational attainment becomes more openly a central effect of expansion, it will be progressively easier to see that the standardization of rules across public and private boundaries serves to systematize and unify activities within the institution. In this respect, states tend to interfere with private schools on two formal rationales: child protection and as a condition for public financing. Interference often has a larger, informal objective. As a state manages the expansion of the institution, it must unify measures and rules across previously respected boundaries. This suggests a liberal turnover in property rights. Property rights are person-held rights of access, use, and trade within an economic, political, or social activity. The demand for expansion of the institution requires a trade off of information, in our present example, local control (the particular) for centralization (the universal). The withering away of local control occurs because institutional expansion—the granting of increased access to higher levels of attainment—carries with it a requirement for more standardized rules of production that must be made by an authority, a governing unit, which has influence over the enlarged zone of trade. This process of change in the structure of property rights proceeds in two phases: (1) a destructive one in which accessions to demands for expansion undercut the legitimacy of the existing order of rules, and result in recognizable institutional failure; and (2) a reconstitution of rules and the governing unit that issues them.

Both the receipt of public money and the gains attributed to the promotion of attainment, act as incentives for private schools to trade within the wider institutional sphere. This allows a state initial entry into the management of the private schools' affairs for the purposes of enhancing the path of universal information needed for expanded trade. Glenn and De Groof (2002), for example, report that a new generation of legislation is "sweeping across Europe as well as the American states and elsewhere, stressing core curriculum, common standards, education objectives and profiles, [and] final attainment targets." Independent schools are far from immune or exempt from this development. For the sake of efficiencies of trade, the direction of information (means and ends) in both public and private sectors is becoming increasingly aligned with lower-in-cost and standardized universals.

State subsidization of nonstate educational systems exists in many Western democracies. Government-distributed subsidies for private schools tend to come with intrusive strings tied to curricula, attendance, admissions, accountability rationales, and, in some cases, the certification of teachers and specific forms of school buildings. In other words, the trade-off for public funds tends to be the price of entering into the universals of the expanding institution as managed by government. In Ireland and Belgium, for example, the receipt of state subsidies authorizes broad regulation of nongovernmental schools. In the Netherlands, state funding of private schools is conditional on state regulation over the content of instruction. In Scandinavia, as in New Zealand, the state subsidizes private schools, though in the former, private schools tend to retain less autonomy and in the latter private schools allegedly retain greater autonomy.

As in most Western democracies, parents in the United States possess a recognized right to choose for their children an independent-private education, which is to say an education that is local and particular in nature. From time to time this right has been challenged by managers of universal information. For example, in reaction to an Oregon statute requiring public school attendance, the U.S. Supreme Court ruled the statute unconstitutional in the case, *Pierce v. Society of Sisters of the Holy Names of Jesus and Mary* 268 U.S. 510 (1925). The court reasoned in part:

> The fundamental theory of liberty upon which all governments in this Union repose excludes any general power of the state to standardize its children by forcing them to accept instruction from public teachers only. The child is not the mere creature of the state; those who nurture him and direct his destiny have the right, coupled with the high duty, to recognize and prepare him for additional obligations.
>
> (268 U.S. at 535)

While government may compel a child to attend school until a particular age (usually 16), parents in all 50 U.S. states have a legal right to choose private education for their children. Concurrently, states retain certain powers to regulate private schools. In *Wisconsin v. Yoder* 406 U.S. (1972), the Supreme Court held that based upon the "high responsibility for education of its citizens, [a state] may impose reasonable regulations for control and duration of basic education" (406 U.S. 205, 213). But government regulatory power over education is not without restrictions. Some 80 percent of private schools in the United States are religiously oriented and are thereby protected (so far) by the First Amendment of the U.S. Constitution as well as by the constitutions and statutes of many individual states (e.g., Alabama, Tennessee).

Where a state has sought to ("excessively" or "unreasonably") regulate a private school's particular preferences, the Supreme Court has thus far renounced such attempts. In *Meyer v. State of Nebraska* 262 U.S. (1923), the court rejected a Nebraska rule that prohibited the teaching of German to elementary school children on the premise that the law unreasonably interfered with the power of parents to control their children's education. In *Farrington v. T. Tokushige* 273 U.S. (1927), the court found that a Hawaiian rule that had state officials regulate the teachers, curriculum, and textbooks of private language schools, exceeded the boundaries of the constitution. More recently, the Ohio Supreme Court ruled against Ohio authorities who had imposed a "minimum standards" rule on private schools. Here, the Ohio court said that the rules were "so pervasive and all-encompassing that total compliance with each and every standard by a non-public school would effectively eradicate the distinction between public and non-public education, and thereby deprive these appellants of their traditional interest as parents to direct the upbringing and education of their children" (*Ohio v. Whisner* 351 N.E.2d [1976] 750, 768).

These U.S. cases appear to reveal at least three principles guiding state regulation of private schools. State rules and laws must (1) respect the fundamental right of parents to direct the education of their children; (2) protect the state's interest in developing an informed citizenry but avoiding interference with religious beliefs unless compelling interests are at stake, and then only in the least restrictive manner; and (3) avoid comprehensive regulation of private education that would deprive parents of any choice in education (U.S. Department of Education, 2000).

Notwithstanding these formidable legal precedents and other constitutional and statutory protections for educational choice, during the 1980s, 1990s, and into the twenty-first century, immense institutional momentum emerged for applying undifferentiated universal information across public and private boundaries. As of 2000, the U.S. Department of Education reported that state-mandated educational requirements accounted for rules for private schools in (1) the length of school year (37 states); (2) teacher certification (13 states); and (3) mandated curricular subjects (36 states). Extending the logic of convergence outward, state oversight of the private domain will increase proportionate to expanded trade and its effect on the division of information. Ergo, it is predictable that government registration, approval, accreditation, and licensing of private schools will likely increase, perhaps dramatically, in the coming decades both in the United States and elsewhere, particularly as voucher schemes gain wider use.

What has seemed to elude theorists until recently are the cost differential and direction to information within the expanding institution and how their effects alter the rationality of education production. While increased competition may serve to increase the flow of information, the specific kind of information generated within systems of education tends to narrow in depth, decrease in quality, and become almost entirely oriented in the direction of standardization. On the institutional level, independent of politics or markets, states or trading organizations standardize competition and educational trade across public and private boundaries, its cost effects continually emphasizing attainment (the universal) over specific and locally informed knowledge and skills acquisition (the particular). The purpose of this universal direction is to manage more trade. Private-independent schools and voucher-receiving parents are unlikely to escape the effects of expansion as had been predicted by some economists and political theorists. Seemingly left intact at the organizational unit of analysis are the libertarian agency of individuals and the decision making of organizations. Under institutional analysis, theorists will over time begin to see that fewer options and directions shape educational activities in politics and private spheres. Uniformity becomes the criterion of institutional rationality. In turn, managers of universal information tend to write off private or local preferences of individuals and organizations as irrational; particulars are perceived as jamming mechanisms potentially inhibiting the formal reach of rules.

As the criterion of rationality is split from realizations of individual liberty in authentic educational choice, what also becomes clearer is that the problem of human capital development will not be resolved from within the present theoretical framework. Neither markets (e.g., the World Trade Organization) nor politics (e.g., the United Nations Education, Scientific, and Cultural Organization) can offer a theoretical framework that ensures the quality of educational environment, one that maximizes the development of human capital in its full complexity. It is a given from 25 centuries of educational history that the production of a complex human good requires as a necessary (but insufficient) condition a sizeable volume, quality, variety, and depth of information exchanged between school and pupil. Indeed, the production of an educated person (students and their teachers) is amongst the most complex and costly type of good that an institution can produce. Yet institutional scale and scarcity will continue over time to have a progressively debilitating and costly effect upon the quality of human capital produced by schools. Apparently absent from concern and agenda are the counterfactual transactions in schools and classrooms that do not take place, which otherwise could take place under a less-hostile framework, as well as in a lower-cost direction to those which actually take place. These privately held preferences of individuals and organizations gone unrealized within the system of production are one of the principal social costs of institutional expansion.

When all relevant causes and effects are considered, institutional expansion and its division of information is ultimately incompatible with the individualized and complex development of human beings. Institutional expansion so alters educational production, orienting information toward uniformity in rules, curricula, and policy, that the human complexities of nature and nurture are at once depleted and simplified. By coupling production to the efficiencies of standardization, human development is grossly affected by shifting the aims of production almost entirely toward collective, homogenous interests. The education good is thereby reducible to the undifferentiated social whole—a criterion familiar to members of the European Union (EU) as "social cohesion." Yet what many social contract theorists seem to misunderstand is that the weight of the collective interest imposes a severe cost on the individual and the individual's complex development (and liberty), substituting fewer options for more options; replacing for individual reason in the choice of ends with the weightier ends assignable to the collective; forcing units of production unlike in talents, interests, and desires into like units of production. At its core, the principle of public-private convergence explains why it is difficult to retain individuality (and negative liberty) within collectivity (and positive liberty) (Berlin 1969).

The theoretical case of voucher-receiving private-independent schools sufficiently illustrates how educational freedom and property rights embedded within particular information are ultimately reconciled to the claims of society in universal or standardized information. We have argued the irregular point that public-private convergence in educational production attempts to resolve problems of scale and scarcity almost universally in the direction of collective interests. This direction toward collective interests tends *not* to harbour advantages thought to exist for voucher-receiving individuals (parents and students) and private-independent schools. What this fact entails is that as institutional rules converge with the particular information of private schools, they become less private, less inclined (or able) to shield their higher quality, locally preferred particular information represented in, for example, the varieties of rich educational exchange needed for individual human development, from convergence.

As we have seen, the problem rears its head especially when a bearer of particular information such as a parent or independent school voluntarily enters into the larger trading environment of education through the receipt of a state-funded voucher. It is at this point that universal or standardized information is provided heightened opportunity to converge with the local preferences of a parent or voucher-receiving independent school. Even within the private sphere of educational production, including schooling occurring at the margins of the greater trading environment, the effects of universal information unconsciously affect the categories of thought by institutional actors. Institutional scale and scarcity so influence trade that virtually all elements of educational trade become oriented around cost, the features of which press conformity under the weight of expansion and its evolving rules and agenda.

It is intuitively plausible that voucher schemes in lower levels of education (primary and secondary schools) are unlikely to reveal significantly substantive alterations of student outcomes when all relevant variables are controlled (Witte 2001). Owing to the failure of the present institutional framework to lodge value in the types of higher-cost exchange activity esteemed, for one example, by Progressives such as John Dewey, individualized preferences become attenuated. In other words, theorists studying the individual-collective problem in education appear to have overlooked the important fact that independent schools necessarily carry out their productive functions within the very institutional framework, and its information network, discounting their higher-cost exchange activities. On the organizational level of analysis, independent schools may appear different from public schools in any number of ways, for example, governance, curricula, teacher input, parent participation (Chubb and Moe 1988, 1990). By focusing the lens of analysis outward to the broader sphere of trade, that is, to the institutional level of analysis, both private and public schools can be seen operating within—even tracking—the expanding institution and its network of information.

The pace at which the division of information occurs may be different in different environments—public or private; but there should be no mistaking that the division of information is present and operates throughout all levels of the institution. With respect to the private school, parents will likely insist that their son(s) and daughter(s) acquire education goods associated with the competitive market. Parents may be unaware, however, that the market's uniformity requirements are shaping their perceptions of the education good in the collectivist direction. The greater market of education under expansion adjusts the means to meet ends, altering the thought and aims of its producers and consumers. Ergo, education goods have in effect been altered by characteristics of universal information. Testing as "high stakes" is seen as an end, not as a means, is one ready example. Recognizing the shift in parents' preferences, private school leaders set their agenda within the framework of universal information. The chief idea here has been that it is very difficult for the private school to operate altogether outside that dominant institutional framework governing educational trade. Even "home schools" are being brought within the framework as states in the United States (e.g., California) and elsewhere find new ways of capitalizing upon the regulation of this activity.

Teacher Education

The Principle of Convergence

The old Bedouin tale of the camel's nose under the shepherd's tent is often told to convey a parable of the incremental momentum of large, intrusive objects, rules, ideas, or beliefs. Told in its usual way, the camel, initially and without permission, sneaks its cold nose under its master's tent. Over time, the camel progressively occupies the increasingly scarce tent space with its master, who discovers that he must soon share the tent with the beast (reducing his autonomy over tent space), or be dislodged by it altogether (effectively eliminating his property right to tent space). The camel effect is what can and often does occur to teacher education in independent colleges and universities when the institution of education expands.

However, there is an economic twist in the usual telling of the parable. In the theoretical case set forth below, the leadership of an independent college or university (the master of the tent) intentionally and voluntarily invites the state and its apparatuses (the camel) into their production activities (analogous to the scarcity of tent space) in order to trade in a specific sector of education. An independent college or university typically does this for two primary reasons: (1) to participate in the production of a public good (the training of teachers), and (2) to participate in a lucrative sector of trade that helps to cross-subsidize the organization's budget. A public entity (a state, including quasi-state accrediting agencies)[2] is invited to interlope into a program's decision making, relative to its means and ends, in order for that college or university to provide a good (trained teachers) and receive due benefits in the form of tuition money that often cross-subsidizes other areas or departments of the organization. Writ large, then, the camel effect is what occurs when education as an expanding institution responds to conditions of scarcity, thus causing an informational public-private convergence that affects (reduces) the autonomous decision-making authority of independent colleges and universities.

As we observed in chapter 2, the state is perhaps one of only a few entities that can manage expansion across markets. Expansion due to scale reacts to resource and information scarcities that require rule making, allowing a more centralized state to impose rules through processes of democratic control where bureaucracies manage educational expansion (trade) and the chaos of conflicting preferences. On the positive side of the ledger, state central planning brings cost-saving efficiencies that encourage a specific direction of production, for example, greater levels of access, participation, specialization, and attainment. More people are getting what they want from educational expansion. Among the several negative effects that follow from expansion and convergence is a threat to the de jure and de facto independence of higher education; specifically, in our present example, a constriction in the flow of information into teacher education programs, thus diminishing their capacity to help solve pressing educational problems, contributing to the underdevelopment of teachers-in-training and, when the logic of the reductio is followed, an underproduction of human capital in schoolchildren.

Historically, education as an institution has been concerned with knowledge and skills production and transfer. In this aim, its purposes have been centered within a human and social capital framework for centuries. It is critical to note that the development of human and social capital requires an adequate volume, breadth, and depth of information. From the time before Plato to the present, we have known that information is a necessary (but insufficient) condition for the development and production of knowledge and skills in any field. Implicit in Aristotle's principle of maximization are the necessary information conditions of education. We also have the accumulated centuries of experience and wisdom to remind us that where the flow of information is in anyway restricted by institutional rules or constraints, formal or informal, in either private or public sectors of trade, the development and production of knowledge and skills is hindered. This can be reliably seen, for example, when one considers what an ideal model of production might have otherwise accounted for in terms of information volume, breadth, and depth. In the complex production of teachers, the ideal may vary greatly. For example, some may see teachers as mere technicians delivering a standardized curriculum without variation. Others may see teachers as knowledge workers who are artists creating the complex conditions of education in the context befitting actual participants. In any case, where constriction of information occurs, the central effect of information asymmetries is an underproduction of the good. In the case of education, there is an underproduction of human capital in the development of teachers and by extension schoolchildren.

It is clear by now that the rise of the state resolves the challenges of scale and scarcity from a division of information, a resolution that radically separates information and emphasizes one form of production over other forms. For example, when a state (or its accrediting agencies) centrally assigns information in a domain or field of knowledge, it incentivizes and, in many cases by proxy, plans production activities for independent colleges and universities, including within the field of teacher education. Even in the seemingly progressive sanctums of higher education, production activities follow institutional incentives. The examples are many. The Office of Scientific Research and Development under the Truman administration linked federal money to scientific research in higher education. The Eisenhower and Kennedy administrations linked money to natural sciences research in defense and space programs. Under President Johnson's Great Society programs, research for the social sciences reached remarkable heights. Under President Bush, the No Child Left Behind Act of 2001 developed new, federally directed incentives in areas of schooling. In Europe, the European Higher Education Area is (by 2010) synchronizing and standardizing highly diverse colleges and universities in response to new market and political incentives.

When responding rationally to these production incentives, higher education consciously makes a certain trade off: in order to secure gains from trade, it often willingly releases significant degrees of independent decision-making authority that otherwise identify and define education goods in that area of production (e.g., the production of teachers). The process requires the incremental trading off of particular (locally held/locally produced information) for universal information (top-down and uniform across boundaries). Over time it gives rise to strict uniformity in the structure of rules. This process proves to be the basis for the least-cost advance of convergence between public and private spheres in the means and ends of educational production.

By virtue of public-private convergence, independent higher education becomes an arm of universal information, an arm—albeit a sometimes skeptical and wary arm—of the state, and must subsume or hold at significant cost their own local and perhaps unique preferences (their own values and ideals of the education good) within that highly regulated domain of information. Instead of exercising local and independent judgment and analysis—as it were, responding to the particularities "on the ground" and closest to the point of exchange—a central coordinating body far removed from the complex contexts of that particular independent college or university does this for them, resulting in a top-down reordering and regulation of educational property rights.

With respect to teacher education, what follows after resignation to the economic trade-off is that much of the flow, volume, and kind of information filtering into an independent college or university's teacher education program are largely controlled by externalities, and not by or within the organization itself. Inasmuch as teacher education now operates under the information domains of behavioral and social sciences, it correspondingly responds to institutional incentives and patterns of information in these fields. Admittedly, this is typically so for other academic disciplines or fields of knowledge in the humanities. The difference with teacher education is that a state is more connected to information, namely, the social and behavioral sciences and thereby has an interest in its utility function and direction. The rise of the social sciences in Germany, Great Britain, and the United States from the 1870s forward assisted both the technical functions of the state and industrial markets. Likewise, the behavioral sciences, as for example, psychology, captured agenda in the United States from the 1920s forward (e.g., in the works of Terman, Thorndike). Both these movements helped to lower costs of technical rationality; it provided instruments (mental and aptitude tests) for the technical manager in industry, the military services, the state, and within the institution of education. A state is usually less concerned about the content and direction of poetry or philosophy or English literature than it is about the content and direction of professions such as education that serve a utility function. Hence decisions in the humanities (e.g., curricula and policy) are more often made locally as influenced or informed by diverse and centuries-old academic traditions, professional customs, and organizational worldviews.[3] This is not true for the production of teachers today.

Today, public-private convergence allows the state, but not higher education, to more thoroughly manage educational access (trade), including the informational inputs and outputs in the production of teachers. For example, from a great distance away the state universalizes the technological information (e.g., the modes and methods of *techne*) of what teachers should know, have experienced, and have attained to be ranked as "qualified" or "highly qualified" teachers. The state sets the rules of production, reviews information from national accrediting bodies, for example, the specialized professional associations accredited by the National Council for Accreditation of Teacher Education (NCATE), in the light of the rules, and then the state determines whether or not programmatic and teacher certification is warranted.[4] Once a consensus regarding universal information is fashioned, then rule bound (standardized), the state sets agenda for the broader aspects of curriculum of virtually all teacher education programs, even those located within *independent* colleges and universities. The top-down agenda setting of rules and production procedures through the government processes positions the state to incentivize one direction of information while imposing a hidden cost on the other direction. Through its signaling function, it is able to remove the noncommon features and properties of information, thus regulating the general curricular decisions of teacher education programs by universalizing a set of standards (information) to which *all* colleges and universities having such programs must conform in order to receive accreditation and secure various gains from trade.

Sidebar 5.1   Accreditation for Market Integration

Relative to higher education in the EU, the United States maintains a quasi-public method of college and university accreditation coordinated by the Council for Higher Education Accreditation (CHEA) and the U.S. Department of Education. The U.S. Department of Education itself accredits (or "recognizes" based upon "criteria for Secretarial recognition") national, regional, and special programmatic accrediting agencies, making these agencies quasi-public and not completely independent. Within its office of postsecondary education, the department maintains an accrediting agency evaluation unit that carries out a variety of functions. The unit conducts continuous review of standards, policies, procedures, and issues in the area of the department's interests and responsibilities related to accreditation; it administers the process whereby accrediting agencies and state approval agencies secure initial and renewed recognition by the secretary of education; and it serves as the department's liaison with accrediting agencies and state approval agencies.[5]

By relying on a two-tiered system, government may set agenda through an informational backdoor. For example, in 1989, the U.S. Department of Education required accrediting agencies, as a condition of secretarial recognition, to begin examining student-learning outcomes. Since then, government requirements have expanded to include the measurement of student academic achievement (Ewell 2001). Though effective, this conditionality is not sufficiently reliable to control the rule structure of the higher education market; a direct approach is more efficient. In 2006, the Department of Education chartered a 19-member Commission on the Future of Higher Education whose initial work attempted to create a national accrediting body with uniform standards.[6] College and university leaders and lobbying groups rallied to kill (at least temporarily) the proposed change, sensing the likely effects that the division of information would have on their respective organizations (Bollag 2006).

Direct control over accrediting and accountability standards would be new but consistent with other types of institutional control. For example, pairing federal funding to accreditation is one indispensable method to ensure compliance by a college or university to the rule structure regulating the larger market. Before receiving Title IV funding eligibility, colleges and universities must be accredited by one of the private or public agencies sanctioned by the Department of Education. There is some history behind this power. For example, in 1952, the Korean War GI Bill for the first time authorized the federal government to link the receipt of the financial aid voucher to *accredited* colleges and universities. The federal string of money accompanies control over certain kinds of information and public policy preferences.

When linked to the processes of accreditation, the term "accountability" often serves as a rhetorical foil for the command over information. Senator Robert Kennedy, presidents Lyndon Johnson and Richard Nixon, and every executive administration since Nixon has used the term (or a derivation) as a means for expanding federal control over the education market (Sirotnik 2004). The term "accountability" is often used in ways that presuppose colleges and universities as a class have not been responsive to their constituencies, and that it is up to government to supply the neutral rules necessary to efficiently regulate market activity. Yet Joseph Schumpeter correctly recognized some time ago that government would naturally expand beyond its expediency in the sense of acting as an information clearinghouse and regulator of rules.[7] Specifically here, the modes, methods, and missions of individual bodies of faculty and their colleges and universities will be required to empirically justify the quality of their work along a common metric and thus be accountable in legible[8] ways to a central agency. Opportunity costs are difficult to calculate, but over time, this conditioning and direction of information will likely influence the knowledge work of faculties in all academic disciplines, some influence readily apparent, some not.[9]

The theoretical bases for accreditation and its accountability movement are several. First, it operates on a positivist assumption, one that supplants questions of complex exchange with questions of discernible and measurable outputs. The information pattern here replicates a trade-off between particular information preferences, especially located within the situated context of the local/individual, and a universal outcome metric, such as outputs located within the broader domain of trade. Second, accreditation and accountability seek information symmetry, that is, one where the "consumer" of educational services might allay investment risk by receiving a reliable signal of organizational quality. This signal is meant to expand trade by expanding the return on investment through further educational attainment. Mitigating the high degree of uncertainty surrounding the exchange of education property rights is vital to suppressing risk and boosting trade.

Third, accreditation and accountability in higher education signals to the larger market of K-12 schools the information patterns that will produce an integrative and expanding market. These include identifying specific knowledge, skills, experiences, and regularities of behavior that a student would invariably need to access increasing levels of attainment and eventual success in the labor market.[10] The hierarchical structure for allocating scarce educational resources works as a pyramid, controlling access to a higher level from the one below. This hierarchical structure greatly influences resource allocation decisions by lower levels, because throughout the hierarchy status is measured in terms of the percentage of students a given level is able to matriculate and move on to the next step on the ladder. By aligning systems of accreditation and accountability across educational levels, making the entire market more common and legible, all parties help to expand participation throughout the system. Less market differentiation lowers costs and facilitates smooth transitions between primary, secondary, and higher education, public or private. The feeling of equality is enhanced by appearances of universal access.

In effect, the state transmits economic costs onto independent higher education where a college or university holds any sort of particular information (say, preferences for producing teachers) that in any way conflicts with (or exists apart from) standards imposed by the state. The state requires that certain information be covered irrespective of whether that college or university believes they can chart a better course for teacher preparation or, say, believes that the excessive, uniform control over information tends to exacerbate social inequalities, produces ineffective schools, or leads to underproduction of human capital (Chubb and Moe 1990). Under the present institutional filter of information, there is little room for entrepreneurs, innovators, or contrarians to operate within teacher education programs; Schumpeter's entrepreneur and Mill's genius and the good they perform are effectively eliminated.

With the rise in scale, that is, expansion, there is a perceptual yielding to universal information, that emerges in the creation of rules, norms, and customs of the institution, all of which direct production away from the diverse agenda and interests of the actors and participants. It is not surprising, then, that teacher education faculty members tend to align their own categories of thought, their professional worldviews, and their ideological lenses within the theater and logic of greater institutional rules and incentives (North 1990; 2005). This is an entirely rational choice of action. However, constriction of the flow, breadth, and depth of information into independent teacher education programs ultimately produces a path-dependent ideology that works to ossify this sector of trade and imposes nontrivial costs on alternative modes of production of teachers. The logical extension of this rationality is that an underdevelopment of human capital ensues at nearly every level of production.

Although centralization has been occurring for many decades, centralization of information in the important sector of teacher education received impressive inertia during the dawn of the Standards movement in the 1980s and has sustained this direction since. For example, shortly after the *Nation at Risk Report* (1983), in 1986, the Carnegie Forum on Education and the Economy; the Holmes Group; the American Association of Colleges for Teacher Education (AACTE); and two major teachers' unions, the American Federation of Teachers and the National Education Association, all called for an end to differentiation in teacher certification and processes of accreditation. Instead, each called for national certification under central control. Many, if not most, of these actors during that period probably sensed an economic opportunity for themselves and their members; they were quite willing to commit to the trade-off inherent in the division of information. Indeed, many actors probably did not thoroughly understand the trade-off, falsely believing that the costs would tend toward zero. And even if they had understood the trade-offs, their decisions would likely have been no different, so powerful were the incentives to expand universal information.

The Four Main Effects of Information Constriction

It is little recognized by educationists that the deeper foundation of inequalities in education is located in the division and distribution of information. Yet it is an axiom not easily subject to dispute that public-private convergence affects information. It tends to both constrict the depth and breadth of information flow and channel it in one direction. The constriction and direction of information into teacher education programs in independent colleges and universities has four main effects.

First, as has already been mentioned, it tends to hinder the discovery, development, and production of knowledge about education, which, in turn, is impeding innovation and progress in educational theory, policy, pedagogy, and curriculum. This makes the likelihood of solving problems of institutional scale (e.g., societal inequalities and the like) virtually impossible from this domain of information. Educationists after Dewey are rarely looked to for such answers owing to their tightly coupled, reifying ideological and methodological commitments to the advancement of universal information. The constricting forces of information so narrows the conception of education—shifting its meaning to state-based schooling and mere attainment—as to virtually ignore the many other important institutions (family, media, civic groups, government services such as park districts, labor, markets, religions, etc.) that contribute to the field of education, and which could otherwise help to resolve issues of inequality.

Second, constriction likewise tends to erect artificial trade barriers that impede information from other disciplines within the academy from having significant influence within departments of teacher education, promoting an insular effect, separating education faculty from their peers, and generally lowering the status of teacher education departments (Labaree 2004). The theologian, political scientist, economist, medical or business academic, ethicist, artist, musician, and others are artificially prevented from importing valuable information into teacher education (and many schools of education), leading invariably to an informational seizure or contraction. The simple truth of the matter is that education as a field or discipline is no longer seen by other departments of knowledge as a liberal art, let alone the culminating locus of all the liberal arts. Rather, it has emerged as a mere, though honorable, professional science but one without the benefit of many of its faculties and students thinking *liberally*. This fact tends to place teacher education departments at odds with the practices and missions of other departments and, in some cases, the greater organization. These differences are tolerated to the degree of budgetary cross-subsidization.

Third, becoming information poor appears to act as a screen to create artificial scarcities in two areas: (1) faculty in teacher education programs; and (2) public school teachers. Scarcities of this nature are often created to bring out employment certainties such as access to jobs, salary, tenure, health care, retirement gains, and other rational, benefit-seeking activities. Specialized forms of information (rules) and sets of experiences act to exclude persons and information from the trading environment. Faculty members not possessing practitioner experience are excluded from holding positions within teacher education. In the narrow sense this screening mechanism might be understandable, particularly if education is strictly equated with schooling (especially public schooling). This is somewhat analogous to police training, which primarily relies upon persons possessing practitioner information (experienced police officers, less so academics who study and research police work) to train new officers.[11] But the training of police officers in the United States is usually done under the auspices of community colleges, just as the training of teachers was once done in "normal" teacher training schools.

Unlike police training, by the 1960s and 1970s, teacher training—and their faculties—had been thoroughly absorbed into the production activities of state and liberal arts colleges and research universities, usually under the general guidance of research-oriented schools of education. Schools of education were the location of inter-disciplinary research in the study of education (broadly defined) and the higher-cost training of scholars. Subordinate faculty of departments of teacher education once used that research (information) to direct practice, including teacher development. As public-private convergence began to reach a zenith in the 1990s and the first decade of 2000, teacher education became more dependent upon state-directed information while at the same time schools of education became increasingly dependent upon teacher education tuition money. Convergence helps to explain this new synergy.

What is clear is that talented people are excluded from teaching in state-run public schools for lack of requisite state-ordered education courses, including well-educated liberal arts graduates, business professionals, civic and military professionals, and thoughtful senior citizens. No matter how qualified on other human capital criteria, those not possessing this credential or certification are viewed as outsiders until run through the universal mill. The process of certification secures the transfer of certain mental frames and dispositions all subject to information patterns and rules.

In public school systems, for example, exceptions are being made at the upper end of the hierarchy in order to bring missing talent to the superintendency. And when there is a teacher crunch, such as in the early and mid-1990s in California during the class size reductions in grade K-3, artificial embargos on formal teacher credentialing are temporarily lifted (with positive and negative effects). Of course, exclusivity may also hold for other areas of professional knowledge (e.g., law and medicine), thus revealing how intimately teacher education—like many of its sister professions—is aligned with universal information and institutional expansion (yet informational flow within law and medicine programs import diverse sources of information into their productions functions). The effects of professional exclusion are obviously not all bad, but can work to exclude talent. Many of today's best college and university teachers would be arbitrarily precluded from teaching full time in public high schools despite their pedagogic mastery and their vast content knowledge.

The irony of this analysis—and what is missing from the orthodox, "professional" view—is that these artificial scarcities do not enhance job security for faculty in teacher education; full-time, tenured, and tenure-track faculty in reality become expendable as the production of education is increasingly centralized and made uniform. Under the present information conditions, faculties of teacher education become clonelike; they become undifferentiated in nearly every respect and full-time tenured faculties are easily replaced by part-time adjunct faculty members.

And fourth, the constriction of information that arises from convergence gives the manager of universal information, bureaucratic apparatuses of the state, significant leverage into the decision making of private, independent colleges and universities. This is possibly the most important effect of convergence. Free and independent higher education is one important citadel for a free and productive society; this is arguably the very reason for the existence of free and independent higher education. In past times and in locations around the world, coercive state leverage into teacher training and other areas of higher education was used for detrimental ideological and propagandist purposes; it was used for the manipulation or control of belief systems, for choking alternative views, and for the denial of civil rights to vast segments of people. In Western democracies, however, its present effect is to make education production highly efficient. At the same time it tends to rob information and lower the cost and quality of exchange between professor and teacher-in-training. In a series of reductionisms, this information conditioning leads to unhealthy patterns that affect the quality of teacher-student exchanges in schools.

Becoming information poor in teacher education retards and pacifies independent decision making, obstructs the production of new knowledge, freezes capacities and incentives for innovation that run afoul of orthodoxy, and shifts the categories of thought surrounding the production of the education good from the complex, higher-cost development of good teachers toward a narrow, state-dictated new-Essentialist agenda whose good is a simplified facsimile of what it otherwise could be. The relevant information becomes unavailable to production, and even teacher education within *independent* colleges and universities has exhibited the same path-dependent pattern as many teacher education programs in state-run higher education. There is very little difference today between the two in mode, method, or mission. In teacher preparation in the United States, public-private convergence has mostly been achieved.

Sidebar 5.2   Schools of Education

The productive activities of schools of education are today oriented mainly around the practical affairs of schooling leaving an impression that theoretical issues that define the framework of operations (its information economy and so forth) either have been resolved or are incapable of being resolved by schools of education.

There is relevant history behind the information direction of education schools. For example, Lagemann (2000) attributes the information problem to a lack of status, production isolation, narrow methods, weak research, and an absence of cross-pollination of information. Yet these are not causes; they are the effects of the division of information discussed in chapter 1. The information signal sent by the initial stages of the Standards movement during the early 1980s cultivated both the Holmes Group (1986) and Carnegie reports (1986), which had called for schools of education to organize along universal lines of information. It was thought then, as it is thought today, that more rules, more centralization, and more planning were needed to emulate a professional model. Two years later, in 1988, two prominent scholars, Geraldine Clifford and James Guthrie, made this recommendation:

> We believe it is time for education schools to face their historic failures boldly, to divest themselves of false pretenses to being miniature models of social science institutes or liberal arts departments. To acknowledge their need to become professional schools and align themselves with their natural constituency of practicing educators is to contribute more intensely than they have at any time this century to the building of a profession of education in the United States.
>
> (Clifford and Guthrie 1988: 366)

Not much has changed in the last 20 years. For example, the Carnegie Challenge of 2002 continued to signal the direction of educational production by tightly connecting it to universal information (Hinds 2002). It does so by efficiently linking schools of education to practitioner concerns and the "clinical" dimensions of school teaching—curriculum, pedagogy, assessment, accreditation—where universal information lies under conditions of expansion.

Such uniformity of rules and information across the public-private market of higher education is likely to continue and expand further under international trade in education. As momentum builds, rules of production are being extended beyond individual U.S. states, beyond even the federal government of the United States, and increasingly across international borders through political membership—United Nations Educational, Scientific, and Cultural Organization (UNESCO)—and through associative bodies of trade—World Trade Organization (WTO). For example, in 1994, the General Agreement on Trade in Services (GATS) sought to mimic trade in commodities and extend this model for trade in services, including higher education. With over 140 member states, the WTO, which replaced the General Agreement on Tariffs and Trade (GATT) in 1995, is responsible for the regulation of GATS. In sectors of politics and markets, these rules are facilitating immense international trade in higher education, with states and markets capitalizing on franchising opportunities. This trend gives strong indication that the division and distribution of information can be found increasing toward the universal, thus facilitating institutional expansion. As scale increases, the extension of transborder rules lowers barriers to trade; it socializes risk by stabilizing trade that, when attenuating the costs of information, makes trade more efficient and increases the capacity to produce more of it.

Irrespective of whether educational trade in higher education is filtered through politics (the public sphere) or markets (the private sphere), trade in teacher education within independent colleges and universities is becoming more like its state counterparts. Consequently, convergence is placing in jeopardy their de jure and de facto claim to "independence." The state is irreconcilably intertwined with the private sphere because, as Fredrich Hayek noted decades ago, virtually every individual (or, in this case, an individual teacher education program) seeks its own economic self-interest. Teacher education faculties are not above exercising (imperfect) rational optimality.

The Special Example of Information Constriction in Faculty Course Evaluations

An example of exercising rational optimality can be readily seen within the actual exchange between faculty and students, and how faculty members specifically respond to informational incentives laid before them. College and university course evaluations in teacher education are often the subject of accreditation by managers of universal information. Faculty members are more or less aware that such evaluations are formative in that they add value (information) to issues surrounding course content and instructor pedagogy. Yet they are also summative in that they contribute information during the process of faculty promotion and tenure evaluation. As with any—and we intentionally use the term "any"—assessment tool, even self-designed tools, particularly standardized ones, course evaluations in both these roles capture a limited quantity and quality of information from a human activity (educational exchange) that is inherently complex, situated, nuanced and, at the same time, intentionally immediate and longitudinal. And since, by nature and context, the educational activity may look different in important respects for each faculty member, particularly across disciplinary territory, it is costly to have both an individually designed formative course assessment and a separate, standardized summative assessment. Issues of diversity and complexity would also seem to hold even within disciplinary territories, for example, a single form for all fields in the social sciences would fail to value or capture all the transdisciplinarity that goes into quality teaching and mentoring.

It is true that a standardized summative course assessment would lower the relative costs (time, etc.) in the evaluation of faculty by peers, administrators, and external accreditors. This is an understandable organizational aim, as all parties have a fiduciary duty to establish a fair and relatively efficient process. However, the trade-off for standardization would impose unseen, perhaps significant (counterfactual) costs in failing to appreciate the diversity and complexity of approaches to teaching and mentoring. These costs would likely be borne in at least three linked areas.

1. The trade-off would likely impose specific, unseen costs on the individual faculty member attempting to capture particular formative and summative information who, out of rational self-interest alone, will consciously or unconsciously begin to align their teaching and mentoring around the new organization incentive lodged within the narrow, flattened criteria set before them, rather than freely teaching and mentoring in thoughtfully complex, diverse, and creative ways, which are relevant, of course, to the context of the situation.

2. Similarly, the trade-off for standardization will impose unseen, but very real costs on the overall educational environment at the college or university, again where many faculty members who are less inclined or able to resist banal conformity will, because organizational incentives are lined up in this direction, alter their diverse, complex, and artistic professional practice and "teach to the form." The risk here is that the assessment tool itself becomes the primary driver of the content, not the other way around.[12] In both lower and higher forms of education this tends to cheapen the environment and constrain faculty of their liberty of professional choices.

3. It is quite likely to impose unseen costs on college and university students, who will arguably have fewer options for providing summative course and instructor feedback, thus constraining student information into the tenure and promotion process, this while increasing the likelihood that students might be treated in a utilitarian fashion, that is, as a mere means by faculty members or college officials to achieve an end (to secure/grant/deny tenure or promotion).[13]

For the argument for such standardization to succeed on merit, it must presuppose that known to us are all of the factors of production, that all of the necessary and sufficient conditions for good teaching and mentoring can be accounted for, distilled, and standardized into a single instrument. But this borders on a category fallacy: the confusion of teaching as more techne than *metis, arête, sophia,* and *praxis.* Praxis, for example, occurs in a complex, contingent, heterogeneous, nonpredictable, nonformulaic type of environment that requires practical knowledge (*phronesis*). We suggest that this view is a thin simplification of educational processes, processes whereby the good must be turned into an amalgamation of perceptible and describable data. It is an understandable impulse of the social and behavioral sciences to "get at" the central variables of good teaching and mentoring so as to homogenize and lower the respective costs to the evaluation of this highly complex activity. But as Fredrich Hayek and Alfred North Whitehead noted some time ago (in response to positivist tendencies of their own day), it is often a misapplication of means to an end; it fails to fully understand the ontological realities of the teaching profession—of what education *is*. Here, Hayek in this regard is prescient to this point in the teacher education's emerging direction.

> The blind transfer of the striving for quantitative measurements to a field [or activity] in which the specific conditions are not present which give it its basic importance in the natural sciences, is the result of an entirely unfounded prejudice. It is probably responsible for the worst absurdities produced by scientism in the social sciences. It not only leads frequently to the selection for study the most irrelevant aspects of phenomena because they happen to be measurable, but also to "measurements" and assignments of numerical values which are absolutely meaningless. . . . "In this respect some recent measurements are of the same logical type as Plato's determination that a just ruler is 729 times as happy as an unjust one."
>
> (Hayek 1952: 89–90)

To be cognizant of the forces of scale and scarcity is to appreciate their informational effects on the institution of education, including the progressive costs imposed onto independent colleges and universities to make a choice: trade-off their quality (located in their particulars), or hold on to their commitment to quality at an ever-increasing cost, or succumb to many of the intrusive externalities "suggested" by well-meaning accrediting agencies. It is a reliable presumption that were there 81 different faculty course evaluations being used at an independent college or university, this fact would, in the first instance, likely give pause to a group of external accreditors. Indeed, it probably would give pause to internal faculty assessment committees within that college or university. Yet, once education itself is understood in its full and inherent complexity, it ought to signal an intimate understanding of the complexities of higher education, not signal a lack of such understanding. Uniformity has no particular claim on multifaceted human activities.

The decision of when and where faculty choose to standardize and simplify important and complex elements of educational production (e.g., the tools of course evaluation) will likely narrow—not broaden—the range of information available to the process. Consequently, it is important to recognize the trade-offs in such a decision. Such economic decisions would incrementally affect, perhaps not right away but over time, conditions of education production.

Issues of higher education *quality* in teacher education are predicated on at least two important questions: (1) How does decision making help to raise or elevate the costs of producing the education good, not lower them? (2) How can their faculties widen the availability of relevant information to such processes, not narrow it?

The Role of Independent Higher Education

It must be admitted that independent colleges and universities have a somewhat different function from state counterparts in higher education; as John Agresto has well said, "For liberal education to survive in a healthy way it needs, first, to recognize its *private* as well as its *radical* nature" (1999: 44, emphasis added). Perhaps their central role is to provide liberal society with independent, nonstate-based conceptions of first- and second-order education goods (e.g., human flourishing, purposes, ways of living, modes and methods of the professions); to provide a contextual basis for varied interpretations of truth, beauty, justice, and human purposes; and to consider and secure diverse sources of knowledge for the understanding of human activity within social institutions and the professions. If the Jeffersonian ideal of free and independent higher education continues to be a condition for a free republic, akin to a free press, then information and knowledge being necessary to this critical social role would seem more emergently (though less efficiently) located in a smaller, more local scale, within spontaneous ordering, organizationally dependent and driven, and should try where necessary to avoid conforming precisely to the external expectations of the centralizing managers of universal information. But this is more difficult to do within the present institutional environment where informational direction, incentives, ordering, etc., all favor increasing degrees of central control and submission thereto. Thus production processes become less able to broaden and enhance the educational experiences; they become less able to satisfy the information demands of complex reality, the diverse interests and needs of the public at large.

Convergence, of course, has an underlying history in democratic theory. At one time, under localism, democracy meant that citizens made decisions, or elected persons who served as their agents. Thus the idea of democracy shifted from one of agency to one of selection. Given enough expansion (and public-private convergence), the meaning of democracy shifts to assent, from individual liberty toward state-determined collective freedom. A lot of information and decision making is off the table (assent only). The benefits expand in the direction set by universal rules. The new rules, in turn, impose costs on preferences not aligned with the rule set, constantly realigning individual self-interest to the collective. And these rules create social cooperation: they allow individuals to pursue their individual interests so that they are compatible with one another, but only if they are attuned to the ordering of collective rules.

But every society which values liberty of thought will place a premium upon a diversity of free educational institutions just as they do for a free press. Under the pressure of institutional expansion, freedom is not a first-order virtue. Many faculty members within independent teacher education programs— even those within liberal arts college programs—seem reticent to acknowledge the possibility that the government authorities might be wrong or in error about how best to achieve the education good in the production of teachers. They seem too willing to assent to the certitude of state rules and standards and appear quick to avoid the hard work of independent investigation and collegial debate by asserting (not arguing) that a consensus exists on the central elements of production, that we know and can modulate all of the necessary and sufficient conditions for quality teacher production. As a concept "consensus," as viewed by some, requires near unanimity of opinion or view concerning an area of information; it also bears an "enormous" cost given that which must be traded off in trying to achieve it[14] (Sowell 1980: 43–44).

There is little doubt that more public agreement exists about the purpose, content, and practice of education at the primary or elementary grades than in middle school, high school, college, and graduate school. It is more difficult to achieve consensus as one ascends the education ladder; hence more conflict. Indeed, the public good aspects of education are more recognizable in the lower grade levels, much less so as one climbs up the education ladder, where education becomes more individually focused and nearer to one's entry into the labor market and responsible citizenship.

Consensus in education is largely achieved on a presupposition of lesser complexity, that is, of fewer qualitative distinctions. This means that as consensus marries scale it must continually rule out the use of higher-cost particular information in production. Yet when the managers of universal information presume that a consensus exists surrounding any but the most settled fields of knowledge, an error of logic is often made. In an area as elusive and complex as identifying the necessary and sufficient conditions for successful transactions between teacher and student, the conditions for effective schooling, and the complexities inherent to the development of human capital, these would seem not to warrant a claim of strict, formulaic consensus. Answers to what it is that makes a good teacher, an effective school, or develops an individual's talents and skills hold a near-infinite set of variables that make it virtually impossible to wrap into a grid, matrix, or formula. At the core, attempting to achieve a condition of lesser complexity is a fallacy of ontological awareness.

But the counterargument might be that our argument is one from tautology. For example, one might suggest: Of course the state manages educational trade in developing schoolteachers; after all, most of these teachers are trained to work in state schools. Inasmuch as independent colleges and universities care to participate in the production of this public good, the cost, so the argument goes, is rightly borne by complying with the universal rules governing this sector of information. But this objection seems to presuppose that a primary function of the state is to govern and conduct (via extension of the rules) the training of teachers who work in public (state) schools. This line of reasoning not only misunderstands the constrained role of the state in a free society, but also comes quite close to equating the state itself with the public good (De Soto 2000), that no private entity may participate in the production of a public good without state sanction or governance.

Three things may be said about the objection from tautology. First, private entities and the private sector in a liberal society frequently participate in the production of public goods absent state interference (e.g., lighthouses in England, see Coase, 1994; Cowen, 2002); they have so throughout much of American history (e.g., on the American frontier, see Anderson and Hill, 2004). Research and development is often a public good that is produced in great quantities by the private sector (in universities, libraries, firms, garages, taverns, etc.). Prior to the emergence of the present technical model of teacher production, people became "public" school teachers from private colleges without inordinate state interference; teacher quality may have once been better than it is today, and information and human capital development less constrained.

Second, if state interference is required, this may be kept to a minimum—as a lubricant rather than as the engine—in order to prevent state ossification of production widely seen throughout socialistic political-economic systems (Friedman 1962). And third, the objection would seem to ignore the larger effects of institutional expansion under the theory of public-private convergence such as:

- economic and social inequalities have been increasing between quintiles for several decades
- institutional scale and its information base are stripping away particular forms of information (e.g., local values, preferences, ideals, aims, and

modes of production) that are linked with a growing asymmetry between educational attainment (more schooling) and an incommensurate level of knowledge and skill; this transmits a distorted signal to the labor market about the distribution of skill and talent in the workforce

- transaction costs are raised in the procurement and delivery of education goods
- competition intensifies in such a manner as to worsen inequalities of educational opportunity
- an undersupply of the education good to society

It is a widely acknowledged axiom in political and economic theory, developed by Max Weber and many others, that the state, by its very regulatory nature, tends to supplant the autonomy of individuals and individual organizations, generates bureaucracy, and seizes opportunities to plan and manage the affairs of expanding institutions such as education (Chubb and Moe 1990; Scott 1998; Drake and McCubbins 1998). Concerning the political economy of education and the state, E. G. West (1994: 295–337) has suggested that much of this state activity is an effort to control the problem of scarcity; that through legislation (rules) and the reordering of institutions scarcities may be resolved. This is largely consistent with theories of social contract. In order that planning and management achieve social efficiency, and be calculable and predictable, in order to meet mass demand for education in conditions of scarcity, the state tends to centralize power by centralizing the levers of information.

The tendency toward uniformity and the central control of education was already well underway, perhaps even irreversible, by the 1920s. Some centralization, of course, has had positive effects (De Soto 2000). During the 1950s and 1960s, centralization of education in the United States arguably worked to enhance the educational property rights of previously excluded communities. However, state centralization alters the meaning of democracy by establishing a powerful, but artificial, path dependency that collectivizes rule sets, marginalizes individual needs for the group, separates out and disqualifies specific kinds of information, and encourages the development of a tentacular, multilayered bureaucracy by which to regulate exchange. The assent of collectivism often emerges as a dominant public philosophy.

The sphere of control over the internal incentive structures of independent colleges and universities evolves and becomes increasingly linked to formal imperatives and informal constraints of the state, eventually forcing the independent college or university into accepting an external regime of regulation. A risk is run here in compromising the individual college's or university's unique mission and role in democratic society. But compromises of this nature are not entirely obvious; they do not occur at a uniform pace, nor is there in a constitutional republic such as the United States, a single defining event that forces compromise, or a dramatic revolutionary break from political foundations. (Elsewhere in the world, there is often a single observable event or set of events that force independent higher education to compromise with the state; forcing particular information into the devouring market of universal information.) In U.S. higher education, the advance of universal information across the trading environment of independent colleges and universities can be incrementally glacial, but momentous in nature. And in order to participate in the development and production of schoolteachers, seen by college and university leaders and boards of trustees as participating in a public good, an independent college or university finds that they must assent to the conditions for such participation, pragmatically believing that they have not and will not sacrifice their individual preferences or mission.

Abdication of an important social role does not appear to exist (or exists less so), for example, in schools of journalism where traditional attitudes of skepticism against the forces and effects of most forms of collectivity remain strong (recent media consolidation notwithstanding). Yet no such view is widely held by professors of teacher education where the triumph of universal information is not viewed as an infringement. Rather, it is embraced as a method of achieving social efficiencies, of gaining status elusive within the organization (Clifford and Guthrie 1988; Labaree 2004), and of securing steady streams of income for those colleges and universities without large endowments. By joining with the teachers' unions in tying initial hiring and teacher salary advancement to certification and educational attainment, the state is thereby positioned to dictate the type of universal information future public school teachers receive in their teacher certification programs. This economic trade-off taps ready-made consumers, teachers-in-training, and routes their substantial dollars to university coffers in exchange for permitting state encroachment, the power of setting the terms of information, certification, accreditation, assessment, and other forms of decision making into independent higher education. Sister disciplines or fields of knowledge within higher education hardly raise an objection to this Faustian bargain because the agreement often cross-subsidizes their own budgets, at least in those organizations where endowments and outside funding (research grants, etc.) are slight.

Cost-Generating Activity

The guiding questions for further theoretical and empirical investigation begin to emerge: What are the costs to information, knowledge, and decision making under convergence? And how might convergence affect the unique missions of independent, autonomous educational organizations? Whatever long-term dangers and informational risks exist in the convergence between the state and an independent college or university, these are seen as outweighed by the short-term volume of rents received. Gains tend to be made by accommodating what at first appears to be benign interloping by managers of universal information. Over time, however, interloping of this nature can (and often does) lead to much more. Many—certainly not all—independent colleges and universities that have such programs readily endure the information costs in order to rent their departments of teacher education to the state in exchange for a reliable revenue stream.

Public-private convergence in teacher education programs heightens the value of attainment—thought by many to improve the objective conditions for professional growth and achievement—a lower-cost production function, over the acquisition of locally developed, individualized knowledge and skills, a higher-cost production function. Attainment in the form of acquiring a credential, more post-BA units of education, and an MA degree, brings virtually instantaneous gains on the school-district salary chart. But it does not necessarily follow that educational attainment by itself makes for a better teacher, especially given the asymmetrical informational problem mentioned earlier. Marking a teacher "qualified" by the mere attainment of lower-cost state licensure, as opposed to some areas of actual performance, is further evidence of the universalizing influences within education; it so misunderstands the complex nature of teaching and mentoring in education as to be near fatal to the development of quality teachers.

The points of interaction between universal and particular information inevitably lead to points of cost-generating processes by the universal onto the particular. Those which fail to comport with the lower cost and simplified realities, identities, and relations derivative from standardization are found wanting in importance and are marginalized or discarded from agenda. Given this kinetic state of affairs, many "independent" teacher education programs in private higher education have voluntarily entered into a bargain. Faculty from these departments can lobby and work within the apparatuses of the state, and they often do. But their loyalties to their host organization remain in doubt because of their prior and possibly continuing work for the state (consulting, regulatory work, etc.). Bureaucratic loyalties often become confused; faculty members in teacher education, by virtue of their past affiliation with the state, are conditioned to promote the advance of universal information, perhaps without even knowing it. Given present incentives, these faculty members are unlikely to resist (even if they knew how) the convergence between the state and independent colleges; or, if intent to protect some of their particular information, they may choose at significant cost to "go beyond" these state-imposed rules and standards. But in either case, they cannot, at the risk of participation in the trading environment, run contrary to them; teacher education programs, no matter the formal claim of independence by their host organization, are not free to embark on a different path of training teacher candidates that has not already been identified and prescribed for them by managers of universal information.

Returning to the earlier metaphor, once the camel representing the institutional rules of universal information as managed by the state gets its nose under the academic tent, specifically through processes of constructed ordering (rules originating from above), systemic encroachment of tent space (decision-making capacity) is likely to follow. Accepting the camel into the academic tent (in many cases encouraging its entry) may, at first, seem a costless, rational decision. Indeed, it might at first appear a tempting way to grow the organization along common lines of production—create demand, create streams of revenue (Kirp 2003). Rippling outward to all levels of education, the instrumental rationality behind these decisions views the individual (faculty members, schoolteachers, and their students) as an asset of consumption, a statistical unit with no definite or durable relations other than those determined by managers of universal information and their allies. The formative mission of the expanding institution of education transmutes to stimulate consumer demand through directing gains toward mere attainment.

The expanding institution is, of course, the clear winner in public-private convergence, with many secondary beneficiaries in the wake. The clear losers, as we have suggested, include independent higher education, teacher education departments and their incapacity to solve pressing educational problems, the underdevelopment of teachers-in-training, and the inevitable underproduction of the human capital of schoolchildren.

Transnational Trade in Higher Education

As with the voucher and teacher education examples, rules are also being extended across international borders through political membership and through associative bodies of trade. In sectors of politics and markets, these rules are facilitating immense international trade in higher education and give strong indication that the distribution of information can be found increasing toward the universal and the promotion of institutional expansion. As scale increases, the extension of cross-border rules lowers barriers to trade which, when attenuating the costs of information, makes trade more efficient and increases the capacity to produce more of it. Our fundamental point in this section is this: irrespective of whether transnational trade in higher education is filtered through politics or markets, the principles of our theory of information within expanding institutions hold.

As the institution of education expands, a seamless transition emerges from the lower levels of the educational hierarchy (individual schools and local school districts) to the upper levels (state boards, federal departments, and regional and global organizations) where the principles of central control are universalizing property rights, creating greater efficiencies in trade, and maximizing production activities through regulation by central authorities. Expanding jurisdiction likewise fosters the unification of measures and broadens the incentive structures such that nation-states, like schools and teacher education departments, will have powerful incentives to trade on these new terms. One important question during the last ten years has turned on whether it is better to advance trade through markets, which some argue tends to advantage wealthier countries, or whether to promote trade through politics, which others suggest tends to advantage— or bring less harm to—underdeveloped countries.

There is, at the beginning of the twenty-first century, great controversy over which international body is going to have preeminent jurisdiction over the regulation of global trade in higher education. Among the prominent competitors are UNESCO, which tends to filter educational trade through politics; the WTO, which tends to filter educational trade through markets; and other organizations such as the World Bank and the International Monetary Fund (IMF), as well as various regional bi-, tri-, and multilateral organizations such as the Organization for Economic Cooperation and Development (OECD). Central to the issues brought forth by these organizations are how to define the good (complex v. simple), in what category of activity should the production of education be placed (public good v. commercial service), to whom should advantage be given in the delivery of educational services (domestic entity v. foreign entity; public v. private), under what economic influence should education be pursued (competition v. cooperation), what role do various stakeholders (e.g., students, unions, governments, the public, business, and entrepreneurs) play in trade access and accountability (strong role v. weak role), and finally what formal structures and constraints will serve to regulate trade and exchange (state-regulated politics v. state-regulated markets)?

Sidebar 5.3 The Bologna Process

The recent Bologna Process concerning higher education in Europe is an example that demonstrates the power of expansion and uniformity of rules. This is so particularly in their effects on convergence at the superstate level of economic activity. From its initial inception in 1999, when 29 countries signed the Bologna Declaration,[15] 45 nations have now expressed a commitment to a European Higher Education Area. Four general rationales underlie the new framework for higher educational trade: (1) quality assurance through undifferentiated, cross-border frameworks (the superstructure of agreement); (2) common and cohesive rules in course offerings, grading, and in transcript analysis that make trade interconnected, which lowers risk in educational investment; (3) enhancement of educational mobility thus ensuring a cross-pollination of intellectual trade through faculty and students; and (4) ensuring a EU emphasis in all sectors of higher education trade, thus diminishing specific market niches or nationalistic educational claims (e.g., the claim that German universities are better than Spanish ones).

This turnover of local information and production preferences, represented in this case at the nation-state level, for more universal information, as represented by the EU level, increases the institutional capacity for expansion. Many previous barriers in Europe for accessing higher education, such as citizenship, residency, subsidies, and financial aid, were virtually eliminated by enlarging the zone of trade.

The Bologna Process has convergence expressly in mind. It is, in one sense, an intentional convergence as specific EU ministers, leaders, and elites desire cosmopolitanism. In another sense, the EU as an institution is merely rationally tracking the division of information priorities of globalization: "The aim of the process is thus to make the higher education systems in Europe *converge* towards a more transparent system which whereby the different national systems would use a common framework based on three cycles—Degree/Bachelor, Master, and Doctorate."[16] A common higher education system helps to ferret out and remove expansion destabilizers located in culture, ethnicity, and nationalism that have threatened European unity for centuries.

An area of controversy for U.S. higher education is how the Bologna Process has structured EU degree requirements. With 45 countries across Western and Eastern Europe standardizing the three-year bachelor's degree, the U.S. Department of Education may have to arrange new

interests of all participants on a mutually advantageous basis and to securing an overall balance of rights and obligations" (Part IV, 1).

Along with identifying the four forms of educational trade that come under the influence of GATS, perhaps the more controversial provisions of the agreement are these two principles: "national treatment" and "most favored nation."[20] The principle of "national treatment" promotes undifferentiated, nondiscriminatory treatment between domestic and foreign service providers. In other words, the internal political rules of a state may not seek to favor domestic service providers over foreign ones or vice versa. The principle of "most favored nation" guarantees equal treatment among all foreign services providers operating within a member country: if a member country grants one service provider from a GATS-member country most favored nation status, all other service providers from GATS-member countries must also receive the same status.

As one may readily see, the GATS rules of trade tend to impose boundaries or constraints upon the political rule making within and between nation-states. This development and its processes has led to no shortage of consternation on the part of left- and right-leaning groups and organizations who believe that such agreements have shut them out as stakeholders. They often argue that they would have had greater access under the democratic processes of UNESCO. Yet other groups argue that competitive markets will provide the wherewithal (predictability, risk-reduction strategies, etc.) that will enhance investment leading to the development of underdeveloped countries.

What about the views of higher education itself concerning the politics–markets dichotomy? In 2001, important higher education organizations of Canada, the United States, and Europe entered into a joint declaration regarding GATS.[21] The principles set forth within this declaration seek to limit market forces concerning transnational educational trade. Among these principles are: education should be viewed as a public good; that its regulation ought come from "competent" state or quasi-state bodies; that education exports should not undermine developing countries' own development of domestic higher education; that the transnational expansion of higher education will likely enhance the quality, relevance, and power of higher education; that transnational trade should operate under a "rules-based regime" (i.e., UNESCO); and that public-private higher education systems are interdependent and cannot be separated as institutional subgroups. Also, in 2001, two of the U.S. higher education organizations, CHEA and ACE, in a letter to the office of the U.S. trade representative, made intrastate efforts to reaffirm and to secure assurances against GATS.[22]

With the addition of the International Association of Universities (IAU), this same group in 2004 put forward a statement of normative principles that, they believed, ought to guide cross-border trade in higher education. Their argument, rooted within the political sphere, suggested that stakeholders ought to (1) respect states' sovereignty for internal policy, implementation, and regulation, yet states must ensure domestic access and equity; (2) promote the aim of assisting developing countries in order to promote global equity; (3) contribute to the broader economic, social, and cultural development of communities within the host country; (4) assure accountability to public, students, and governments; (5) minimize the barriers to mobility of faculty, researchers, and students; and (6) make educational trade transparent at the national and international levels.[23] Their concerns over the (alleged) commodification of transnational trade in higher education have moved higher education organizations in North America, Europe, and elsewhere to coalesce and recommend an alternative set of universals (standards) grounded chiefly in principles set forth by UNESCO. In other words, higher education groups to date have tended to favor the political approach governing institutional expansion over a market-based one. This initial alignment with the political apparatuses of states is unlikely to change over the coming decades.

Once again, the larger picture under view is that whether through markets (e.g., WTO) or through politics (e.g., UNESCO), few will suggest that the institution of education not expand. Virtually all stakeholders view expansion of the institution not only as inevitable, but also as the preferred direction. What is not widely recognized is that international treaties and global trade agreements that subject education to market forces, as well as associative political bodies that tend to filter the production of education goods through politics, both perform their respective regulatory functions through the division of information. While nearly all the regulatory work is oriented toward expansion, all competition is being filtered through the institution. In other words, the WTO, UNESCO, EU, and others continue to operate within and under the same information constraints.

The shift in emphasis toward the collective and away from the individual tends to change the nature and production of the education good. Under national and international measures, education goods as represented in the work done in schools and higher education are altered and become linked to economic and social productivity. More education (attainment) is soon correlated with greater economic productivity. This circularity feeds a bubble where a significant trade-off occurs: individual human beings, individual organizations, and, over time, individual nation-states become standardized products of expansion with less and less room for higher cost differentiation.

Notes

1. Framed in economic terms, particular information, as represented by individual and local preferences in missions, curricula, resource allocation, organizational structure, and property rights, are largely circumvented by scale, scarcity, and the division of information. The division of information is trading off particular information for universal information. The process is initiated by an expanding institution with the demand for sameness adjoined by universal information. This has two primary characteristics that join it to the logic of expansion or large-scale production: (1) its cost effectiveness—that is, its ease (lower relative cost) of handling or processing; and (2) its capacity for developing cooperation and trade on an impersonal level. Expanding institutions prefer universal information because it has the characteristic and function of lowering the cost of production; it consists of properties that are mostly measurable, predictable, consistent, and order generating—attributes that tend to make communication easier, that enable calculation and trade to move forward toward complex impersonal exchange.

2. "Quasi-state" is a term of art apropos when the National Council for American Teacher Education (NCATE)—for example, develops a "symbiotic relationship" with state licensing boards on agenda (Vergari and Hess 2002). More generally, since 1965, the federal government has made accreditation of colleges and universities a requirement for receiving federal funds. Although many accrediting agencies are nongovernmental, the symbiosis exist under state or federal oversight, for example, standards as defined by the Department of Education.

3. Through secondary education programs, however, rules are progressively intruding into the production preferences of academic disciplines in the humanities via teacher education. State content standards impose curricular ordering onto the college or university in these areas; even when an English, history, or modern language department will want to emphasize x, the state may impose y. The college or university then has a decision to make: align its curricular content with state standards of information or terminate secondary teacher certification in that area, thus effectively terminating the connection between the state and that specific academic department.

4. NCATE is one of the central accrediting agencies in the United States.

5. U.S. Department of Education, "Accreditation in the United States," www.ed.gov (accessed August 21, 2006).

6. Robert Dickeson, "The Need for Accreditation Reform," Issue Paper: Fifth in a series of issue papers released at the request of Chairman Charles Miller to inform the work of the Commission on the Future of Higher Education, 2006. Dickeson, a former president of the University of Northern Colorado, wrote that the higher education accreditation system is "a crazy quilt of activities, processes, and structures that is fragmented, arcane . . . and has outlived its usefulness" (p. 1).

7. Schumpeter (1975). Speaking on the subject of a central board, such as a central accrediting agency for higher education, Schumpeter notes that it "would

unavoidably act as a central clearing house of information and as a coordinator of decisions—at least as much as an all-embracing cartel bureau would. This would immensely reduce the amount of work to be done in the workshops of managerial brains and much less intelligence would be necessary to run such a system than is required to steer a concern of any importance through the waves and breakers of the capitalist sea." Schumpeter identified the two-edged sword (the trade-off) for central planning and control. In the dynamic environment of higher education, central control over information would necessarily impact teaching (conditioning the exchange) and knowledge production (giving it certain orientation).

8. Scott (1998: 183) suggests that legibility entails "a condition of manipulation. Any substantial state intervention in society . . . requires the invention of units that are visible. The units in question might be citizens, villages, trees, fields, houses, or people grouped according to age, depending upon the type of intervention. Whatever the units being manipulated, they must be organized in a manner that permits them to be identified, observed, recorded, counted, aggregated, and monitored."

9. Ingersoll (2004: 190–216) suggests that in one view, the central control over teacher education and teachers themselves leads to an inevitable disempowerment and de-professionalization of a vast segment of U.S. knowledge workers. In this view, the term "accountability" is therefore a tool that wrenches the connection of control ever tighter.

10. It is important to note that the level of these knowledges, skills, experiences, and regularities of behavior does not necessarily (nor even reliably) correlate with traditional notions of educational attainment as we note in detail in chapter 3.

11. Though the training of new police office officers does involve other knowledge professionals, including attorneys, judges, police and forensic scientists, sociologists, psychologists, and the like.

12. Individually designed course evaluations permit faculty members to take measures to avoid this phenomenon.

13. This, of course, assumes that college and university students are competent and mature enough to evaluate a highly complex activity. Some scholars believe that such an assumption is unworthy of quick assent (Sowell 1980).

14. Consensus, particularly when arrived at lazily, can blend with custom and conformity. Mill illustrates the hidden costs: "I do not mean that they choose what is customary, in preference to what suits their own inclination. It does not occur to them to have any inclination, except for what is customary. Thus the mind itself is bowed to the yoke: even in what people do for pleasure, conformity is the first thing thought of; they like in crowds; they exercise choice only among things commonly done: peculiarity of taste, eccentricity of conduct, are shunned equally with crimes: until by dint of not following their own nature, they have no nature to follow: their human capacities are withered and starved: they become incapable of any strong wishes or native pleasures, and are generally without their feelings of home growth, or properly their own. Now is this, or is it not, the desirable condition of human nature?" Mill (1986: 70).

15. "The Bologna Declaration on the European space for higher education: an explanation," Confederation of EU Rectors' Conferences and the Association of European Universities, February 29, 2000.
16. The Bologna Process: Next Stop Bergen 2005 (http://ec.europa.eu/education/policies/educ/bologna/bologna_en.html) accessed August 4, 2006. Emphasis added.
17. For a summary of these conventions, see "Higher Education in a Globalized Society," *UNESCO Position Paper, 2003.*
18. Convention on the Recognition of Qualifications concerning Higher Education in the European Region (1997).
19. *General Agreement on Trade in Services,* 1994. The GATS agreement emphasizes expanded trade liberalization: "The General Agreement on Trade in Services (GATS) is a relatively new agreement. It entered into force in January 1995 as a result of the Uruguay Round negotiations to provide for the extension of the multilateral trading system to services. With a view to achieving a progressively higher level of liberalization, pursuant to Article XIX of the GATS, WTO Members are committed to entering into further rounds of services negotiations. The first such Round started in January 2000." See the WTO website for further details surrounding this agreement.
20. GATS, Part II, Article II.
21. Joint Declaration on Higher Education and the General Agreement on Trade in Services, 2001. The declaration was signed by representatives of the Association of Universities and Colleges of Canada (AUCC), the American Council on Education (ACE), the European University Association (EUA), and the CHEA.
22. *CHEA and ACE Letter*—"Comments about Inclusion of Higher Education Service in Pending World Trade Negotiations," June 2001.
23. Sharing Quality Higher Education across Borders: A Statement on Behalf of Higher Education Institutions Worldwide, January 2005. Joint statement found at http:// www.chea.org/pdf/StatementFinal0105.pdf (accessed on September 1, 2006).

CHAPTER 6

Market Failure in the Preservation of Liberty

Rationality begins where individual liberty ends. By employing this principle as a major premise, leading theorists from the Enlightenment onwards, men such as Hobbes, Locke, Spinoza, Rousseau, Saint-Simon, Comte, Hegel, Marx, and their modern successors, were able to put forward a coherent vision and model of social existence. Though they differed profoundly on many other crucial issues, this was common ground. Indeed, to all of them, the final measure of rationality was independent of individual freedom.[1] Whether consciously or not, this was the tactical step that enabled them to project a future of total harmony, the ultimate unity of human ends, a world of perpetual gain, and one of "true" liberty.

The relevant point about the logic used by these theorists is that it reflects a basic similarity to that which is active in markets. By this we mean simply that expanding markets give rise to conditions (i.e., rules, beliefs, and demands) that work to separate the concept of individual liberty from that of rationality. And it is a fact of considerable importance that the pressures from this narrowing of rationality lead to radical changes in the system of values and to distorted assessments of market growth.

That this problem has so far escaped notice is undoubtedly due to the influence of the tangible benefits that accompany market expansion. It is hard not to see and be impressed by the enormous gains in efficiency, improved ideas and technology, rising prosperity, and so forth. To all appearances, market growth puts together a freer and a more stable state of affairs; the general atmosphere seems to reduce risk, remove the uncertain, and provide the system with a greater capacity for cooperation. It is difficult to overstate the extent to which this appearance has strengthened the reputation of growth and development as a progressively positive process. And the implication that many have been tempted to draw from this is that as markets grow, society makes progress toward perfection—that is to say, it tends to zero costs. The belief, which appears to be widely held, is that we shall get nearer to the social optimum, to the right rules and right distribution of resources, and to a compatibility of plans and values, by way of increasing the volume of output.

However, we can find no adequate grounds for affirming the view that expanding markets, or the influential theories cited above, tend to move or have moved the social system toward a situation in which equilibrium prevails. Indeed, in all such instances, the apparent progress to zero costs is illusory. To admit this is merely to recognize that market growth conceals from us the fact that it raises the cost of individual freedom by divorcing it from rationality, and that this process of separation places on society a steadily growing burden of cost from which it attempts to extricate itself by means of further expansion. Perhaps the best way of concisely stating our main thesis is to say that the evolving rule structure of market expansion is on net balance a cost-increasing mechanism, in that it makes individuals less free to choose.

We know of no more vivid way to bring out the wide contrast in which the traditional view of market expansion stands to our own view than by examining the central assumptions of some of the most influential technical and social models of our own era—specifically those expressed in the theory of games and the social choice and contract theories of Amartya Sen, John Rawls, and Jurgen Habermas. For it is in these systems of thought that we find a common stance and dependence on the very logic and formula that acts to raise costs in expanding markets. A fuller argument will make clear the particular nexus between these theories and the underlying logic of the economy. It will show how the use of this formula, both in politics and in markets, adjusts human beings to nonindependence and to antirealism, that is, to a false sense of equilibrium, to a distorted synthesis, and to a unity that eliminates from consideration the greater part of what we know to be the human experience. It will, in fact, make clear how the evolving standard of rational action and thought reduces individual liberty and thereby raises the total sum of costs in the socioeconomic system.

Freedom: True and False

In consideration of the fact that freedom has been discussed from almost every conceivable standpoint, we will venture to offer something new on the subject. In this attempt we reaffirm the certainty, and take it to be self-evident, that liberty is good for us and that we ought to desire it; that it is an ultimate end and value pursued for its own sake; that it is not a contingent concept, but an unqualified right; that it needs no justification, but is itself the nonviolable source of justification for human relations. We shall assume also that the capacity for choice is intrinsic to rationality and to the dignity and status of the human individual. Indeed, the freedom to choose between possibilities is one of the essential demands of human nature and is part of the very conception of what it is to be a normal human being. It follows that to contract the area of choice is to degrade the true essence of man and the idea of persons as self-directed beings. If such a claim is conceded, then we shall have to admit that to confine individual liberty to an ever-limited range, that is, to decrease the sum of individual freedom, is to transmit an unredeemable cost onto the individual and society. And no amount of efficiency, output, or trade—indeed, no other factor—can compensate for its loss.

In saying this we are mindful that paths to human realization may obstruct one another. And thus there will always be a need to balance the interests at issue and weigh the claims of the widest possible choice against the claims of other social needs and values. In other words, freedom may, on occasion, have to be curtailed to gain things such as justice, equality, security, happiness, or peace; or one area of freedom may increase by losing it in another. Certain values or conditions may, at a given time, demand a higher priority than freedom; hence its importance and place on the scale of human values can vary with the circumstances. However, on no account must it be sacrificed or suppressed permanently. Under normal conditions it is to be regarded as a supreme and irreplaceable value and must not be surrendered.

The concept of freedom begins with the individual and then proceeds to the social. True freedom as a property or relation[2] is, in the first place, obtained in a formula of individualism or individualist precepts. A theory of freedom must account for the ontology of the human being before aggregating its dimensions outward to collectives of human beings. Linking freedom first to the irreducible entity that is the individual allows freedom and its constituent elements to be identified concretely before political and economic trade-offs occur that dilute, subordinate, or abstract this most valuable of principles, in Rousseau's term, to the "general will."[3] If as suggested by the consent tradition of liberty (Rousseau, Locke, Kant, Mill) natural rights, such as the "natural right of freedom,"[4] exist, then they exist first and foremost at the individual level of existence. Owing to what it is that a human being is qua the natural condition, individual rights by nature and logic precede the social contract. Whether collectivity or individuality, it is the value of the particular, a people, a tribe, a culture, a nation that must be understood first by its individual constituents.

Plato signals to us that the highest state of reality, on which all members of a certain class of beings, properties, relations, or states of affairs depend, is predicated upon—or centered in—the most basic unit itself (Plato 1986). In other words, a form necessarily precedes its class, by which exemplifications of the class become more intelligible; collective instantiation follows an individual one. This would appear to hold both for substances (e.g., human beings) and associated properties and relations (e.g., goods such as liberty). In the case of numbers, the number "one" makes all other numbers intelligible; numbers and their functions are meaningless without this antecedent and cardinal understanding of the number "one." Knowing the form of a good helps to make known both its properties and its relations; knowing the form of a good also helps to manifest understanding around appropriate domains or ranges of equilibrium when competition ensues for its acquisition.

Concerning human goods, the individual of course is the most basic unit of analysis relative to the form human; knowing the form human will allow a more thorough understanding of properties and relations associated with that form as well as foster greater accuracy in knowing how various goods affect aggregates of the class (collectives). Once one understands what a human being is in substance (its constituent nature) then intelligible dimensions of liberty, as a property and relation, would appear to make more sense. In the case of freedom (a real state of affairs but one without precise measurable magnitudes), individual freedom is the most intelligible form of this class of good. For it is only in the form of individual freedom that collective freedom can find its legitimacy: no individual freedom, no legitimacy in collective freedom. The question of what it is that individual freedom consists of and entails is ontologically prior to the collective notions of freedom.

Understanding that the analysis of liberty begins with its relation to the individual human being does not (automatically) negate liberty as applied to and by collectives. We accept Plato's warning in the *Republic* that excessive individual liberty—as represented, for example, in Athenian democracy—can lead to anarchy and tyranny.[5] It would be a mistake of utmost importance to be misunderstood on this point: hale and hearty liberty first begins with (and is maintained by) the individual, but true freedom also consists of its social existence, on which we shall comment shortly. It is clearly a basic human need to belong to some group, to find an acceptable place in society, to be meaningfully integrated into communal life. The group is a reality and in its political organization has a warranted claim to some part of freedom. Thus we assent to the well-worn assertion that no man is an island, that human identity and purpose possess both an individual and social component.[6] Consequently, both individual and social liberty are necessary but by themselves insufficient conditions for true liberty. However, the clear burden of proof rests with those who would in part or in whole exempt individual liberty for a social one.

If we examine the ideal of individual freedom with any care we see that there are no simple or sure tests for appraising it. The difficulty we encounter is that the concept is many-sided; there are multiple criteria and many shades of meaning involved. It is the complex nature of freedom that makes it difficult or impossible literally to arrange on a precise scale of magnitude or compare degrees of it in a quantifiable way. Thus, as with other values, the concept of freedom has been subject to a wide variety of interpretations.[7] These interpretations and their various subjective (not necessarily wholly subjective) expressions reflect an enduring pattern of differences that have persisted across large stretches of history. Indeed much of the current intellectual debate about liberty can be traced to the different ways in which it has been conceived, expressed, and advanced by diverse societies and cultures and by leading thinkers of the past and present. But this indeterminism does not mean that we are unable to draw clear distinctions among the different facets of freedom. The discovery that there are certain fundamental elements related in a certain logical manner, and that certain key aspects and premises lead to opposite conclusions, has permitted scholars concerned with the subject to distinguish between two major conceptions of freedom—namely, negative freedom and positive freedom.[8]

The central meaning of negative freedom is freedom from outside interference, from man-made obstacles that prevent human action, from government, from civil authority, from the rules and institutions of society. This form of freedom entails the right not to be infringed upon within a certain minimum area, the right and opportunity to act as well as not to act, to choose and not to be chosen for, whether anyone likes it or not.[9] It is a zone of existence in which the individual person can freely choose between various possible outcomes of action, an area that lies beyond the realm of external control or supervision, an area where one may desire neither to rule nor to be ruled.[10] We agree with Isaiah Berlin's basic position that "the fundamental sense of freedom is freedom from chains, from imprisonment, from enslavement by others. The rest is extension of this sense, or else metaphor."[11]

No full account of freedom can exclude the concept of positive freedom, or what has been called the freedom to; the basic sense of which is the freedom to shape, to make the best of ourselves, to achieve a definite condition. It is generally conceived as active participation, to alter things in a certain way, the individual or collective conquest of that which obstructs you.[12]

Freedom thus defined is conserving of both its positive and negative forms. These forms of liberty, in whatever combination they occur, exist in complex relation and are necessary preconditions for the success of individual endeavors and for successful (virtuous or ideal) human existence.[13] These principles seem to hold no matter where or how the "individual" or "group" is represented in the social hierarchy: an individual person, an individual community or locality, an individual nation-state; likewise, a collective community, a collective nation-state, a collective transnational agency. The terms "individual" and "collective" are relative to context, and this appears to hold, too, for the exercise of agency and liberty.

However, if the argument advanced thus far is right, it implies that the incentive effects of expansion bias markets to represent the positive vision of liberty as fundamental, as constitutive of true freedom, and the negative vision of liberty as something of a less-important, antiquated species. This becomes evident when we reflect that expansion brings about a division of information, which, as we have already seen, is the key constraint that leads to changes in society's productive base, and these changes in their turn contribute to price movements in the two forms of freedom. The consequence is that the logic of expansion demands a freedom that more readily passes the test of universalizability, that can be put in the service of a common cause and purpose, and that will not slow or weaken the durability of expansion; which means it demands a freedom that possesses a relatively cost-effective (universal) information structure.

This requirement necessarily consists of the need to remove from the model of freedom the basic concepts and categories of individualism, that is, to dispense with the less-stable, less-predictable, hard-to-control paths to human fulfillment, those on which the notion of negative freedom primarily relies. To put it another way, an expanding system must simplify the complex edifice of freedom; it must thin the influence of the personal essence, the peculiar, the nonsocial; it must dismantle the home of separateness and dissent, of that which seeks independence, of that which seeks to put up walls, the home of the polarizing vicissitudes of living as I like and doing as I like.

Day in, day out, this process takes the form of the creation of laws, policy measures, property rights, and norms of conduct that progressively extend the category of general interest and replace private rule with public rule. The steady buildup and prosecution of these rules through government agencies and institutions provides a framework within which the emphasis is necessarily on the perceivable qualities and useable measures of freedom. As an issue of practical politics and economics it becomes important to increase investment in a more uniform and legible kind of freedom, one that can add to order and stability, which is less susceptible to conflict and internal contradiction, a positive freedom that is to a high degree advantageous to the pursuit and attainment of growth.

The most harmful effect of expansion is not that its rules serve to increase the accepted primacy of positive freedom, but that the propagation of this order inevitably leads to the delegitimation, and hence to the overpricing, of the information base of negative freedom, which makes it too costly either to defend or maintain in the social system.[14] Every step made in this direction means depreciation in the content, scope, and meaning of freedom. Indeed, every move in this direction drives us on to accept as the basis of our proceedings an assimilationist view of freedom, a freedom deprived of its individualist essence, or, what amounts to the same thing, a subversive and false vision of freedom.

The main insight we must hold onto is that the increased tendency toward the acceptance of a false view of freedom is expressive of the alignment of the forces of expansion and the division of information. As paradoxical as it may seem, the trend here is such that the two forces in combination gradually produce a framework of institutions and traditions wherein human liberty coincides with compulsion and subservience to authority. The circumstances that contribute to these results are to be found in the evolving realm of the general outlook and behavior, which includes the tendency to (1) advance a doctrine that does not recognize the status of the individual as independent from the group; (2) increase the discretionary powers of government to regulate the rendering of services and make rules to determine what the people shall get; (3) believe that general rules of development possess the capacity for neutral objectivity; (4) accept as true the notion that all rational interests can be brought into line and final harmony; (5) look for liberation in the provision of public benefits and technical advances; (6) assign individual freedom the status of a preference (or a normative value) with no necessary priority over other preferences; (7) seek the kind of freedom that appears to effect reconciliation between the individual and organized existence; (8) obscure the lines of distinction between universalism and individualism, between authority and autonomy, between freedom and the means for the use of freedom; (9) regard freedom as valuable not for being intrinsic to the nature of the human being, but for providing more opportunities to achieve the things we rationally value; and (10) dissolve the connection between true individual freedom and rational thought and action.

It strikes us that the logic in use here is not different from that found in the work of the noted economist Amartya Sen, inasmuch as it expresses an impersonal vision of human life and suggests a nondeclining liberty under growth. Sen becomes crucial at this point for addressing the perennial question of how to accommodate liberty and rights in social welfare decisions. In answering this question he has challenged the pessimism of Kenneth Arrow's impossibility results of social choice[15] and replaced it with the optimism of a social choice possibility.[16] In essence, he claims to have found a way of satisfying the priority of freedom while developing an adequate framework for welfare judgments for society as a whole. Another way to say this is that he has conceived of a system that moves from individual preferences to satisfactory social preferences without compromising freedom.[17]

In *Rationality and Freedom* (2002) Sen seeks to establish the notion that this workable social system arises from the principle of information broadening. He is sure that the resolution of the problem of social aggregation lies in broadening the information base available to social choice.[18] When Sen speaks of information broadening (also information widening or enrichment), he is using it as a premise for a process of taking account of people's differences in well-being, in their opportunities, capabilities, freedoms, real incomes, education, health care, employment, and so on for the purpose of social and economic evaluation. This choice process, which he and others call "interpersonal comparisons of utilities or overall advantage," relies on the give and take of open discussion, on finding points of solidarity, on the exercise of reasoned public dialogue, and on the scrutiny of the capability to achieve a certain kind of lifestyle.[19] Consensus building, the full public airing and weighing of the issues, seems to be the central point of his entire thesis; it functions to bring forth an adequate information base for the provision of social opportunity, the social ordering of preferences, and sustained improvements in human liberty.

But everything leads us to think that this account of social choice, in which reasoned public discourse and welfare assessments work to bridge the gulf between the one and the many, is not merely untenable but conceptually incoherent. The model that Sen unfolds is inadequate because: (1) it is non-conserving of information; rather than broadening the information base available to social choice, it reduces the number of variables that must be taken into account; (2) it sets up a conflict between the conditions for the formation of a rational framework of social choice and the requirements of human nature; and (3) it destroys freedom through the violence of aggregation.[20]

The first thing to notice is that for Sen the natural unit is the social whole. In speaking of the individual he does not refer to the order of being separate from the group. His system deals with the class, with the chosen sample, not the individual. Though he couches his argument in the persuasive terminology of individualism,[21] he seems determined to exorcise the illusion of the independent self, the solitary will, the individual as separate from the impulse and continuum of the social nexus. Sen rejects the entire notion that the person exists for his own sake, that he is an end in himself, that he exists in an individuate state. The individual and the collective are not just joined together; they are one.

But now the main problem appears. By arguing that the parts do not exist independent of the whole, that is, by subsuming the individual into the group,[22] Sen reduces the individual to an abstract element and engages in nothing less than the division of information.[23] It is here that his model falls and never regains balance. For it restricts the informational content to a specified social or aggregated context over which individuals exist and have preferences. This is a system in which the social alone has genuine significance and reality, in which the claims of society are supreme. It is everybody except the individual. Thus, on the one hand, it increases the environment's capacity to carry universal (collective) information, and on the other it marginalizes and rules out the use of particular information (the actual human being and the variety of human desires) in production and exchange. From this very move the priority of individual liberty becomes implausible, and the attempt to resolve the social choice dilemma cannot but end in failure.

It is well to realize that starting from this kind of distortion, with system-wide substitution in the universal direction, Sen gives expression to his vision of perpetual improvement. The vision he sets forth is one of progressively solving problems, of a world marching forward toward unity, stability, better technology, rational arbitration of conflicting values, and getting smarter about making rules. It is a view of moving toward one organized union of reason, the association of wills that in the course of time bend in the same direction. Growth in right proportions—the reasoned concentration of (human and material) resources toward intelligible and progressive purposes—is the objective good and goal.[24]

The remarkable thing about Sen's argument is not that he sees all this within the limits of human possibility, but that he sees society ascending to this level by means of enlightened public discussion. He seems driven by an unreserved confidence in naked human reason to bring about a unified structure of institutions—laws, habits, language, and standards—by which to comparatively judge all matters of welfare, to pile up facts, to equalize the distribution of benefits, to even out the respective capacities to live well, and to provide the maximum number of opportunities for satisfying human needs and desires. Sen's conclusions stem from his belief that out of this discourse will emerge informed convictions of right and wrong, of good and bad, of true and false, of reality and appearance; and out of this will come correct social adjustments and interventions in terms of the provision of various social safety nets, such as housing, health care, education, employment, income supplements and so forth, which offer the best hope and basis for creating a more perfect conception of freedom, justice, and a life worth living (Sen 1999: 40).

But it must be realized that what makes such a far-reaching vision seem possible in the world is that it does not depend on maintaining contact with common human experience. Sen's model works in theory by sealing itself off from the constraints of reality, that is, it works by removing a priori the experience of wholly opposed ends and values, of constrained options, of moral failure, of the manipulator, of the corruptions and arrogance of power, of the very fragility of civilized life. Implicit in this vision is the notion that deceit does not find its way into public policy, that individual and property rights are secure, that an institution can be neutral in its allocation of resources, that there is reason in the unified wills of the people, that human beings know what they want, that their modes of transmission and apprehension are equal, that everything is enforceable, and that all conflicts can be contracted away.

Hope and optimism we need, to be sure. But these assumptions should be abandoned as being too distant from reality. At this point we may ask: Who decides what constitutes a minimally acceptable life? Who is entitled to give orders? How do we determine who is happy and who is not? On what basis does the collective proceed so that its judgments will not be arbitrary? How do different people gain access to the same data? How do subjective data become objective data? How do we discover the cost-minimizing inputs? When must one depart from the standards of society? Where do we find the basis for a system of values?

Behind these questions lies the weakness of Sen's argument. For a little reflection will show that his system of social choice leaves us with no sufficient base, no ultimate standard or point of unity, by which to know and be certain of the external world, to achieve consensus, and to judge the collective and its actions. It is a system that knows only relative entities and opinion. On every level the good equals the pragmatic. The criterion of value seems to be nothing other than the presence of public satisfaction and the absence of its dissatisfaction. It is, in essence, a morality of public achievement and power, an ethic of sociological averages, a widely sensed impulse, a belief in the ability of human beings to rise to a sufficiently high level of virtue and knowledge needed to secure happiness, justice, equality, and freedom.

Sen does make an effort to point out the need for an ethical structure, for a class of generally acceptable values (not determined formally) on which to base social choice.[25] But this is as far as he goes. For his entire line of thought conveys the idea that truth and other values change with the evolution of our mental mechanisms, with our collective cognitive development.[26] The implicit premise is that all values, including freedom, are a matter of convention, relative to time and place, and almost wholly a matter of conditioning, custom, and law. In other words, values arise out of an evolving schema of interpretation ("the exercise of reasoned judgment," as he says), reflective of the fashions of the day (Sen 2002: 290). In this respect as well, freedom is a product of human creation, a property of language, and almost always subject to pragmatic adaptation and schemes of rhetoric and power; it is an open question, a potential, and can be described in terms of existence relative to other contingent objects and values (Sen 1999: 261).

To achieve what he wants—namely, a social choice possibility—Sen has devised a system geared to controllable forms of information, to chosen samples and similarities, and to the aims and interests of growth. Understanding this point is crucial to any effort to preserve freedom. For it involves a necessity in terms of expanding the public character of freedom to the diminution of its private character. In keeping with the logic of expansion, Sen has created an order that turns away from the notion of freedom in its individual sense, which in his view is devoid of true liberating effects, and attaches freedom to a collective conceptual base.[27] He invites us to think of freedom as a collective achievement, as achieving preferred results for specific groups. We are set free by others shaping and guiding us, by the development of good government and right rules, by obeying the laws of reason, by being in step with the general pattern of development.

This kind of freedom fulfills the claims of reason because it coincides with the public project, with law and authority, and because it responds effectively to society's material wants and needs. A fair statement of Sen's model is that it appears to extend the area of free choice by substituting other values for freedom, and by establishing equivalences between the concept of freedom and the conditions of its exercise. For instance, he equates freedom with harmonious activity, capability, welfare, with the expansion of opportunities and social services, and the emergence of the "right outcome." In Sen's system, all these distinctions break down. Liberty becomes identical to its accessibility, to power, to restraint, to participation in decision making, to the elimination of obstacles to human will, and to valuations of liberty itself (Sen 2002: 417).

But could it not be maintained that here freedom belies its name, that Sen stretches human freedom to the point of depriving it of its true meaning and significance? Could it not be maintained that he has created a world in which the notion of freedom is in sufficient harmony with the activist and interventionist state, a society in which public authority progressively assumes control of the context of freedom, in which the ruling powers decide which freedoms will be respected and denied, in which individual actions will increasingly be by permission only?

By invoking an aggregative approach to social choice Sen provides freedom with what appears to be a fuller characterization. But what actually occurs in this case is a drastic scaling back of individualized (particular) information. The truth is that Sen's maximizing model factors fewer differences into the meaning of freedom. It is a system that rests upon a deficiency of information and the elimination of too many necessary things. If we may recall once again our point that beginning with the impersonal, with the interrelated social whole, there is no rational basis for the individual person's freedom. The individual is nothing and cannot exist without the group, the community, the state, the nation, and so forth.

This is the context, then, in which we should understand Sen's system. And as mentioned before, he ties all this to a growth solution. That is to say, his argument rests upon the view that human and material growth function to broaden the information base available to social choice, and that this will, in due course, enhance civic capacities and thus extend liberty in all directions. But as we have shown, the tendency of an expanding market is to divide the flow of information, to set a least-cost direction to production, shifting it to an impersonal (collective) plane. And yet this is the very trend that leads to a higher balance of costs in the social system, in which the informational demands of freedom, in its true individual sense, cannot be met.

By dissolving the concrete individual into the abstraction of the class, by prescribing universal goals to all agents, by emphasizing collective reason in the choice of ends, Sen extends the frontiers of the collective against the rightful claims of the individual. In so doing, he forces the individual and the individual's freedom into a model that is in conflict with our basic categories of thought and action, with our recognition of what it means to be a person. While he repeatedly stresses the importance of protecting the domain of individual liberty, the term has been reformulated and is never conceived as an isolated being. Human freedom is necessarily social; it is a formula of aggregation, and the correct means of its attainment is through united public action, political effectiveness, and the integrative force of the state and its institutions. If Sen is right about what the human being is, to seek freedom in private directions, to assert private principles, to create a private life and desire to withdraw from or resist the direction of society, is to abandon rationality and exist in a state of non-freedom.

Game Theory

The trade-offs inbuilt to market expansion and social cohesion are not without economic costs for human liberty and possess other, perhaps more invidious ontological implications for human relations. Joseph Schumpeter recognized some years ago that information is produced through sets of human relations influenced by diverse cultures, and whose range of relations over time are conditioned and must conform to the prevailing rationality of productive activities (1975: 121–130). As institutional rules bias universal information as factors of production, people operating within institutions tend to evolve in their relations toward a lower-cost, universalist (and utilitarian) path-dependent pattern. Inasmuch as incentives are ordered in this direction, their move along this path is often and in large part voluntary.

This, then, seems to be the problem for the institution: namely, that its evolving method of production fails to capture that which is most human— all the existential nuances of individuality and its value in the social sphere. The problem in turn leads to a logical challenge for the technical functions of expansion such as in the game theoretical framework: a category mistake in the application of the technical model that attempts to arrogate, encompass, or simplify the whole of human activity and choice.[28] In order to successfully regulate relations between the individual and group, cohesion seems to require the pragmatic marginalization of information considered to be too personal, too costly to maintain, and re-classifies this as extraneous. But it is often extraneous information (the particular) that is most valuable in understanding a culturally influenced set of relations between persons, or between persons and institutions, or between persons and spheres (e.g., social or moral). The volume, kind, quality, and depth of information are also at the very core of the healthy *demos*. Thought to have been coterminous, liberty and rationality[29] and democracy and growth[30]— as these terms were once understood—are now incompatible.

The main problem in game theory, in any variant of game theory, is that the rule of maximization is subject to an information constraint. In other words, it casts all the relevant relations and choice sets of the game into a universal or quantitative mold. In order for this "rational" (least cost) state to obtain, it becomes necessary, a priori, to raise costs on particular information, that is, to place the modifying influences of individual values and preferences, as well as other portions of human reasoning and forces of place and time, in the area of nonreason. This requisite imposition of cost means that the rules and preference orderings express information that has an artificial scarcity attached to it. Hence at every strategic level they express a restraint on the range of the variables and a restriction in the size of the opportunity set open to the agents. And it is the multiple equilibria and unstable outcomes of the various game models that reveal the existence of this cost or scarcity.

Part of the case against game theory, whether in its standard or extended form, is that it proceeds on the assumption that the problem of the means-ends relation is technical, and not economic, in nature. It disregards from the outset the basic scarcity of means, manifest in the differential cost of information, which biases the game model toward (lower cost) universal information. This initial bias, or disequilibrium, is the dominant constraint of game theory; it impinges on all explanation; it limits the possibilities of analysis and specific prediction; it gives preeminence to the collective; and it leads to distorted judgments of progress. Given the nature of this constraint, we can, at the very least, say that the game innovation offers no sufficient base for being sure about human actions; its activation leaves only approximations and no certainty of continuity or correlation between subject and object, between what is real and unreal. As a viable base for decision making, for knowing what really exists, and as a means to true equilibrium, it will not do (Kreps 1990; Dixit and Skeath 1999; Samuelson 2002).

It should be apparent that the game construct shares structural parallels with the framework of an expanding institution (Bowles 2004). Each is a version of the technical model—one is in full form, the other tends in that direction. As such, they both work to compress all the facts into universal rules and relations, a process that leads to quantifiable experiences and categories of thought. In both these models the superior system is one that aligns rationality with social unity, one, in other words, that gives the appearance of tending to zero costs. The salient issue is similarity; it alone seems to be relevant. For just as the institution expands on likeness, not difference, the game model calculates from likeness, not difference.

The point is that the rational is not necessarily real. Game theory may be formally true, but materially false. As a technical model, it is there to simplify complex interactions and the problems of rational choice through the division of information. It is there to standardize and create uniformity, to form a common base and a coherent world of cause and effect. Thus it cannot but seek to lay down a course of action that is free from internal contradiction, free from the incursions of individual desires and the illusive information of individual will. That this method is an effective force for integration is obvious enough. That it also creates an air of optimism about rules may be less clear. Yet, such is the case. In fact, it may be said that it gives rise to the notion that rules can be so devised as to arbitrate between mutually exclusive ends, that they can bridge the gulf and resolve the tension of instability between the individual and the group. Such logic tends to reinforce the conviction that we can succeed in uniting the progress of growth with that of individual freedom. It keeps alive the hope that through precisely defined sets of rules we can make the common good, that it is a product of rational human design, and that we can demonstrate this logically.

However, as we have shown, the technical model achieves stability through the division of information. This means, in essence, that the system achieves balance by creating an imbalance; it achieves the universal by excluding the particular. Synthesis is what it desires, but it must play favorites (raise costs) to get it. It must suppress individual differences and eliminate from productive agenda the greater part of complex human reality.[31] If our thesis is correct, this division of information is the obstacle to the notion of a stable solution, to finding the "right rules" or a just order whereby all competing claims will reach a state of rational cooperation. Which leads us to a conclusion of crucial importance. A theory of equilibrium consistent with the division of information is not possible.

Collective Visions of Rationality

Rationality and individual liberty are increasingly incompatible. Today rationality is more and more confined to virtues arising from expanding markets and politics, in the code and measures of globalization, and in the collective ordering of social goods: efficiency, social cooperation, reduction of risk, greater certainty of information and its direction, less friction (cost) in trade, standardization of rules, flattened communication, and more secure property rights.

This is all seemingly true: it is rational to be on the side of institutional expansion; work and development on behalf of nation-states, cosmopolitan political bodies, and trading organizations proceed on this assumption. However, a more thorough philosophical analysis reveals that political expansion, as with market expansion, inflicts a heavy ontological price relative to the individual and the individual's libertarian agency. Such agency entails the property of uncoerced choice in the set of life's potential realities. Constriction of choice and the thinning of potential realities imposed by collectives over individuals are meant by contract theorists and elites to avoid the chaotic condition.[32]

If the rules of the economic and political game confer property rights, distributed and governed somehow by neutral referees, how should these rules be structured in order that a "fair" allocation of scarce resources and political and economic rights be aggregated and imputed to groups, factions, and individual claimants? The initial problem with such a question is that it seems to presuppose that rules may be conceived in such a way as to neutrally regulate competing claims on rights and resources. This of course presupposes the further belief, widely held among contract theorists, that transaction costs are zero or at least negligible, that a scheme of compatibility between diverse human ends—and the means to achieve them—may be discovered, and that important components of institutions matter little in analysis. In spite of these noteworthy deficits of belief, it is this initial question regarding the supraordinate rules of social contract (their structure, force, and rationality) that has occupied much of political philosophy since before Mill.

Perhaps the "fair allocation" scheme is the wrong initial question. As Berlin and others have correctly recognized, conflict between means and ends, between various ideas of ends, between the claims of the individual and those of the collective, between the principles of individual liberty and those of social conceptions of justice, are inevitable and unlikely to be resolved even within an ideal scheme.[33] While inevitable, such conflict today is in fact often resolved through the trade-off processes of expanding institutions, in politics as in markets. What is little understood is that conflict is resolved at an ever-increasing cost. As we have demonstrated, institutional expansion and its division of information inevitably predispose outcomes to the advantage of collectives, not of individuals; to the universal and not to the particular; to the global and away from the local. For the reason of cost, if for no other, perhaps the more fundamental question for institutional theorists (if not contract theorists) is how much individual freedom must be traded off in order to achieve a social conception of justice?[34] How, in fact, is liberty separated from rationality?

Inasmuch as individual freedom is imagined by elites to be an impediment to growth, it becomes a criterion of irrationality within social conceptions of justice. Expressions of personal context must yield to the general pattern, logic, and uniformity of the social whole. Given the often very visible and tangible bonus realities inherent in expanding institutions, for example, the various goods efficiently and profitably produced under the forces of scale, scarcity, and the division of information, the obvious or rational way to order the scope of social control through institutions is an accompanying turnover of property rights. Under the press of aggregation, then, freedom becomes rational only when prearranged (schematized) through collective lenses.[35]

Any political observer in the examples of political philosophers John Rawls and Jurgen Habermas readily sees the incompatibility of individual liberty and rationality. In order to try to position persons roughly equally in the distribution of life's lottery, Rawls—whose line of thought had twentieth-century forebears in John Dewey, John Nash, and the game theorists—conceived of an a priori move whose (ontological) tenets are entirely consistent with institutional expansion, principally within politics but applicable to markets as well. These consist of purposively depreciating particular information, divesting personal preferences from the calculus of exchange and social choice, through a set of categorical principles and procedures and the highly conscious biasing of universal, collective information.

Specifically, Rawls fashioned a "veil of ignorance" from which to achieve an original position in the process of institutional ordering. Positioning all persons (especially citizens and their representatives) behind the "veil of ignorance" before talents, resources, and rights are distributed leaves all persons initially wondering about their respective lot—a combination of self-interest coupled with a there-but-for-the-grace-of-neutral-rules-go-I principle. Rawls is frank in this a priori maneuver: "Somehow we must nullify the effects of specific contingencies which put men at odds and tempt them to exploit social and natural circumstances to their own advantage. In order to do this I assume that parties are situated behind a 'veil of ignorance'" (Rawls 1971: 36). What the "veil" is supposed to conceal from actors is information—desires, native talents, education, relations, original holdings, etc.—that tends to influence decision making, thus liberating actors from the temptations born of egoism, tribalism, and ethnonationalism.

Of course, neither Rawls nor those who follow his view would find the principles of justice derived from the "original position" (behind the veil) as inimical to individual freedom. But the question is not what Rawls or his followers believe is the case; rather, it is the actual working effect of the "veil of ignorance" that matters. And the veil has two central effects that make for valuable examination: (1) it is supposed to conceal information from persons in order to bring about the "original position" (especially as citizens); (2) it conditions the remaining information and—as social contracts are prone to do—gives it a collective or universal orientation.

In the original position, Rawls's expectation was that these principles of justice will be capable of reaching an "overlapping consensus" among individuals with different moral identities. However, in representational democracy, what is it that ultimately gets traded off in the overlapping concentric circles of consensus? Some information loses agenda and other information wins agenda. This is the high cost to consensus described elsewhere, for example, by Thomas Sowell (1980). In order to reach Rawlsian consensus or social cohesion—the very object of his principles—it is the preferential heightening of principles of justice that require the trade-off of certain freedoms (e.g., public moral groundings). For example, Rawls is enough of a pragmatist to suggest that religion in the public square must be sorted (excluded) because such information is too divisive, nonconsensual, and a violation of his general rules. Yes, people are allowed to *be* religious; but they ought not to allow religion to publicly inform their citizenship.

Rawls's idea of liberty is closer to a "republican" conception of freedom: the focus of his theory is not the private individual with a comprehensive set of moral doctrines, but the public citizen and the citizen's representative, whose concerns are comparatively narrow. But again, one must press the question: What is the informational difference between the person and the citizen? This is a fundamental question concerning what information is necessary to life, how informational preferences are justified, and what serves as the criterion. The person has a comprehensive set of information and preferences and possesses the right, according to Rawls, to retain these.

However, the citizen behind the veil is expected to make conscious or unconscious trade-offs, which modifies (alters) the citizen's preferences in order to accommodate others' interests. This is a favorable, perhaps even necessary, condition to a contract. But let's not pretend that there are no costs being raised against the individual and the individual's liberty and freedom of options. Over time, it becomes less rational and more irrational for persons acting in the public domain (citizens) to retain particular information priorities that are in conflict with social preferences (whatever these turn out to be).

The a priori nullification of particular information (Rawls's "specific contingencies") is a necessary condition for the evolutionary advance of universal information, necessary before expanding political processes or market forces can mediate trade-offs through an evolutionary turnover in rules and property rights. Calling on persons to eliminate their particularisms, Rawls and others attempt to resolve the tension between the individual and collective in an environment of scarce resources, particularly those intensified by the greater progress of scale. A growth in scale requires the extended reach of the new rules of rationality to mark the direction of communication and exchange.

Rationality becomes lodged within the voluntary restraints exercised by the people, as they become citizens and their representatives under the auspices of the principle of "public use of reason." In order to secure political stability, pluralistic conceptions of social goods require the avoidance or subordination of private reasons (e.g., those informed by contentious religious or metaphysical information, what Sowell referred to as "cosmic visions") for action in the public sphere. The liberal, pluralistic society requires procedural public reasons for action, reason informed by and grounded in secular consensus surrounding a social conception of justice—the algebra of the moral and political world that the contract represents.[36] Principles of justice, liberty, and rationality each take on the subtle and catholic tokens of cosmopolitanism. Nothing publicly legitimate should lie outside the superintending medium of the social contract.

This move seems to be intuitively conscious of the information costs intrinsic to the division of information, though Rawls would likely argue that the trade-off tends toward zero cost—and a more rational, but arguably less-free society results. Under our theory, it remains clear that biasing the universal transmits an undeniable and unredeemable cost onto particular information that, in turn, fosters the expansion of trade within political or market institutions. This necessarily turns an institution's rules, incentives, policies, and property rights incrementally away from the individual and toward the collective, away from individual liberty to a collective ordering. For example, the new rules and property rights impose externalities on the old rules and property rights, which deliver "a unique evolutionarily stable equilibrium" (Skyrms 1996: 11).

What is important here is that Rawls's "original position" behind the veil calls on all individuals and groups to rationally bargain for finite and scarce resources without the benefit of knowledge (information) otherwise necessary for complex social arrangements. It is important to again note that Rawls appears to suggest that such a framework is without cost or at least that costs to individuals can be recompensed through the improved social order.[37] Indeed, the highly conscious idea of aligning rationality with social cohesion at nearly any conceivable institutional level requires a concomitant subordination of private desires and inclinations that cannot be fully synthesized to the prevailing criterion of rationality. Such bargaining conforms to the pattern of expansion and tends to be a risk-reducing strategy, endorsing seemingly reliable and stable notions of certainty in the allocation of political goods. Reflective equilibrium is supposed to deduce the perpetual voluntary cooperation of all persons in society, particularly its leaders (Plato's guardians), lessening the plausible use of coercion. Eliminating particular information at the outset helps to purge perhaps the greatest obstacle to social cohesion: individual claims to liberty.

Social equilibrium and planning, then, depend for their viability upon public reasons for relations among and between human beings and their institutions; they work to extend the reach of institutional rules. In reality, however, the strategy imposes nontrivial costs intended to disadvantage individual liberty (seen as a jamming mechanism) in favor of collective notions of freedom. It clearly exacts a high price on freedom and the ethical framework relative to the individual and the individual's ability to operate in life with significant libertarian agency. The planning process, in fact, results in a skewed (or false) equilibrium between the individual and the collective—ultimately infringing upon the former for the advantaging of the latter—in the division of scarce resources and allocation of property rights.[38] Over time, political expansion tends to exacerbate the price of (social) rationality, which creates patterns of injustice and inequalities, but does not resolve them.

Rawls of course wrote his epoch *A Theory of Justice* (1971) at a time during the late 1960s when political institutions, characterized by the border-bound nation-state, were losing their grip over the expansion of markets. Since the 1960s, market expansion has significantly outpaced the capacity of individual nation-states to match scale. This brings us to Habermas's political theory.

Habermas has recently suggested that global markets endanger the social state and the self-direction of the *demos* (Habermas 2003). Global markets rob a nation-state's capacity to act sovereignly to protect political and cultural particularities, including exercising democratic autonomy; they extinguish capacity not only to uphold the "local" preferences of a nation-state, but also to protect its people and borders from nefarious externalities such as crime, pollution, epidemics, unfettered immigration, and unbalanced trade. (Here, Habermas is witness to our theory of information under scale.) There is strong empirical evidence that impersonal global markets have in fact outgrown and are threatening to replace the personal, local, and particular politics of border-bound or territorial nation-states. These expanding markets, according to Habermas, have necessitated the urgent expansion of democratic control in order to inform and direct the relations of human exchange and the commercial conditions for investment capital. Since the expanding market genie cannot easily be returned to its proverbial bottle, Habermas's solution is to likewise expand transborder democratic control to eventually subordinate markets to "legitimate" politics. Politics must become as integrated as markets, but must do so under a new political entity that is married to the processes of democratic legitimation.

It is important to note that any notions of attaining transborder political institutions without incurring the individual-collective, particular-universal trade-offs, clearly assume that a near-zero cost is achievable. Our theory shows why this is a mistaken belief.

There is no small degree of irony at work here. The demos is harmed when decision making is filtered through intergovernmental trade agreements because these typically do not fall under the scrutiny of individual citizens or "democratic opinion and will formation, which remain anchored in national arenas" (Habermas 2003). Habermas correctly observes that democracy is being traded off for market growth. Yet it is concurrently alleged that the demos is neither harmed nor disadvantaged by the expansion of politics, such as under a proper or rational rendering of the European Union (EU).[39] In the one sense, Habermas appears to employ against the control of expanding markets a critique of positive liberty exercised under market expansion, one that has "effectively disempowered . . . the loss of state capacities for control, the growing legitimation deficits in decision-making processes, and the increasing inability to provide legitimate and effective steering and organizational services" (Habermas 2003: 88–89). And in another sense, one on behalf of political control, he appears to invoke an argument from negative liberty.

In many European countries, the displacement of politics by markets manifests itself as a vicious circle of rising unemployment, overburdened social-security systems, and shrinking taxpayer contributions. The nation-state is confronting the dilemma that the more necessary economic stimulus packages and higher tax rates on moveable property become for its exhausted public budget, the harder it becomes to carry out these measures within the state's own national borders.

(Habermas 2003: 91)

Once again, this is a both/and argument. Political control is thought to protect the very particular information that is undemocratically (ergo illegitimately) sorted from choice by expanding markets. What lies waiting to be discovered is that neither the expansion of markets nor the expansion of politics appears to possess the capacity to fix value, legitimacy, or rationality in traditional notions of the demos, that is to say, if the demos represents the common people, their culture (localism), and protected spheres (rights) for individuals.[40] In order to grow political or market institutions, rationality under any conceivable scheme of expansion will predictably be separated from philosophies of individual liberty. In this sense, it is clear that Habermas has accurately calculated the cost of market expansion while at the same time presuming that the cost to political enlargement tends toward zero.

What is interesting about the present European institutional framework is that it unequivocally advantages a social or collective sense of freedom by biasing a specific direction of information through confederated fiat. This was Habermas's critique: there was not enough democratic legitimacy to the EU's early bureaucratic arrangements. Too much particular information was fleeced from policy considerations. For Habermas, the form of a transborder confederacy requires a constitution, a networked educational system, a multivocal media, and a collective consciousness ("civic solidarity"), which somehow promotes collaboration in recognizing common interests, "but without damaging cultural distinctiveness" (Habermas 2003: 97–98). Yet Habermas appears to be double-minded here, a point to which we now turn.

To believe that individual freedom, as represented in particular information and distinctions of culture, will remain a central element of democracy is to assume that the standard of rationality will remain the same as political and economic activities transition from small to large scale. Political expansion creates a new species of democracy. As Dahl notes, "Size matters. Both the number of persons in a political unit and the extent of its territory have consequences for the form of democracy" (1998: 105). Habermas believes that he is expanding democratic legitimation within certain market pressure, but democracy in his scheme becomes increasingly oriented toward the universal, in terms of rules (institutions) and its conceptions of freedom, rationality, and human nature. Far from giving safe harbor to "cultural distinctiveness," local culture (even at the nation-state level) and its particular information set must be traded off under the distorting processes of the division of information. Local culture is a threat to political expansion. Therefore, the demos must be separated from its culture and reconstructed on new universal terms of contract.

How, practically speaking, does the demos become separated from its culture? The answer is through formal and informal processes of the division of information under expansion. The demos depends for its identity on all the truth-bound history of culture, on all the lessons learned from trial and experiment, and on the trial and error observation that leads to behavioral consequences (e.g., war, economic prosperity and depressions, social unrest, or advancement). It also depends on local institutions, such as the family, the neighborhood, the village, and the like.[41] Over a long period of time, a people figures out what works based on observing the particular consequences of various lifestyles and actions. This knowledge is passed on from one generation to another principally through procedural knowledge, for example, history, cultural slogans and song, arts and entertainment, and local understandings about how to consider limitations and risk.

This procedural knowledge of the cause-and-effect relationships between actions of the past and their respective consequences is vital particular information for any culture. Nevertheless, the demos become progressively attenuated through processes of market and political expansion. Under expansion the meaning of democracy changes owing to the separation from the demos of its local history and procedural knowledge. The older understanding of democracy of the tightly knit community (e.g., as expressed in the town hall) gives way to third-party representative democracy.[42] Consequently, points of commonality that once bound a demos shift from the particular information found within the culture(s) of a local community (or a nation-state) toward an emerging form of commonality derived from new structures of mass communication and its "deep language"[43] (Ellul 1965; Mayhew 1997). The social influence of mass media replaces in importance the complex, intimate, and daily human exchanges that occur within the local barbershop, town hall, coffee house, the church, and park.

The influential nature of mass communication is an integral element in the shift toward the saliency of the collective and transforms the very meaning of democracy. Today's universal communication displaces culture through sophisticated and often subtle informational techniques, which supplant local conduits of information and provide an artificial social solidarity that helps to create new sets of beliefs concerning rights and obligations; it helps to alter categories of thought and establish links to new social alliances and identities.[44] It exemplifies a path-dependent pattern that occurs in the changing rule structure, which over time redirects people's perceptions of costs associated with political and economic choice.

Put another way, universal communication is social influence entailed within political and market communication (e.g., opinion polling, push-polling, market research) as well as evolving administrative power (e.g., its coercible law, the facility of public accounting techniques). Habermas suggests that these processes of universal communication move interpersonal understanding forward. In essence, they advance the new social life on principles of universal rationality: "Our first sentence expresses unequivocally the intention of universal and unconstrained consensus" (1971, quoted in Mayhew 1997: 35).

In the EU and elsewhere, societies are being integrated not on the division of labor, as Emile Durkheim believed, but through new structures of information and mechanisms for its communication that use common symbols of language, words, measures, and icons. In short, the universal information that attempts to tie highly diverse societies together is advanced through the language and techniques of public relations. The words and symbols of public relations help to dislodge the pesky particular information embedded within cultures. For example, EU cosmopolitans ask the French people to trade off (privatize or otherwise subordinate) certain informational preferences, for instance, to limit certain aspects of their *Frenchness*, a characteristically French way of life, for the greater good of union expansion. Initially, the French people will reject this trade-off. In the end, Frenchness will bear too high a cost and will likely yield to the trade-off.

It is evident that supra-state political expansion is not building member consensus around the particular cultural information located within individual nation-states. This was clear, for example, when EU members, with several exceptions (including Poland and Italy), rejected any mention of centuries of Christian heritage (Catholic or Protestant) in the preamble of the EU Constitution. Because particular information is often an impediment to integration into a cosmopolitan order, the rationality of new communication separates the discussion of the polity from past, present, and future consequences of action.

It works in the short term because it breaks up words, language, images, and feelings from particular information. The aim is to align rationality to the activity of institutional expansion. Its messages are attractive and farsighted, suggesting that the cosmopolitan age is different, that societies are beyond the laws and normative values of the past, that culture is stuck in the old ways of old people, that the future can transcend the past, that the uncertainties of globalization can be assuaged through the linguistic gymnastics of public relations and its use for social reconstruction. The appeal to vanity and ego, to playing the smart role of vanguards of destiny, all suggest the denial or trivialization of the trade-offs at work in this division of information. The posture of contract theorists holding this view appears to presuppose that negligible costs are being raised against the particular actors, peoples, and nation-states.

Often certain forms of communication also rely on an antirealism of denial. History offers many examples. In one example, Plato's point in the *Protagoras* was that the demos of Athens, because of a bad education, could not distinguish between the teachings of Socrates and those of Protagoras. The demos had difficulty drawing distinctions between realism and antirealism, between the pursuit of wisdom and understanding located in the dialectic and the propaganda of mere rhetoric. If Plato's view is to be believed, the demos of Athens at that time was constructed around wide swaths of sophistry (propaganda) that relied on hubris about the future and a denial of past mistakes—the Peloponnesian war being one consequence of hubris and denial.[45]

What we are discussing is the logic of collective interests under expansion as they separate from and displace the experience of the individual (or local) by means of new channels of communication. As Habermas suggests, processes of political integration are mediated through "public communication that transcends the boundaries of the thus far limited national public spheres" (1998: 160). However, we suggest that over time, collective interests alter the meaning of democracy itself under the aegis of public communication. This too can be seen in history.

As we have witnessed, at one time, under localism, democracy meant that citizens made decisions, or elected persons who served as their agents. A competitive, elite model of representation replaced this late-eighteenth century idea of democracy. No longer did citizens run the government or elect agents to do their bidding, but instead they chose a leader. Different leaders proposed different agendas, and the citizens acted democratically by electing the most preferred leader (and presumably his agenda). Thus, the idea of democracy shifted from one of agency, to one of selection. Public communication and the growth of technology tracked these political shifts as evidenced by the rapid rise of political consulting and lobbying, the dramatic increase in the use of social science techniques for political purposes (e.g., polling, focus groups), and the expansion of various media and political think tanks (Mayhew 1997: 209–35).

Given enough institutional expansion and state centralization, the meaning of democracy shifts to assent only, paralleling the shift from individual to collective freedom. While the pace of this shift is never uniform, the meaning of freedom itself changes as individuals adjust their self-interest to the realities of institutional change. As we have seen, the new rules create social cooperation: they allow individuals to pursue their individual interests so that they ultimately become compatible with one another. However, they do so by shaping preferences and conceptions of self-interest in ways that deny individual purpose and ends grounded in individual experience. It is in this manner, based on the volition of the individual to choose the collective direction, that freedom itself becomes identified with the institution and its direction. And the respective institution, in one sense, represents the aggregated demand for universal information.

The division of information mechanism sufficiently explains both the incentives behind and in what manner the particular is traded off for the universal. The United States is an apt example. At its beginnings, individual states with varying cultural distinctives came together to form a union of United States. At first, the union was managed by a weak system of national government. Shortly after its founding, the principle of federalism was established in order to ensure equilibrium between the individual states (states' rights) and a stronger national government. Eventually states' rights were traded off for a stronger national government. A civil war pushed the matter along, as did the Great Depression and United States' involvement in both World War II and then the Cold War. Underlying many decisions during these eras was the choice between localism and growth and the principle of security that growth seems to ensure. Growth required rules that transcended state boundaries exemplified by the Fourteenth Amendment to the U.S. Constitution and expanded interpretations of the Interstate Commerce Clause of the constitution by the Hugo Black-led 1930s Supreme Court. These rules constituted an externality on states' rights, shifting the fulcrum of governance toward the national.

Unlike the United States, which has reached the advanced stages of market and political integration among its diverse states, the EU is in the early stages of this trade-off process, but is suffering through fits and starts similar in nature to the U.S. states. What must be known, however, is that once the problems of ethno-nationality are eased (or limited) through an enlarged system of rules, the union of nations in Europe may enjoy a prolonged period of rising prosperity, as these universal rules tend to increase trade and production.

Following a line of thinking originated by Kant, Habermas figured out how a shared system of values could supersede ethno-national differences. As a modern cosmopolitan, Habermas sees the expansion of the EU as a merging set of political institutions, one that requires the denial—not the preservation—of local information (experience, law, etc.). (Recall that, on the one hand, Habermas expressed a concern to preserve distinctions in culture, yet on the other hand, he appears to know that such preservation acts as a an obstruction against expanding normative cosmopolitanism.) The EU requires a categorical imperative of universal rationality. While Kant in his own advocacy of early cosmopolitanism could not see (or simply chose not to see) that particular information would in fact be traded off for universal information, Habermas does not appear to make the same error. Instead, according to Habermas, trading off particular information will cash out in greater collective freedom, an ever-greater universal rationality.

Specifically, Kant was interested in preserving the particular (localism) while having the force of the universal. In his idealism, Kant believed that principles of the categorical imperative should lead a nation-state to order its domestic rules in so rational a manner as to allow them to become compatible with a global legal order, thus offering the potential for a functioning global equilibrium.[46] The "league of nations," for example, is a Kantian invention that might serve to avoid war, bring about peace, and expand trade all under conditions of mutual self-interest. Under Kant's *moral* conception, a league of nations would generate voluntary (noncoercive) nation-state compliance primarily through weak appeal to enlightened rationality that mutual association might bring. In theory, then, a nation-state could protect its sovereignty and informational preferences by not integrating (not expanding) its institutions with the institutions of other nation-states.

Habermas obviously recognizes the problem of incompatibility with Kant's compatibilist scheme.[47] Habermas is not interested in the weakness of a *moral* conception of the EU, especially if it relies upon voluntary nation-state assent. Essentially, he believes that nation-state sovereignty (and its particular information) cannot and should not be preserved in the federal union of European nation-states, especially if it is to have a chance of unifying conceptions about the collective good. Nation-state sovereignty and the particular informational, cultural ties that bind it must be traded off; provincialism must give way to cosmopolitanism. Yet in contrast to Kant's nonbinding moral appeal to a loose confederation of states, Habermas calls on today's European nation-states to advance a binding *legal* framework, a multinational law and set of institutions that retain coercive police power.

Cosmopolitan law must be institutionalized in such a way that it is binding on the individual governments. The community of peoples must be able to ensure that its members act at least in conformity with the law through the threat of sanctions. Only in this way will the unstable system of states that assert their sovereignty through mutual threats be transformed into a federation with common institutions that assume state functions, that is, which legally regulate the relations between its members and monitor their compliance with these rules. . . . Cosmopolitan law is a logical consequence of the idea of the constitutive rule of law. It establishes for the first time symmetry between the juridification of social and political relations both within and beyond the state's borders.[48]

The internal-external symmetry that Habermas seeks imposes a quite severe cost against the individual, against the local, against the particular, and against the individual nation-state. In order to bring about the rational political assent of diverse peoples to the universal direction, and in the process separating them from their individual preferences and ways of life, Habermas, like Jacques Ellul before him, suggests that political socialization is brought about through educational institutions. The polity can then be rebound on these new terms and within these educative institutions after the demos and all that it represents is weakened. Social influence serves this function. The instruments of communication evolve and network as new words, language, symbols, images, and slogans substitute the old ways rooted within local culture (the old public) for what Mayhew calls "the new public" (1997). What is clear is that growth and integration both deny that which is part and parcel of a viable demos and channels political and market communication in the collectivist direction.

Perhaps the early Enlightenment view of the German philosopher Johann Herder best exemplifies the trade-off occurring within Habermasian political expansion. "The love of humanity is a noble sentiment, but most of the time we live our lives by smaller solidarities. . . . [It] reflects the fact that we learn to love humanity not in general but through its particular expressions. . . . The savage who loves himself, his wife and child, with quiet joy, and in his modest way works for the good of his tribe [is] a truer being than that shadow of a man, the refined citizen of the world, who, enraptured with the love of all his fellow-shadows, loves but a chimera" (Herder 1791: 309).

Democracy, Law, and Rationality

The question of whose rules and system of law will govern political enlarge-ment is an interesting cultural question for the EU and other transborder political groups.[49] In recent years, greater scrutiny has been given to coun-tries' origins of law and its relationship to political freedoms and the relative security or insecurity of property rights.[50] One thesis carried recently is that the common law countries of British origin or under British influence (e.g., through colonialism, imperialism, or voluntary participation in the Commonwealth) tend to more thoroughly secure political liberties and property rights than the civil law countries of Scandinavian, German, or French derivation. Indices of judicial independence, democracy, human rights, banking operations, employment laws, law enforcement in general, and creditor rights all mix to suggest the principle of liberty to act politically or economically, and without significant government or market subterfuge, is best secured by the traditions of Anglo-American institutions. This analysis has been helpful from a historical perspective concerning the growth and maturation—or their opposites—of various economies and political systems. It has fittingly considered the institution in determining the factors of political and economic action. Institutional structure and its information base set the context for decision making, incentives, and reform or resistance to reform.[51]

However, as institutions expand and rules covering economic and political activity become increasingly universal, the nuances of legal origins, small or large, will over time matter proportionately less, as these will continue to be superseded by exogenous transnational economic agreements. The historical differences in legal traditions between, say, France (a civil law country) and Britain (a common law country) will remain historical accounts.[52] Previously disparate legal systems such as those between France and Britain, or those between the United States and Mexico, will continue to undergo a single-track of integration. For example, major legal differences are being kneaded out through common legal instruments from political associations such as the EU or through economic trade agreements such as the North America Free Trade Agreement (NAFTA), making commerce commensurable, property rights seemingly more secure, and assuring a greater sense of stability of economic activity. While local economic customs and cultural practices may continue to function at the margins of production and exchange, and secondary and black markets may even flourish in some localities, the formal constraints and differences between political and market institutions, which once erupted from the disparate legal origins of countries, will become increasingly assuaged by an evolutionary top-down turnover in universal rules and property rights.

In the arena of markets, for example, the Lisbon Strategy of the EU is worth mentioning. In 2000, the heads of state and government of the EU met in Lisbon to set forth a strategy of institutional reform whose chief goal was to make the EU "the most dynamic and competitive knowledge-based economy in the world, capable of sustainable growth with more and better jobs and greater social cohesion" by 2010. Notwithstanding the unanticipated slow progress toward this aim in the face of Spartan eruptions of ethno-nationalism, the strategy consisted in part of establishing efficient and integrated financial markets among member countries that attempt to transcend previous native barriers to trade.

The original Lisbon Strategy—affirmed again by members in its mid-term review in 2005—seeks to thoroughly and rapidly develop a single, coherent internal market between member states that does the following and much more. The strategy: (1) eliminates barriers to investment in pension funds; (2) establishes better functioning of bond and equity markets through transparency on debt-issuing calendars; (3) improves functioning of cross-border sale and repurchase markets; (4) brings coherence and comparability to companies' financial statements and market regulations; (5) adopts the International Accounting Standards Regulation in order to better secure financial transparency and higher degrees of investor and trading partner confidence; and (6) makes property rights more secure by universalizing patent protection, professional licensure, and ensuring cross-border labor mobility. At its core, the strategy is designed to unify and expand institutions under a single internal EU market and political framework, thus lowering transaction costs commonly associated with cross-border goods and services exchange.[53]

It is also noteworthy that the EU has established the Court of Justice of the European Communities. The court's jurisdiction extends to all member countries and entails de jure review of violations of EC law by states or institutions. The court (as of 2006) consists of 25 (proclaimed) independent-minded judges and 8 advocates-general, all legal experts appointed by common accord by member countries, and who serve reelectable six-year terms of office. The transnational actions that the court may take up concern failure to fulfill obligations, actions of annulment, issues of failure to act, and applications of compensation. The EU's Court of Justice has emerged as the transcendent legal force in Europe, "the supreme guardian of Community legality," while also recognizing that lower-level national courts may also apply community law. Under one line of thought, a strong and independent judiciary is a necessary condition (a net plus) to secure individual liberties and property rights for a healthy demos. This line of thought seems to rely upon the optimistic belief that *stare decisis* (lit., "to abide by"), which once bound constitutional review to a theory of original intent of domestic and common and statutory law (i.e., a historical-grammatical principle of textual interpretation), will continue to provide a reliable method of legal analysis.

Having generated decades of relative certainty surrounding constitutional hermeneutics, this legal thought is now subject to a newer, expansive phenomenon of consciously importing international sources of law into American judicial review. For example, the U.S. Supreme Court's growing use and citation of international sources of law to interpret a domestic constitution seemingly negates some of the validity girding the belief that property rights are more secure under such legal systems. This is so because such action used with any measure of frequency and determinative force tends to make a domestic constitution significantly less rigid, less reliable in meaning, less reliant upon domestic precedent, and more subject to the highly selective ideologies of judicial inspiration.

These examples indicate that the expanding institutions of law, markets, and politics in Europe and elsewhere possess dynamic traits of character, which alter previous conceptions and characteristics of national sovereignty and culture. Under the logic of expansion, nation-state trading partners and political associations will continue to emphasize the benefits of collective freedom under the logic of social cohesion, benefits that tend to make human exchange uniform, predictable, and more governable, but tend also to lessen the capacities and choices in the realm of individual action. As the EU's Lisbon Strategy declares, social cohesion is its preeminent goal. But as many other political and economic philosophers have recognized, social cohesion requires a common faith, a vision of future perfection, a set of consensual and overarching principles and conventions. These cannot afford to be obstructed by the particularities inherent in locally held belief systems (individual, community, state, or national, as the case may be) about legal, market, or political institutions.

Thus, the once-dramatic differences between British, French, German, and Scandavian institutions of law, markets, and politics are being roughly worked out through intentional and unintentional forces of expansion and central control. So too, is this taking place between nation-states in the Americas and Asia. And in order to aggregate preferences under scale, the costs associated with individual freedom must be raised proportionate to the lowering costs of collective action. This turnover in universal rules and property rights tends to reduce rather than enhance the universe of individual choice and action. In order to guarantee the security of values and their compatibility, rationality must be divorced from individual ideas of liberty.

As inherently dissipative systems, expanding institutions suffer the loss of information during the give-and-take trade-off processes occurring between the particular and the universal. We have shown that this loss of information typically occurs on the particular side of exchange and production, bringing syndetic advantages to notions of collectivity but significantly weakening individual capacities of choice and production (unless these align with expansion). These processes shift the sense of balance toward positive freedom, that is, an extension of liberty granted by a sovereign for person P to choose x, and away from negative freedom, that is, the natural right of person P to choose x (or non-x) without interference or coercion, even when choice x is deemed irrational by the collective. We would suggest that person P's choice of x is not bound by equivocal senses of rationality or self-interest, rather by the moral sphere and nonviolable conceptions of respect for others' individual freedoms. Moreover, what is also clear to the canons of common sense is that choice x may in fact represent or become oriented around either collective or individual goods: person P may rightly decide whether or not to participate and when, where, and under what conditions, in the production or exchange of collective goods.

It was Mancur Olson who recognized the paradox of individual-collective action under self-interest. "If members of a large group rationally seek to maximize their personal welfare, they will *not* act to advance [the collective interest] unless there is coercion to force them to do so, or unless some separate incentive, distinct from [the collective interest] is offered to members of the group individually on the condition that they help bear the costs or burdens involved in the achievement of the group objectives" (Olson 1965: 2, emphasis original). Even under a scheme of coercion or incentives where, say, individual incentives are tightly coupled with collective interests, it remains correct to say that person *P* ought to have some measure of freedom to choose *x*, but the costs associated with choosing *x* if *x* lies outside the social good might be inordinately high. It is also critical to note that the very term "freedom" becomes equivocal. For reasons of cost and equivocation alone, it is a kind of freedom that is never found to depart far from the criterion of social goods and collective interests.

These comments bring us to this brief conclusion: The economist has assured us that institutions make simplifications of the world for the sake of efficiency, and that the expansion of institutions indicates the movement of markets from less-than-optimal to optimal states. This book warns us that expanding institutions generate information costs, and that the existence of these costs leads to the progressive loss of individual liberty.

Notes

1. It is worth remarking in this connection that each of these visionaries would likely be exceedingly offended at such a characterization of their views, inasmuch as they all (in their different ways) expressed a genuine concern for freedom and regarded themselves as true advocates and great defenders of it. Yet what is perhaps most striking about their theories, as many critics and scholars have correctly pointed out, is that in practice they all lead ultimately to various forms of statism and dependence. By consigning the specific beliefs, feelings, and volitions of an individual life to the category of the insufficiently rational, the trend in these collectivist systems is to propagate fatally distorted views of freedom and democracy.

2. A property is generally considered an attribute or quality that a substance (and often its class) is said to possess. In other words, properties are *had* by substances; a human being (a substance) is said to be free when it *has* the property of liberty. Thus a property is often a real nonspatiotemporal entity and can remain that way even when exemplified in a particular substance (or class). A relation can be the connection of a property to a substance. The property of

red is *in* the ball. The property of liberty is *with* an individual human being when *x* conditions are satisfied. Freedom may be considered a relation, for example, between an individual and a collective.

3. See Rousseau (1987).

4. See Simmons (1979) for a helpful discussion concerning natural rights.

5. See books eight and nine of Plato's *Republic* (1986).

6. Hayek is prescient and balanced on this point: "That true individualism affirms the value of the family and all the common efforts of the small community and group, that it believes in local autonomy and voluntary associations, and that indeed its case rests largely on the contention that much for which coercive action of the state is usually invoked can be done better by voluntary collaboration need not be stressed further" (1948: 23).

7. Abraham Lincoln was reported to have once said, "We all declare for liberty; but in using the same word, we do not mean the same thing."

8. These forms of freedom are dichotomized with the recognition that their origins are not entirely dissimilar nor are they easily disentangled. Each kind of freedom plays a part in the machinery of the world, each may claim its limited authority in human affairs, and each may claim its legitimacy as an ultimate end. The two are not equivalent. Yet there is, no doubt, in practice, some overlap and interdependence between them, and the distinction in many cases cannot be too sharply drawn.

9. It is helpful here to consider the view offered by David Held: "Rights define legitimate spheres of independent action (or inaction). They enable—that is, create spaces for action—and constrain—that is, specify limits on independent action so that the latter does not curtail and infringe the liberty of others. Hence, rights have a structural dimension, bestowing both opportunities and duties" (1996: 302).

10. This view of freedom has been at the heart of the liberal tradition since the time of Enlightenment and Reformation. See in particular the works of J. S. Mill, Adam Smith, Benjamin Constant, F. A. Hayek, and R. Nozick.

11. See Berlin (2002: 48).

12. The classical statements on this subject are found in Aquinas, Locke, Spinoza, Hume, J. S. Mill, T. H. Green (1881); and something like this has been asserted by more recent writers. See, for example, Dworkin (1978) and Sen (1988).

   John Dewey defined liberty (in its positive sense) as "the effective power to do specific things" (1935).

13. The most illuminating exposition of the distinction between positive and negative freedom was probably that given by Sir Isaiah Berlin in his *Four Essays on Freedom* (1969). Yet another illustration of this distinction is in *The Works of T. H. Green* (1881).

14. In agreeing with the view held by Adam Smith, R. H. Coase said, "The extent to which we follow any course of action depends on its cost" (1994: 99).

15. As Sen (2002: 329) noted, Arrow started the modern discipline of social choice. His impossibility theorem states that if there are at least three distinct social states and the set of individuals is finite, there is no social welfare function satisfying

conditions U ("unrestricted domain"), P ("Pareto principle"), I ("Independence of irrelevant alternatives"), and D ("non-dictatorship"). See Arrow (1963).

16. Sen considers his formal analysis to be part of a wider intellectual effort "that has helped dispel some of the gloom that was associated with earlier social choice and welfare economics." See Sen (2002: 86).

17. Essentially this is an effort to overcome the conflicts of the Liberal (Sen's) Paradox, also known as the Impossibility of the Paretian Liberal, which basically argues that no social decision function with unrestricted domain can satisfy both the principle of minimal liberty and Pareto optimality or efficiency. See Sen (1979).

18. Sen makes his position on this quite clear. "In general, informational broadening, in one form or another, is an effective way of overcoming social choice pessimism and of avoiding impossibilities, and it leads directly to constructive approaches with viability and reach" (2002: 96). And in an earlier work he said, "Indeed, through informational broadening, it is possible to have a coherent and consistent criteria for social and economic assessment" (Sen 1999: 253).

19. According to Sen, "Once interpersonal comparisons are introduced, the impossibility problem, in the appropriately redefined framework, vanishes" (2002: 273). This happens, as he said, because "the additional informational availability allows sufficient discrimination to escape impossibilities of this type" (2002: 80). Hence the idea of interpersonal comparisons of individual utilities figures prominently in Sen's theory. However, the way it is stated can easily mislead. It must not be taken to mean an actual side-by-side comparison of the utilities of individual persons, that is, an assessment of preference and well-being at the base level of the single person. What Sen is in fact referring to here is intergroup comparisons, statistical averages, and approximations; it is the act of aggregative comparison and evaluation. Though he pleads convincingly for broadening the information base of social choice, his overall pattern of information broadening proceeds in the universal (aggregative) direction. Thus what appears to be information broadening is in reality information narrowing. The main point to understand is that his rational solution construct is purchased at the price of individualized forms of information.

20. Our theory suggests that social aggregation takes place not through a broadening of the information base, as Sen has argued, but through a narrowing (dividing) of it. However, as we have shown, this narrowing of information results in higher overall costs, in that it leads to a reduction in the range of individual choice.

21. It is apparent that much of Sen's analysis of freedom rests upon an equivocation of language—that is, the terms employed in argument undergo a change in meaning.

22. See for example Sen's use of Adam Smith's observation of the relationship between the individual and society in *Development as Freedom* (1999: 271).

23. The real objection to Sen's model is that it has the effect of reducing the human species to the level of raw material, to functioning, manipulatable parts in the social machinery.

24. The suggestion implicit in Sen's theory is that growth (i.e., development) is a manifestation of rationality because it is the act of projecting ourselves together in a certain direction, because it breaks down barriers between people and brings unison and association. In both *Rationality and Freedom* (2002) and *Development as Freedom* (1999), Sen seems to suggest that what this process resolves is necessarily rational and therefore proves that it is just.

25. See *Rationality and Freedom* (Sen 2002: 626).

26. It is clear that Sen sees error elimination in social and political arrangements along with sweeping improvements in the evolution of preferences as the solution to the problem of social choice. As he said: "The point can be made that ultimately the guarantee against conflicts of the kind that the Liberal Paradox identifies has to lie in the evolution of preferences that respect each others' freedom to lead the kind of life each respectively has reason to value. The evolution of such preferences can result from natural selection over time, but they can be helped also by conscious reflection on the nature of the problem that the Liberal Paradox tried to identify, combined with public discussion of these issues" (2002: 454).

27. According to Sen, "Freedom is an irreducibly plural concept" (2002: 585).

28. Hargreaves-Heap and Varoufakis (2004: 21) show how the concept of game theory relates to the larger issues and debates of social science. They suggest that the central problem of game theory "may not be unconnected to the model of persons at its foundations."

29. See, for example, Sen (2002).

30. See, for example, Bhawati (2002: 151–162).

31. Hargreaves-Heap and Varoufakis (2004: 266) bring their book to a close this way: "In short, we conclude that not only will game theory have to embrace some expanded form of individual agency, if it is to be capable of explaining many social interactions, but also that this is necessary if it is to be useful to the liberal debate over the scope of the State."

32. See, for example, Sen (1970).

33. See, for example, the section "The One and the Many," in *Four Essays on Liberty* (1969). "This ancient faith rests on the conviction that all the positive values in which men have believed must, in the end, be compatible, and perhaps even entail one another. . . . It is a commonplace that neither personal equality nor efficient organization nor social justice is compatible with more than a modicum of individual liberty, and certainly not with unrestricted *laissez-faire;* that justice and generosity, public and private loyalties, the demands of genius and the claims of society, can conflict violently with each other. And it is no great way from that to the generalization that not all good things are compatible, still less all the ideals of mankind" (167).

34. Rawls is unequivocal in the direction entailed by rationality: "Social justice is the principle of rational prudence applied to an aggregative conception of the welfare of the group" (1971: 21). Hayek famously challenged the notion of social justice as an illusion, seen as a costly trade-off between individual freedom

and collective order. "[If] 'social justice' is to be brought about, the individuals must be required to obey not merely general rules but specific demands directed to them only. The type of social order in which the individuals are directed to serve a single system of ends is the organization and not the spontaneous order of the market, that is, not a system in which the individual is free because bound only by general rules of just conduct, but a system in which all are subject to specific directions by authority" (Hayek 1976: 85).

35. This question, of course, presupposes that the terms "just" or "humane" can be negotiated from a framework of common conceptions about human beings, their nature, attributes, aims, purposes of human capital, etc. Given the plurality of world-views, common conceptions surrounding philosophical universals are next to impossible to achieve, making the question a difficult but ultimately necessary one to answer.

36. See "Reconciliation through the Public Use of Reason" in Habermas (1998: 49–74).

37. Rawls suggests that "even though the parties are deprived of information about their particular ends [by adopting a priori principles of justice], they have enough knowledge to rank the alternatives. . . . Guided by the theory of the good and general facts of moral psychology, their deliberations are no longer guesswork. They can make a rational decision in the ordinary sense" (Rawls 1971: 123).

38. A classic accounting of this skewed equilibrium may be found in the U.S. Supreme Court decision, *Kelo et al. v. City of New London et al.* (June 23, 2005), wherein a 5 to 4 court majority extended the power of government to condemn or "take" real property from the possession of an individual party for "public use," where the terms "public use" within the Takings Clause of the Constitution (Fifth Amendment) has now been widened under a collectivist notion of rationality. The court's jurisprudence has been on this path since at least the 1930s under the Hugo Black Court.

39. See, for example, "Is There a Future for the Nation-State?" in Habermas (1998: 105–164).

   Habermas elsewhere is highly critical of the EU's current bureaucratic structure in Brussels, Belgium: "Today the European Union is a regime of continental magnitude that is very thickly networked horizontally via markets while maintaining relatively weak political regulation vertically though indirectly legitimated authorities" Habermas (2003: 94).

40. For a thorough discussion in this area, see Hayek (1948: 1–32). Berlin is equally prescient here: Freedom is "the absence of obstacles to possible choices and activities—absence of obstructions on roads along which man can decide to walk. Such freedom ultimately depends not on whether I wish to walk at all, or how far, but on how many doors are open, how open they are, upon their relative importance in my life, even though it may be impossible literally to measure this in any quantitative fashion. The extent of my social or political freedom consists in the absence of obstacles not merely to my actual, but to my potential choices— to my acting in this or that way if I choose to do so" (Berlin 1969: xxxix).

41. For an apt illustration of this, see Vidich and Bensman (1958).

42. Dahl has called this phenomenon "the law of time and numbers: The more citizens a democratic unit contains, the less that citizens can participate directly in government decisions and the more that they must delegate authority to others" (Dahl 1998: 109).

43. We are not speaking here of the vulgar type of propaganda used by the Nazis, which tried to fuse the antirealism of propaganda to culture, but a much more sophisticated and subtle kind that displaces cultures through the technology of mass communication. Nazi propaganda attacked but did not crush German culture. For example, the German people began a retreat from Hitler after the military collapse at Stalingrad.

44. See, for example, Jowett and Odonnell (1999). The conditioning of human thought may occur with or without intentionality. Our argument tends to emphasize the unintentional side of the debate. However, we do not deny the role that mandarins and elites play in the reconstruction of society or its institutions.

45. It is true that Ellul, in contrast to Plato, suggested that successful propaganda requires a well-educated populace. Yet it is sufficient for now to point out that Plato's conception of education differs from Ellul's. We will bracket the nature of this difference for another occasion.

46. See Kant, "The Contest of Faculties" and "Perpetual Peace" in *Kant's Political Writings* (1970).

47. See Habermas, "Kant's Idea of Perpetual Peace," in *The Inclusion of the Other: Studies in Political Theory* (1998: 165–201).

48. Ibid., p. 179, 199.

49. Philosopher John Dewey insightfully suggested that "the problem of freedom of cooperative individualities is then a problem to be viewed in the context of culture. The state of culture is a state of interaction of many factors, the chief of which are law and politics [etc.] and, finally . . . the system of general ideas used by men to justify and to criticize the fundamental conditions under which they live, their social philosophy" (1989: 25).

50. See Rafael La Porta et al. (1998; 2002a; 2002b). Any empirical analysis of freedom does demonstrate that such investigations are methodologically bounded; these modes tend to lead with a quantitative model and, as a result, can only approximate in lesser degrees the reality of the situation. As Hayek understood so well, trying to explain complex phenomena, systems, and spheres such as freedom within relations between individuals and institutions can only produce pattern predictions, not precise predictions. The empirical method will not allow recognition of the deeper qualitative questions and realities occurring within the realm of freedom. Because the method of investigation is comparatively narrow, it must simplify the goods and relations under view, reducing to the category of nonimportance all of the bona fide ontological questions and categories inherent in notions of freedom. As with game theorists trying to reduce the very real complexities of choice and exchange to formulas of math, all empirical attempts to evaluate the real status and conditions of freedom,

positive or negative, individual or collective, are likely to be inadequate and suffer from a fallacy of category.

51. See, for example, William Heller, Philip Keefer, and Matthew McCubbins, "Political Structure and Economic Liberalization: Conditions and Cases from the Developing World," in Drake and McCubbins (eds), *The Origins of Liberty: Political and Economic Liberalization in the Modern World* (1998: 146–178).

52. In *Measures and Men* (1986: 226), Witold Kula supports the point with this interesting observation: "Writing a hundred years ago of the ancien régime, de Tocqueville was amazed to note that 'virtually all Europe had the same institutions.' For the historian today, this is still more amazing because more recent studies of institutions, especially legal institutions, paint a false picture of their infinite variety; behind that picture, however, the forms of human relations in the different countries are fundamentally identical."

53. Regarding the institution of education and its property rights, the Lisbon Strategy likewise seeks to lower educational trade barriers by ensuring the following: (1) greater percentages of educational attainment for its laborers (relying upon the assumption that attainment and knowledge and skills development track symmetrically); (2) uniform credential recognition that fosters labor mobility; (3) the expansion of virtual schools through the Internet; (4) the emphasis of technological skills; and (5) opportunities for lifelong learning according to changes in technological demand. As we mentioned in chapter 4, the expanding institution of education is rapidly standardizing on a global scale both access and services across informational boundaries and geographic borders. So far, the European rationale for expanded educational trade is premised upon a theory of human capital at odds with the realities and complexities of individual freedom; it is based upon the utility-value of human beings in competitive environments for scarce resources.

Bibliography

Agresto, John. 1999. "The Public Value of the Liberal Arts." *Academic Questions* 12, no. 4 (Fall): 40–44.

Alchian, Armen. 1950. "Uncertainty, Evolution, and Economic Theory." *Journal of Political Economy* 58, no. 3: 211–221.

Alder, Ken. 1995. "A Revolution to Measure: The Political Economy of the Metric System in France." In *The Values of Precision,* edited by M. Norton Wise. Princeton: Princeton University Press.

Amsterdam Treaty of 1999. http://www.eurotreaties.com/amsterdamtext.html (accessed October 5, 2005).

Anderson, Terry, and Peter Hill. 2004. *The Not So Wild, Wild West.* Palo Alto, CA: Stanford University Press.

Arrow, Kenneth. 1974. *The Limits of Organization.* New York: W. W. Norton.

———. 1963. *Social Choice and Individual Values.* 2nd ed. New York: Wiley.

Ayittey, George. 2005. *Africa Unchained: The Blueprint for Africa's Future.* New York: Palgrave Macmillan.

Barzel, Yoram. 1989. *Economic Analysis of Property Rights.* New York: Cambridge University Press.

Becker, Gary S. 1964. *Human Capital: A Theoretical and Empirical Analysis, with Special Reference to Education.* New York: Columbia University Press.

Berlin, Isaiah. 1969. *Four Essays on Liberty.* Oxford: Oxford University Press.

———. 2002. *Liberty.* Edited by Henry Hardy. New York: Oxford University Press.

Bhawati, Jagdish. 2002. "Democracy and Development: Cruel Dilemma or Symbiotic Relationship?" *Review of Development Economics* 6, no. 2: 151–162.

Bollag, Burton. 2006. "Federal Panel Floats Plan to Overhaul Accreditation: College Leaders Decry Replacing Regional Boards with a National System." *Chronicle of Higher Education* 52, no. 32 (April 14): A1.

Bowles, Samuel. 2004. *Microeconomics: Behavior, Institutions, and Evolution.* Princeton: Princeton University Press.

Brighouse, H. 2000. *School Choice and Social Justice.* Oxford: Oxford University Press.

Buchanan, James, M. 2003. "Public Choice: Politics without Romance." *Policy* 19, no. 3 (Spring): 13–18.

Buchanan, James, and Gordon Tullock. 1962. *The Calculus of Consent.* Ann Arbor: University of Michigan Press.

Callahan, Raymond, E. 1962. *Education and the Cult of Efficiency: A Study of the Social Forces That Have Shaped the Administration of the Public Schools.* Chicago: University of Chicago Press.

Card, David, and Alan Krueger. 1996. "School Resources and Student Outcomes: An Overview of the Literature and New Evidence from North and South Carolina." *Journal of Economic Perspectives,* no. 10: 31–50.

Carnegie, Andrew. 1886. *Triumphant Democracy.* New York: Scribner's.

Carnegie Task Force on Teaching as a Profession. 1986. *A Nation Prepared: Teachers for the Twenty-First Century.* New York: Carnegie Forum on Education and the Economy.

CHEA and ACE Letter. 2001. http://www.chea.org/International/papovich_wto.html (accessed September 2, 2006).

Chesterton, G. K. 1956. *Saint Thomas Acquinas: The Dumb Ox.* New York: Doubleday.

Chichilnisky, Graciela, ed. 1999. *Markets, Information, and Uncertainty: Essays in Economic Theory in Honor of Kenneth J. Arrow.* Cambridge: Cambridge University Press.

Chubb, John, and Terry Moe. 1990. *Politics, Markets, and America's Schools.* Washington, D.C.: Brookings Institution.

———. 1988. "Politics, Markets, and the Organization of Schools." *American Political Science Review* 82, no. 4: 1065–1087.

Clifford, Geraldine, and James Guthrie. 1988. *Ed School: A Brief for Professional Education.* Chicago: University of Chicago Press.

Coase, Ronald H. 1994. *Essays on Economics and Economists.* Chicago: University of Chicago Press.

———. 1974. "The Lighthouse in Economics." *Journal of Law and Markets* 17, no. 2: 357–376.

———. 1960. "The Problem of Social Cost." *Journal of Law and Economics* 3: 1–44.

Constant, Benjamin. 2003. *Principles of Politics Applicable to All Governments.* Edited by Etienne Hofmann. Translated from the French by Dennis O'Keeffe. Introduction by Nicholas Capaldi. Indianapolis, IN: Liberty Fund.

Convention on the Recognition of Qualifications Concerning Higher Education in the European Region. 1997. http://www.bologna-berlin2003.de/pdf/Lisbon_convention.pdf (accessed July 20, 2005).

Cowen, Tyler. 2002. "Public Goods and Externalities." In *The Library of Economics and Liberty: The Concise Encyclopedia of Economics.* Indianapolis, IN: Liberty Fund. http://www.econlib.org/library/ENC/PublicGoodsandExternalities.html (accessed August 31, 2006).

Cremin, Lawrence A. 1962. *Transformation of the School: Progressivism in American Education, 1876–1957.* New York: Knopf.

Cubberly, Elwood P. 1914. *State and County Educational Reorganization.* New York: Macmillan.

Curley, Edwin, ed. and trans. 1994. *A Spinoza Reader: The Ethics and Other Works.* Princeton: Princeton University Press.

Dahl, Robert. 1998. *On Democracy.* New Haven: Yale University Press.

David, Paul A. 2001. "Path Dependence, Its Critics, and the Quest for 'Historical Economics.'" In *Evolution and Path Dependence in Economic Ideas: Past and Present,* edited by Pierre Garrouste and Stavros Ioannides. Cheltenham, UK: Edward Elgar Publishing.

Demsetz, Harold. 1967. "Toward a Theory of Property Rights." *American Economic Review* 57, no. 2: 347–359.

Denison, E. F. 1962. *The Sources of Economic Growth in the United States and the Alternatives before Us*. New York: Committee for Economic Development.

De Soto, Hernando. 2000. *The Mystery of Capital: Why Capitalism Triumphs in the West and Fails Everywhere Else*. New York: Basic Books.

Dewey, John. "Science, and Society." In *The Collected Works of John Dewey, 1882–1953*. Vol. 6, 1931–1932. Edited by Jo Ann Boydston. Carbondale: Southern Illinois University Press.

———. 1938. *Experience and Education*. New York: Macmillan.

———. 1989. *Freedom and Culture*. Buffalo, NY: Prometheus Books.

———. 1985. *The Later Works 1925–1953*. Vol. 6. Edited by Jo Ann Boydston. Carbondale: Southern Illinois University Press.

———. 1935. "Liberty and Social Control." *Social Frontier* 2, no. 2 (November): 41.

———. 1973a. "Philosophy and Civilization." In *The Philosophy of John Dewey: Volumes I and II*, edited by John McDermott. Chicago: University of Chicago Press.

———. 1929. *The Quest for Certainty*. New York: Minton, Balch.

———. 1973b. "The School and Society." In McDermott, *The Philosophy of John Dewey*.

Dickeson, Robert. 2006. "The Need for Accreditation Reform." Issue Paper. Washington, D.C.: Commision on the Future of Higher Eduction.

Dixit, A. and S. Skeath. 1999. *Games of Strategy*. New York: Norton.

Donovan, Frank R. 1970. *Prepare Now for a Metric Future*. New York: Weybright and Talley.

Drake, Paul, and Matthew McCubbins, eds. 1998. *The Origins of Liberty: Political and Economic Liberalization in the Modern World*. Princeton: Princeton University Press.

Dworkin, Ronald. 1978. *Taking Rights Seriously*. London: Duckworth.

Eaton, William Edward, ed. 1990. *Shaping the Superintendency: A Reexamination of Callahan and the Cult of Efficiency*. New York: Teachers College Press.

Eggertsson, Thrainn. 2001. "Norms in Economics, with Special Reference to Economic Development." In *Social Norms*, edited by Michael Hechter and Karl-Dieter Opp. New York: Russell Sage Foundation.

Ellul, Jacques. 1965. *Propaganda: The Formation of Men's Attitudes*. New York: Vintage Press.

European Higher Education by 2010. http://ec.europa.eu/education/policies/2010/lisbon_en.html (accessed August 8, 2005).

European Union Constitution Draft. 2005. http://europa.eu.int/eur-lex/lex/en/treaties/index.htm (accessed September 2, 2006).

European Union Constitution. http://europa.eu/constitution/en/lstoc1_en.htm (accessed September 2, 2006).

European Union Constitution. Articles 1–6. http://europa.eu.int/eur-lex/lex/en/treaties/index.htm (accessed September 2, 2006).

Europol Convention of 1995. http://europa.eu/scadplus/leg/en/lvb/l14005b.htm (accessed October 5, 2006).

Ewell, Peter. 2001. "Accreditation and Student Learning Outcomes: A Proposed Point of Departure." Washington, D.C.: Council for Higher Education Accreditation.

Friedman, Milton. 1962. *Capitalism and Freedom.* Chicago: University of Chicago Press.

———. 1955. "The Role of Government in Education." In *Economics and the Public Interest,* edited by Robert Solo. New Brunswick, NJ: Rutgers University Press.

Gauch, Hugh G., Jr. 2003. *Scientific Method in Practice.* Cambridge: Cambridge University Press.

General Agreement on Tariffs and Trade (GATT). http://www.gatt.org/ (accessed July 20, 2005).

General Agreement on Trade in Services (GATS). 1994. http://www.wto.org/english/ tratop_e/serv_e/gsintr_e.doc (accessed September 2, 2006).

Glenn, C., and J. De Groof. 2002. "What Next for School Vouchers?" In *Educational Freedom and Accountability: An International Overview.* Conference at Kennedy School of Government, Harvard University, October 17–18. http:// www.ksg.harvard.edu/pepg/PDF/events/WNConfPDF/WNAttendees.pdf (accessed on September 1, 2006).

Green, Thomas Hill. 1881. "Liberal Legislation and Freedom of Contract." In *The Works of Thomas Hill Green.* Vol. 3. Edited by R. L. Nettleship. London: Longman's, Green, 1891.

Habermas, Jurgen. 1998. *The Inclusion of the Other: Studies in Political Theory.* Cambridge, MA: MIT Press.

———. 1971. *Knowledge and Human Interests.* Boston: Beacon Press.

———. 1988. *On the Logic of the Social Sciences.* Translated by S. W. Nicholsen and J. Stark. Cambridge, MA: MIT Press.

———. 2003. "Toward a Cosmopolitan Europe." *Journal of Democracy* 14, no. 4 (October): 86–100.

Hallowell, A. Irving. 1943. "The Nature and Function of Property as a Social Institution." *Journal of Legal and Political Sociology,* no. 1 (April): 115–138.

Hanushek, Eric A. 1989. "The Impact of Differential Expenditures on School Performance." *Educational Researcher* 18, no. 4 (May): 45–51.

Hargreaves-Heap, Shaun P., and Yanis Varoufakis. 2004. 2nd ed. *Game Theory: A Critical Text.* New York: Routledge.

Havnevik, Kjell. 1993. *Tanzania: The Limits to Development from Above.* Sweden: Nordiska Afrikainstitutet.

Hayek, F. A. 1960. *The Constitution of Liberty.* Chicago: University of Chicago Press.

———. 1952. *The Counter-Revolution of Science: Studies in the Abuse of Reason.* Glencoe, IL: Free Press.

———. 1948. "Individualism: True and False." In *Individualism and Economic Order.* Chicago: University of Chicago Press.

————. 1976. *Law, Legislation and Liberty: Volume II; The Mirage of Social Justice.* Chicago: University of Chicago Press.

Hegel, Georg Wilhelm Friedrick. 1929. *Hegel's Science of Logic.* Translated by W. H. Johnston, and L. G. Struthers. With an introductory preface by Viscount Haldane of Cloan. New York: Macmillan.

Held, David. 1996. *Models of Democracy.* 2nd ed. Palo Alto, CA: Stanford University Press.

Herder, Johann. 1791. "Ideas for a Philosophy of the History of Mankind." In *J. G. Herder on Social and Political Culture,* edited and translated by F. M. Bernard. Cambridge: Cambridge University Press, 1969.

Hinds, Michael. 2002. *Carnegie Challenge: Teaching as a Clinical Profession: A New Challenge for Education.* New York: Carnegie Corporation.

Hobbes, Thomas. 1997. *Leviathan: An Authoritative Text, Backgrounds, Interpretations.* Edited by Richard E. Flathman and David Johnston. New York: W. W. Norton.

Holmes Group. 1986. *Tomorrow's Teachers: A Report of the Holmes Group.* East Lansing, MI: Holmes Group.

Holtom, Duncan. 2005. "Reconsidering the Power of the IFIs: Tanzania & the World Bank, 1978–1985." *Review of African Political Economy,* no. 106: 549–567.

Horn, Raymond A. 2002. *Understanding Educational Reform: A Reference Handbook.* Santa Barbara, CA: ABC-Clio.

Hume, David. 1740, 1888. *Treatise of Human Nature.* Edited by L. A. Selby-Bigge. Oxford: Oxford University Press.

Ingersoll, Richard. 2004. *Who Controls Teachers' Work? Power and Accountability in America's Schools.* Cambridge: Harvard University Press.

International Monetary Fund. Created in 1944–45. Article I sections 1 and 3. http://www.imf.org/ (accessed July 1, 2006).

Joint Declaration on Higher Education and the General Agreement on Trade in Services. 2001. www.aucc.ca/_pdf/english/statements/2001/gats_10_25_e.pdf (accessed September 2, 2006).

Jowett, G. S., and V. Odonnell. 1999. *Propaganda and Persuasion.* Thousand Oaks, CA: Sage Publications.

Kant, Immanuel. 1998. *Critique of Pure Reason.* Translated and edited by Paul Guyer and Allen W. Wood. Cambridge: Cambridge University Press.

————. 1784. "Idea for a Universal History from a Cosmopolitan Point of View." In *On History,* translated by Lewis White Beck. New York: Bobbs-Merrill, 1963.

————. 1970. *Kant's Political Writings.* Edited by Ciaran Cronin and Pablo De Greiff. Cambridge: University of Cambridge Press.

Katz, Michael. 1975. *Class, Bureaucracy, and Schools: The Illusion of Educational Change in America.* New York: Praeger.

Kiondo, Andrew. 1992. "The Nature of Economic Reforms in Tanzania." In *Tanzania and the IMF: The Dynamics of Liberalization,* edited by Howard Stein and Horace Campbell. Boulder, CO: Westview Press.

Kirp, David. 2003. *Shakespeare, Einstein and the Bottom Line: The Marketing of Higher Education.* Cambridge: Harvard University Press.

Knight, Frank H. 1921. *Risk, Uncertainty and Profit.* New York: Hart, Schaffner, and Marx. Reprint, New York: Harper and Row, 1965.

Kreps, D. 1990. *Game Theory and Economic Modeling.* New York: Oxford University Press.

Kuhn, Thomas. 1996. *The Structure of Scientific Revolutions.* 3rd ed. Chicago: University of Chicago Press.

Kula, Witold. 1986. *Measures and Men.* Translated by R. Szreter. Princeton: Princeton University Press.

Labaree, David. 2004. *The Trouble with Ed Schools.* New Haven, CT: Yale University Press.

Lagemann, Ellen. 2000. *An Elusive Science: The Troubling History of Educational Research.* Chicago: University of Chicago Press.

La Porta, Rafael, et al. 2002a. "Government Ownership of Banks." *Journal of Finance* 57, no. 1 (February): 265–301.

———. 2002b. "Guarantees of Freedom." *Harvard Institute of Economic Research.* Discussion Paper 1943 (January).

———. 1998. "Law and Finance." *Journal of Political Economy* 106, no. 6: 1113–1155.

Linklater, Andro. 2002. *Measuring America: How an Untamed Wilderness Shaped the United States and Fulfilled the Promise of Democracy.* New York: Walker Publishing Company.

Lisbon Strategy of EU. http://ec.europa.eu/education/policies/2010/et_2010_en.html (accessed September 2, 2006).

Locke, John. 2003. *Two Treaties of Government; and a Letter Concerning Toleration.* Edited and with an introduction by Ian Shapiro; with essays by John Dunn, Ruth Grant, Ian Shapiro. New Haven, CT: Yale University Press.

Manuel, Frank E. 1956. *The New World of Henri Saint-Simon.* Cambridge: Harvard University Press.

Marx, Karl, and Frederick Engels. 1999. *The Communist Manifesto: With Related Documents.* Edited with an introduction by John E. Toews. Boston: Bedford/St. Martin's.

Mayhew, Leon. 1997. *The New Public: Professional Communication and the Means of Social Influence.* Cambridge: Cambridge University Press.

McCloskey, Robert G. 1964. *American Conservatism in the Age of Enterprise.* New York: Harper Torchbooks.

Mill, John S. 1986. *On Liberty.* Buffalo, NY: Prometheus Books.

Mincer, J. 1958. *The Illusion of Equality: The Effect of Education on Opportunity, Inequality, and Social Conflict.* 1st ed. San Francisco: Jossey-Bass.

Monk, David H. 1996. "Resource Allocation for Education: An Evolving and Promising Base for Policy-Oriented Research." *Journal of School Leadership* 6, no. 3 (May): 216–242.

Mussa, Michael. 1997. "IMF Surveillance." *American Economic Review* 87, no. 2 (May): 28–31.

Nash, John. 1950. "The Bargaining Problem." *Econometrica* 18, no. 2: 155–162.

A Nation at Risk Report. 1983. A Nation at Risk: The Imperative for Educational Reform; A Report to the Nation and the Secretary of Education. United States Department of Education by the National Commission on Excellence in Education, April 1983. http://www.ed.gov/pubs/NatAtRisk/index.html (accessed August 8, 2005).

Niskanen, William A., Jr. 1971. *Bureaucracy and Representative Government.* Chicago: Aldine.

No Child Left Behind Act of 2001. Public Law 107–110, January 8, 2002, U.S. Statutes at Large 115 (2002): 1425–2094. http://www.ed.gov/policy/elsec/leg/esea02/index.html (accessed August 8, 2005).

North American Free Trade Agreement. 1994. http://www.nafta-sec-alena.org/DefaultSite/index_e.aspx (accessed September 2, 2006).

North, Douglass C. 1990. *Institutions, Institutional Change and Economic Performance.* Cambridge: Cambridge University Press.

———. 1991. "Institutions." *Journal of Economic Perspectives* 5, no. 1 (Winter): 97–112.

———. 2005. *Understanding the Process of Economic Change.* Princeton: Princeton University Press.

Nozick, Robert. 1973. "Distributive Justice." *Philosophy and Public Affairs* 3, 45–126.

Nyerere, Julius K. 1974. *Freedom and Development. Uhuru na Maendeleo. A Selection from Writings and Speeches 1968–1973.* London: Oxford University Press.

Olson, Mancur. 1965. *The Logic of Collective Action: Public Goods and the Theory of Groups.* Cambridge: Harvard University Press.

Oxford English Dictionary. 1989. 2nd ed. Edited by J. A. Simpson and E. S. C. Weiner. Oxford: Clarendon.

Perkinson, Henry J. 1995. *The Imperfect Panacea: American Faith in Education.* 4th ed. New York: McGraw-Hill.

Peterson, Paul E. 1985. *The Politics of School Reform, 1870–1940.* Chicago: University of Chicago Press.

Pickering, Mary. 1993. *Auguste Comte: An Intellectual Biography.* New York: Cambridge University Press.

Plato. 2004. *Protagoras and Meno.* Translated with notes and interpretive essays by Robert C. Bartlett. New York: Cornell University Press.

———. 1986. *The Republic.* Translated by Benjamin Jowett. Buffalo, NY: Prometheus Books.

Polanyi, Karl. 1944. *The Great Transformation.* New York: Farrar & Rinehart.

Popper, Karl R. 2002. *The Logic of Scientific Discovery.* London: Routledge.

Posse Comitatus Act of 1878. United States Code, Title 18, Part I, Chapter 67, § 1385.

Ravitch, Diane. 2000. *Left Back: A Century of Failed School Reforms.* New York: Simon & Schuster.

Rawls, John. 1971. *A Theory of Justice.* Cambridge, MA: Harvard University Press.

Rousseau, Jean Jacques. 1987. *Rousseau's Political Writings.* Edited by Alan Ritter. New York: W. W. Norton.

———. 1997. *The Social Contract and Other Political Writings*. Edited and translated by Victor Gourevitch. Cambridge: Cambridge University Press.

Samuelson, L. 2002. "Evolution and Game Theory." *Journal of Economic Perspectives,* no. 16: 47–66.

Sax, Joseph L. 1983. "Some Thoughts on the Decline of Private Property." *Washington Law Review* 58, no. 3: 481–496.

Schengen Agreement of 1990. http://www.europe.org.ro/euroatlantic_club/1990_Convention_applying_the_Schengen_Agreement.php (accessed September 2, 2006).

Schmidt, Christian. 1996. *Uncertainty in Economic Thought.* UK: Edward Elgar.

Schultz, T. W. 1993. *The Economics of Being Poor.* Cambridge, MA: Blackwell Publishers.

———. 1961. "Investment in Human Capital." *American Economic Review* 51, no. 1 (March): 1–17.

Schumpeter, Joseph. 1975. *Capitalism, Socialism and Democracy.* New York: HarperPerennial.

Scott, James C. 1998. *Seeing Like a State: How Certain Schemes to Improve the Human Condition Have Failed.* New Haven, CT: Yale University Press.

Sen, Amartya K. 1970. *Collective Choice and Social Welfare.* San Francisco: Holden-Day.

———. 1999. *Development as Freedom.* New York: Anchor Books.

———. 1988. "Freedom of Choice: Concept and Content." *European Economic Review* 32, nos. 2–3: 269–294.

———. 1970. "The Impossibility of a Paretian Liberal." *Journal of Political Economy* 78, no. 1: 152–157.

———. 2002. *Rationality and Freedom.* Cambridge, MA: Belknap and Harvard University Press.

Simmons, A. John. 1979. *Moral Principles and Political Obligations.* Princeton: Princeton University Press.

Sirotnik, Kenneth. 2004. *Holding Accountability Accountable.* New York: Teacher's College Press.

Skyrms, Brian. 1996. *Evolution of the Social Contract.* Cambridge: Cambridge University Press.

Smith, Adam. 1776. *An Inquiry into the Nature and Causes of Wealth of Nations.* Republished. Edited by R. H. Campbell and A. S. Skinner. Oxford: Clarendon Press, 1976.

———. 1790. *The Theory of Moral Sentiments.* Oxford: Clarendon Press. 1976.

Sowell, Thomas. 1980. *Knowledge and Decisions.* New York: Basic Books.

Statement on Behalf of Higher Education Institutions. 2004. http://www.chea.org/pdf/StatementFinal0105.pdf (accessed September 2, 2006).

Stein, Howard. 1992. "Economic Policy and the IMF in Tanzania: Conditionality, Conflict, and Convergence." In *Tanzania and the IMP: The Dynamics of Liberalization,* edited by Howard Stein and Horace Campbell. Boulder, CO: Westview Press.

Stiglitz, Joseph. 2003. *Globalization and Its Discontents*. New York: W. W. Norton.

Strik, Peter. 2005. "The Westpahlian Model, Sovereignty and Law in Fin-de-siecle German International Theory." *International Relations* 19, no. 2 (June): 153–172.

Toulmin, Stephen. 1990. *Cosmopolis: The Hidden Agenda of Modernity*. Chicago: University of Chicago Press.

Treaty on the European Union. 1993. http://europa.eu.int/eurlex/lex/en/treaties/index.htm (accessed September 2, 2006).

Treaty of Rome. 1957. http://www.eurotreaties.com/eurotexts.html (accessed September 2, 2006).

Tyack, David. 1974. *The One Best System: A History of American Urban Education*. Cambridge: Harvard University Press.

Tyack, David, and Elisabeth Hansot. 1982. *Managers of Virtue: Public School Leadership in America, 1820–1980*. New York: Basic Books.

UNESCO Position Paper. 2003. "Higher Education in a Globalized Society." Chief, Section for Reform, Innovation and Quality Assurance, Division of Higher Education (France: UNESCO, 2004). http://www.unesco.org/education/higher_education/quality_innovation (accessed July 3, 2005).

U.S. Department of Education, 2000. "State Regulation of Private Schools," June, Washington, D.C.: Office of Nonpublic Education.

Vergari, Sandra, and Frederick Hess. 2002. "The Accreditation Game," *Education Next* 2 no. 3 (Fall): 48–57.

Vidich, Arthur, and Joseph Bensman. 1958. *Small Town in Mass Society*. Chicago: University of Illinois Press.

Vienna Action Plan of 1998. http://ue.eu.int/ueDocs/cms_Data/docs/pressData/en/ ec/00300-R1.EN8.htm (accessed September 2, 2006).

Vreeland, James. 2003. *The IMF and Economic Development*. Cambridge: Cambridge University Press.

Weber, Max. 1949. "'Objectivity' in Social Science and Social Policy." In *The Methodology of the Social Sciences*, edited and translated by Edward A. Shils and Henry A. Finch. Glencoe, IL: Free Press.

West, E. G. 1994. *Education and the State: A Study in Political Economy*. 3rd ed. Indianapolis, IN: Liberty Fund.

Wheeler, Donald J. 1993. *Understanding Variation: The Key to Managing Chaos*. Knoxville, TN: SPC Press.

Whitehead, A. N. 1938. *Modes of Thought*. New York: Macmillan.

Wise, M. Norton. 1995. "Precision: Agent of Unity and Product of Agreement Part I—Traveling." In *The Values of Precision*, edited by Norton Wise. Princeton: Princeton University Press.

Witte, J. 2001. *The Market Approach to Education: An Analysis of America's First Voucher Program*. Princeton: Princeton University Press.

Zupko, Ronald Edward. 1990. *Revolution in Measurement: Western European Weights and Measures since the Age of Science*. Philadelphia: American Philosophical Society.

Index